Germany Debates Defense

The NATO Alliance at the Crossroads

Germany Debates Defense

The NATO Alliance at the Crossroads

*Edited by Rudolf Steinke
and Michel Vale*

*With an Introduction
by Rudolf Steinke*

WITHDRAWN

Published in Collaboration with
the Committee
for a Nuclear-Free Europe

M. E. SHARPE, INC.
Armonk, New York/London

Copyright © 1983 by M. E. Sharpe, Inc.
80 Business Park Drive, Armonk, New York 10504

All rights reserved. No part of this book may be reproduced in any form without written permission from the publisher. German sources of the articles translated in this volume can be found in the Acknowledgments, p. viii.

Published simultaneously in *International Journal of Politics*, Vol. XII, no. 1-2.

Translated by Michel Vale.

Library of Congress Cataloging in Publication Data

Main entry under title:

Germany debates defense.

    Includes bibliographical references.
    1. Germany (West)—National security—Addresses, essays, lectures. 2. North Atlantic Treaty Organization—Germany (West)—Addresses, essays, lectures. 3. Europe—Defenses—Addresses, essays, lectures.
I. Vale, Michel. II. Steinke, Rudolf, 1948-
UA710.G46 1983   355'.033043   82-195539
ISBN 0-87332-243-6 (lib. bdg.)

Printed in the United States of America

Contents

List of Abbreviations   vii
Acknowledgments   viii
Introduction   *Rudolf Steinke*   ix

Part I: The Soviet Threat—Is It Real?

Introduction to Part I   *Rudolf Steinke*   3

What Is a Military Threat?   An Analysis of an Ambiguous Concept   *Christian Krause*   5

The Unfathomable Arms Modernization   *Stephan Tiedtke*   16

"One Day We Americans Will Have to Consider the Destruction of Europe"   *Ekkehart Krippendorff and Michael Lucas*   33

Military Détente and Differences on Military Policy within the Warsaw Pact   *Stephan Tiedtke*   44

Part II: The "German Question" and European Security

Introduction to Part II   *Rudolf Steinke*   65

Bearing Responsibility for Germany: Twenty Years of the Wall—Ten Years of the Four-Power Agreement   *Egon Bahr*   69

The Relevance of the German Question for Peace in Europe   *Herbert Ammon and Peter Brandt*   83

A Peace Policy for Germany   *Günter Gaus*   97

The Political Background of the Rapacki Plan of 1957 and Its Current Significance   *Ulrich Albrecht*   117

Part III: Alternatives

Introduction to Part III   *Rudolf Steinke*   137

Peace: A State of Emergency   *Egon Bahr*   141

The Alliance Is to Be Modernized—Reflections on a European Defense Organization   *Klaus Bloemer*   155

Principles and Problems of Alternate Peace Strategies   *Andreas Buro*   173

Five Proposals for a New Security Policy   *The Committee for Basic Rights and Democracy*   179

Horst Afheldt's Defensive Response Model   *Thomas Trempnau*   187

Technocommando Units or Social Defense? A Comparison   *Theodor Ebert*   197

About the Authors   204

List of Abbreviations

ABC — Atomic, biological, and chemical weapons
CDU — Christian Democratic Union (conservative; FRG)
CSU — Christian Social Union (Bavarian wing of CDU)
FDP — Free Democratic Party (liberal; FRG)
MBFR — Mutual and Balanced Force Reduction
NPD — National Party (FRG)
SALT — Strategic Arms Limitation Talks
SED — Socialist Unity Party (GDR)
SPD — Socialist Democratic Party (FRG)
START — Strategic and Tactical Arms Reduction Talks

Acknowledgments

The articles in this collection are translated from edited versions of the German originals with the permission of the authors and the following sources:

Christian Krause, "Was ist militärische Bedrohung?" *Die Neue Gesellschaft*, 1982, no. 4.
Stephan Tiedtke, "Unergründliche 'Nachrüstung,'" *Vorgänge*, no. 51, and "Militärpolitische Differenzen zwischen den Warschauer Vertragsstaaten und die militärische Enstspannung," *DGFK-Jahrbuch*, 1979-80.
Ekkehart Krippendorff and Michael Lucas, "'Eines Tages werden die Amerikaner über die Zerstörung Europas nachdenken müssen.' Die USA und Westeuropa," *Weltpolitik: Jahrbuch fur Internationale Beziehungen I*, edited by Ulrich Albrecht, Klaus J. Gantzel, Ekkehart Krippendorff, et al. (Frankfurt: Campus Verlag, 1981).
Egon Bahr, "In Verantwortung für Deutschland. Zwanzig Jahre Mauer—zehn Jahre Vier-Mächte Abkommen," *Alternativen europäischer Friedenspolitik*, edited by AK atomwaffenfreies Europa, Berlin, 1981, and "Den 'Ernstfall Frieden' leben," *Vorwärts*, 1982, no. 22.
Herbert Ammon and Peter Brandt, "Die Aktualität der deutschen Frage für den Frieden in Europa," *Frieden in Deutschland*, edited by Hans A. Pestalozzi (Munich, 1982).
Günter Gaus, "Friedenspolitik für Deutschland," *Berliner Stimme*, November 1981.
Ulrich Albrecht, "Die politischen Hintergründe des Rapacki-Planes von 1957 und seine heutige Bedeutung," *atomwaffenfreies Europa*, 1982, no. 1.
Klaus Bloemer, "Das Bündnis sollte modernisiert werden. Überlegungen zu einer europäischen Verteidegungsorganisation," *Die Neue Gesellschaft*, 1982, no. 3.
Andreas Buro, "Prinzipien und Probleme alternativer Friedensstrategien," *atomwaffenfreies Europa*, 1982, no. 2.
The Committee for Basic Rights and Democracy, "Kritik der NATO;—Sicherheit," *Weltpolitik. Jahrbuch für internationale Beziehungen I*, edited by Ulrich Albrecht, Klaus J. Gantzel, Ekkehart Krippendorff, et al. (Frankfurt: Campus Verlag, 1981).
Thomas Trempnau, "Afheldts Konzept einer defensiven, reaktiven Verteidigung," *antimilitarismus information*, 1981, no. 9.
Theodor Ebert, "Technokommandos oder soziale Verteidigung," *antimilitarismus information*, 1981, no. 9.

Introduction

This anthology provides a modest overview of the security debate in the Federal Republic of Germany. A number of more specialized points in that controversy are left out, while primary emphasis is placed on the spectrum represented by the Social Democratic and Liberal parties and the new peace movement. This is justified when one considers that the present debate, which extends far into the ranks of those two parties and even into the camp of the new conservative government, was originally begun, and in its essential features shaped by, the new peace movement.

This movement consciously distinguishes itself from the older peace movement, which was extremely one-sided: it is an international movement that is as critical of the Eastern European states as of the West.

The present security debate takes the NATO decision of December 12, 1979, as its point of departure. At that time Helmut Schmidt, then Federal Chancellor, came out in favor of filling the gap left in the deterrence system after the SALT II negotiations with new American medium-range weapons (albeit sea-based). The new peace movement emerged in the aftermath of and as a response to this NATO decision. In former years it would never have been able to give birth to a mass movement of such scope in terms not only of numbers but of political issues as well.

The background factors are many and complex. The NATO decision of December 12, 1979, remains only the external point of reference. Thus whether the campaign against the NATO decision succeeds or fails, the movement will continue. The reasons for its emergence and growth in the late seventies and eighties in the Federal Republic can be summed up in the following points:

1. The breakdown of the popular image of a communist enemy cultivated in the fifties and sixties, the reasons for which are to be sought in the détente policy pursued by the SPD/FDP coalition in the early seventies. 2. The emergence of a popular movement against the peaceful use of nuclear energy, destruction of the environment, and capitalist industrial economic growth.

The impulses toward the current peace movement were already present in embryo in this earlier popular movement: (1) the fact that it embraces several generations; (2) it is both extraparliamentary as well as nonparty; and (3) the emerging bloc confrontation, triggered by the Soviet invasion of Afghanistan, the "revolution" in Iran, the American hostage incident in Iran, and the failed attempt to rescue the hostages. These events produced a wave of anxiety in Europe that found expression in a strong grass-roots movement outside the established parties and institutions.

The dynamic and explosive form the movement took, however, had its roots in American foreign and security policy, beginning with the turn, taken in the last half of Carter's term of office, toward a strong anti-Soviet position, later to be reinforced by the policies of the Reagan administration, with their emphasis on an arms buildup and power politics. A primary objective of this confrontation course with the Soviet Union is to undermine, or at least seriously to obstruct, the links that have been forged between Western Europe and the Eastern European bloc (consider, for example, the dispute over the gas pipeline, credits to Poland, etc.).

The anxiety in *central* Europe has been especially fueled, however, by American arguments that a limited nuclear war in Europe could be waged and won. This, specifically, was the factor that triggered the fundamental reexamination of security policy in Western Europe which today goes far beyond the peace movement and has even struck roots within conservative

Introduction xi

circles and the new right-wing government. But it is within the Social Democratic and Liberal parties that the debate has taken its most extensive and interesting form. Let us now trace the history and shape of that controversy.

Background of the security debate

In its brief history the Federal Republic of Germany has witnessed three fundamental debates on its security and foreign policy. The first of them, the discussion on rearmament and Western alignment, was of major importance.

The second big domestic debate took place against the background of the decisions on rearmament and NATO membership at the end of the '50s and was marked by the "antinuclear movement." Broad segments of the population were mobilized by this movement (which reached its high point in July 1958 with over 300,000 people participating in demonstrations). It was officially supported by the Social Democratic Party (SPD) and its trade unions (the Deutsche Gewerkschaftsbund, with six million members) and had essentially three aims:

• to prevent equipping the Bundeswehr with weapons capable of carrying nuclear warheads;

• to retract the agreement to store atomic warheads on the territory of the Federal Republic;

• to prevent the stationing of American short- and medium-range missiles in the FRG.[1]

The third major debate began with the acceptance by the SPD and its trade unions of alignment with the West and the abandonment of the antinuclear movement of the '50s. It got a dramatic boost from the building of the Berlin Wall in 1961 and reached its high point in 1969-72, after a decade of laborious reorientation and the shaping of a new policy on the German question and détente by the Social Democrats: The landmarks here were the first Social Democratic–Free Democratic (FDP) government coalition, the Four-Power Agreement on Berlin, the treaty on the basis of relations (*Grundlagenvertrag*), and the attempt from conservative quarters to halt this policy by overturning the Brandt-Scheel government in 1972.[2]

Today we are probably on the threshold of a fourth debate on principles. It will be of an importance comparable to that of the first debate in the early '50s—on alignment with the West and rearmament.

The current controversy stems from present American foreign and security policies and is marked by a growing awareness of the need for a more independent security policy in the Federal Republic now that the economic and political importance of the FRG relative to the United States has undergone appreciable changes compared with the '50s and '60s.[3]

To the extent that the current debate goes beyond a mere criticism of the NATO modernization decision and outlines proposals for a new European security policy, it recalls the position of the SPD in the 1950s.[4] A brief description of that position will therefore be useful.

Disengagement and a collective European security system

As an alternative to the security policy of the Adenauer government, the SPD suggested creating a collective security system in Europe in which a reunified Germany would find its place and its security.[5] Erler, one of the leading Social Democrats in 1945, argued for "security for and from Germany,"[6] as distinct from military alliances. "A military alliance is aimed at a power outside of the alliance; a collective security system includes the potential aggressor as well. It works by all members of the system pledging themselves to stand together against anyone who violates the peace."[7] The resemblance to the "joint security" model worked out by the Palme Commission on behalf of the United Nations is obvious. There is, however, one fundamental difference. In the 1950s concept of a collective security system, ending the partition of Germany played a central role.

> As a member of a collective security system, Germany would be neither neutralized nor neutral in the classic sense. It would simply not be a member of any military alliance. A neutralized country, whose neutrality was guaranteed and overseen by others, would have to accept the intervention of the guarantor powers, something that would be unacceptable in view of Soviet infiltration. A reunified Ger-

Introduction *xiii*

many would not be neutral because it could not defend itself against an armed attack with its own forces alone but would have to rely on the assistance of all its partners in the security system. A reunified Germany would thus be neither neutral nor "neutralized" but merely without military alliances.[8]

Thus Fritz Erler in 1954.

This model received its first comprehensive, programmatic dress in the Ollenhauer plan of 1957 (Ollenhauer was then SPD chairman), which outlined the essential features of a collective European security system:

1) members: reunified Germany and its neighbors to the east and west;

2) mutual declarations of nonaggression;

3) mutual pledge of assistance;

4) arbitration;

5) arms limitations and control;

6) regional system in accordance with the UN statutes;

7) declarations of guarantees from the Soviet Union and the United States.[9]

The declaration of guarantee was meant only for a transitional phase until the security system stabilized. On March 18, 1959, the SPD presented its most specific formulation, accompanied by a precise plan of stages for achieving German reunification and a European security system. This "Plan for Germany" was unanimously ratified by the party Executive Committee and the Bundestag faction and was used by an SPD delegation in intensive consultations in Moscow. But after a long series of disillusionments owing to the Cold War and the reluctance of the Western allies and the Adenauer government, it became clear to the SPD in a few months that the Soviet Union as well had no interest in such a policy, given its aims of a reunified and neutral Germany.[10]

The Social Democratic concept of a collective security system in Europe did not obtain the hoped-for response in Europe among either the West German or the Western European public.[11] Instead, ideas and plans for a "policy of disengagement" steadily gained ground.[12] Between 1957 and 1959 about sixty different plans were presented by the West and about twenty different plans by the East.[13]

The most prominent proposals from the West were the plans by the two Labor politicians Hugh Gaitskell and Denis Healey[14] as well as the one by George Kennan. The proposals from the Soviet sphere of influence assumed various forms, particularly the 1955 offer (conclusion of a treaty on permanent neutrality with Austria) and the 1958 proposals for a peace treaty settlement. However, the plan by the Polish foreign minister, Adam Rapacki, remained the most important, although his proposals have all too facilely been presented as Soviet controlled or Soviet inspired. Today it is clear to serious students that Rapacki's proposals were a specifically Polish offensive to relieve pressure after the Hungarian uprising in 1956.

Rapacki's proposal[15] provided for the creation of a nuclear-free zone to include Poland, the GDR, the FRG, and Czechoslovakia, ideas that were implicit in the plans of Gaitskell, Healey, and Kennan. In the Federal Republic the Rapacki plan was zealously supported by the SPD and the trade unions, which saw it as a first step in a number of respects:

- It was a "limited disarmament step" on which further comprehensive disarmament negotiations could follow, setting an example.
- It was a concrete step toward détente, which could only further efforts for a reunification of Germany.[16] The call for a withdrawal of foreign troops from the nuclear-free zone was present in every declaration by prominent SPD politicians without exception, while Gaitskell and Healey assumed that Soviet troops should withdraw beyond the eastern border of Poland, i.e., to Soviet territory.

This pursuit of a collective European security system, which lay at the base of all plans for disengagement, the aim of demilitarizing the whole of Germany, and efforts to achieve a reunified Germany, betokened the undisputed political direction of the SPD and the trade unions. The Social Democrats thus made clear their disagreement with any neutralization of Germany.

The peace movement and Social Democracy in quest of a new security policy

Thus the way was paved for a radical turn in security and foreign policy and for the CSU-SPD coalition of 1965. Détente and the new *Ostpolitik* followed during the SPD-FDP coalition of 1969 and 1972. Systematic incorporation of the FRG into the Western alliance proved for the next decade to be the historical prerequisite for a new relationship with Eastern Europe, the Soviet Union, and in particular, the GDR. German reunification was abandoned as an immediate goal and put off to a time in the unforeseeable future, when the question of Europe as a whole would be settled. Of course, the SPD never renounced reunification as such, since the Basic Law prescribes it as a mandatory pursuit; as time passed, however, its status declined to that of a general postulate, far removed from the concerns of the hour.

The official program of Social Democracy today, the Godesberg Program, still spells out the following goal:

> The Social Democratic Party shall strive for the inclusion of the whole of Germany in a European zone of détente and controlled arms limitations; foreign troops will be withdrawn from this zone as a consequence of the restoration of the unity of Germany in freedom, and no nuclear weapons and other means of mass destruction shall be either produced or stored or used in it.

Although after 1960-61 this goal receded to the fringes of consciousness among the SPD membership and party officials, the new peace movement disinterred reunification as a goal in a number of key appeals and general formulations, and it has once again made demilitarization and disengagement an issue.[17] Formal party endorsement has so far been lacking, but by all indications this too is only a matter of time. What is more, a small but aware group of intellectuals in the movement has linked the question of reunification to the demilitarization and "denuclearization" of central Europe. But the criticism of the current NATO arms buildup finds considerable support even in the established parties where it points out the incompatibility of European détente and disarmament with reunification (see the articles by Bahr, Gaus, and Albrecht in this volume).

A survey carried out in May 1980 shows, however, the extent of popular support for the neutralization or demilitarization of the two German states: 45 percent of the West German population saw "military neutrality of the Federal Republic and the GDR" as conducive to a lasting peace, while only 34 percent were opposed. But this position has as yet found no political advocacy and, indeed, could become a real political issue only if endorsed by the SPD and the trade unions. Nevertheless, for the first time in more than a decade, leading figures in the SPD have once again addressed the idea of disengagement in approving terms, and Egon Bahr has stated the case radically, directly, and programmatically in the minority opinion of the Palme report: "All nuclear weapons shall be withdrawn from those states in Europe which do not possess them."[18]

The current security debate in the Federal Republic

The NATO decision of December 12, 1979, to station Pershing II and cruise missiles in Europe triggered a broad debate on security. At its party meeting in December 1979 in Berlin, the SPD established that: "The goal of negotiations (between the United States and the Soviet Union in Geneva) is to render the introduction of additional medium-range weapons in Western Europe superfluous by reducing the number of Soviet medium-range weapons and by agreeing on a joint East-West limitation on medium-range weapons in Europe as a whole."[19] The United States' current pursuit of an arms buildup and its insistence on negotiating terms that the Soviet Union cannot accept will in all likelihood mean that the SPD will declare itself against the stationing of these missiles at a special party meeting sometime in 1983.

To give English-speaking readers a clearer idea of the debate in the Federal Republic, we will now attempt to summarize it briefly. The general position advanced in this volume is more or less accepted in common by all distinguished critics of current NATO security policy. The arguments may differ in detail, but they all agree on the key points.

1. Now that the Soviet Union has achieved a balance with the United States in strategic weapons—with the statement of a strategic stalemate in the SALT II agreement as its tangible expression—the U.S. nuclear guarantee has become doubtful and noncredible because an attack on the Soviet Union with strategic nuclear weapons to protect Europe would necessarily

Introduction xvii

mean the destruction of the United States. Indeed, the West German government has been guided by this consideration in its political actions, and it was one of the factors behind Helmut Schmidt's "discovery" of the "missile gap" at the medium-range level (see below).

To restore the credibility of the nuclear guarantee, and of the ability to protect Europe from an attack by the Warsaw Pact, land-based medium-range Pershing II and cruise missiles are to be stationed in Western Europe (if, as per the NATO decision of December 12, 1979, negotiations with the Soviet Union yield no satisfactory results). The assumption (and this is a key point in the criticism of the West German government's position) is that the USSR would accept a U.S. nuclear counteroffensive from Western European soil without responding with a strategic nuclear strike against U.S. territory. Furthermore the stationing of the new weapons is intended to demonstrate U.S. readiness to accept the risk of its own annihilation to protect Europe. A Soviet attack on the launching sites of the new weapons would be interpreted as a strategic attack against the United States, which would then respond with its own strategic weapons. This "liability" (security guarantee) is meant as a tangible guarantee of the United States' function as a guardian nuclear power.

2. The arguments made in support of the "modernization decision" are regarded as totally self-contradictory by West German critics for the following reasons:

If the Pershing II and cruise missiles are strategic weapons (since they threaten the Soviet Union and would force the Soviet Union to respond to their stationing with a counterthreat in kind), the credibility of the American nuclear guarantee for Europe remains questionable even at this Eurostrategic level. In other words, in the case of conflict the U.S. president would be no more inclined to fire a Pershing II or a cruise missle against the USSR than he would an intercontinental missile of the Minuteman II type, for example. Furthermore the Soviet Union knows this, so that the effect seems to be more one of self-deterrence than a greater nuclear security guarantee for Europe.

When the German Federal government argues that the U.S. nuclear guarantee has lost its credibility in the case of strategic weapons, it must also logically concede that the nuclear guarantee is just as lacking in credibility in the case of Eurostrategic weapons.

If, however, the new weapons supposed to restore the credibility of the U.S. nuclear umbrella are in fact superior, then there is no obvious reason why this guarantee should not also exist in the case of strategic weapons. The Soviet SS 20 medium-range weapons (which actually are not strategic because they do not threaten the United States) could therefore still be deterred by the U.S. strategic potential. Thus modernization would not be necessary.

3. If, however, we assume that the decision to modernize is not based on a contradiction, then other reasons that have been kept from the public must be sought. It is quite clear that:

a. the new weapons are meant as a counterstrike force (a model for nuclear warfare developed after 1974) for use against "hard" targets in the Soviet Union on the assumption, or rather the speculation, that the Soviet Union would not retaliate with strikes against targets in the United States because the risk of unleashing a strategic "holocaust" would be too great. Presidential Directive 59 is open to such an interpretation;

b. the new land-launched weapons are first-strike weapons, mainly because they can easily be destroyed by Soviet short-range nuclear weapons, i.e., they are purely tactical. Their stationing on Western European soil would be meaningless on any grounds other than their first-strike capability, i.e., use before a Soviet preventive strike.

4. It must be assumed that the United States has a vital interest in limiting a nuclear war to Europe, including the western Soviet Union, to prevent nuclear strikes against U.S. territory. On the other hand, it is up to the Soviet Union to convince its adversaries that such expectations are unrealistic. Thus the interests of the Western European NATO allies and the Soviet Union converge on this particular point: neither can be very interested in limiting a nuclear war to Europe plus parts of the Soviet Union while leaving the United States intact. In the perverse logic of the deterrence system, it follows from this common interest that the Western Europeans and the Soviet Union must find desirable limited nuclear superiority by the USSR.

Introduction xix

This would fit in with the basic idea of a flexible response strategy, i.e., the institutionalized need to escalate to the use of U.S. strategic weapons to protect Western Europe (see the essay by Stephan Tiedtke in this volume).

5. The argument by the West German government for stationing the new weapons on West German soil is that the nuclear risk to the United States must be shared by its allies. The critics reject this argument as absurd for the following reasons:

a. In NATO's own escalation model, Western Europe would be totally devastated by nuclear short-range weapons before the new weapons or intercontinental missiles could even be engaged. In a war in Europe the European NATO members would bear the brunt of the risk of annihilation.

b. The new U.S. model of a limited nuclear war in Europe means a reduced risk for the United States but not for Europe.

c. A preventive strike by the Soviet Union against the launching sites of the new weapons would cause vast destruction in those countries but would not touch the United States.

6. The proposed stationing of the new weapons on European soil strengthens the suspicion that the United States regards a limited nuclear war in Europe as conceivable and, moreover, in its own interests. It can be interpreted as a signal to the USSR to avoid a strategic war. This suspicion would be dispelled if the new weapons were sea-based, since then the Soviet Union could not draw a distinction between them and strategic weapons. This point is finding increasing acceptance even among the conservative critics of modernization. Conservative intellectuals and left-wing critics join ranks here because the fate of Europe and Germany is being decided over the heads of both in an objective accord between the superpowers.

Stationing these weapons at sea would be more in consonance with the Western European interest in keeping the fate of the United States tied to that of Europe through NATO.

Placing the new weapons in Europe would undermine the two key doctrines of NATO security policy for the following reasons:

a. "Flexible response"[20] would be undermined because the new weapons are first-strike weapons. The modernization decision stipulates that strategic weapons will be used even before tactical nuclear weapons as per the flexible response strategy and NATO's own escalation model.

b. Deterrence would also be undermined. Rather than deterring, the new weapons could even provoke a Soviet preemptive strike because the risk of their use would be unacceptably high for the USSR, while the risk of a strategic confrontation with the United States entailed in the destruction of the launching sites seems smaller and more calculable by comparison. The political function of nuclear weapons, namely, mutual deterrence, would be nullified for two reasons: the constraint on the United States to use them as soon as possible, and the constraint on the Soviets to knock them out even sooner.

The most probable scenario, however, would be a nuclear war limited to the European NATO countries and the Soviet Union. This must be regarded as a probability so long as the two superpowers have a secured nuclear second-strike capacity. However, the stability of this situation is only middle-term (e.g., up to 1992-95) because of the development of strategic defense weapons (space weapons using laser or particle beams, total submarine position finding, etc.). As things stand now, it must be presumed that the two superpowers will not allow a tactical nuclear war to escalate into a strategic conflict and thus choose the "suicide option," thereby acting against their own vital national interests.

Given this situation, a tactical nuclear war limited to Eastern and Western Europe would be a "rational" option for the two superpowers in the traditional sense (i.e., a continuation of politics by other means). For the Europeans it would mean the end. For them there is no difference between a tactical nuclear war and a strategic war. Thus the "flexible response" theory is an absurd military categorization of a very probable conflict.

8. A security policy which if deterrence failed would mean the end of Europe, and probably even the end of all higher forms of life on the planet, is militarily, politically, and ethically irresponsible, unrealistic, and devoid of legitimacy. If so, the respective allies of the two superpowers have a common interest in fashioning an alternative to that policy. "Security models" or strategic options that would in the first instance destroy those countries in both East and West which have no nuclear weapons themselves and, moreover, no say in their use by the super-

Introduction xxi

powers, are quite simply grotesque. It is incumbent on the countries of Europe, therefore, to redefine their security interests within their respective alliances and to defend those interests more resolutely (see the articles by Bahr and Tiedtke).

The nuclear debate: "the battle for the mind of Europe"

Burns, the American ambassador in Bonn in late 1981, described the nuclear debate as a "battle for the mind of Europe."[21] Trenchant enough, but it does not get to the root of the issue. Security is no longer the main point, and indeed, it was never the only issue. The current nuclear debate merely reflects the dilemma of German-American and American-European relations. Something new, something more fundamental seems to be at stake than merely one of those "normal" conflicts of interests, despite the assurances of former Foreign Minister Genscher and Federal Chancellor Schmidt to the contrary, even in the light of the U.S. embargo on the gas pipeline deal (see Krippendorff's article). That is, there is a growing disagreement on the political and economic priorities of the West worldwide in meeting the political and economic challenges that are becoming graver with each passing day.

The differences are showing up over an ever wider range of economic, security, and foreign policy issues and are quite clearly the result of the continuing waning of U.S. hegemony.[22] The conflict in the economic domain has already provoked serious concern. Europe's economic recovery sharpened competition among the capitalist nations, while the mere existence of the Common Market has meant a practically unceasing trade war between the United States and Western Europe. The United States was, however, able to meet the European challenge by expanding its trans-Atlantic economic ties and by a massive export of capital, while to discipline its Western European allies it shifted some of the burden of the alliance to their shoulders, thereby subordinating Western Europe to its own economic and political goals. Despite all the conflicts, down through the '60s and into the early '70s, the fact of mutual dependence was generally recognized. As the NATO "Harmel Report" of 1967 put it, a privileged German and American alliance system ("a bigemony") had been created in military power and détente, as two equal poles of Western security policy preventing the development of an anti-American bloc in Western Europe as a continuation of Gaullism.

The situation changed abruptly in the late '70s. Western European relations deteriorated in every respect. After the second oil shock of 1979-80, which hit the Western European and especially the West German economies harder than that of the United States, the depth of the world economic crisis became clear. Institutions built up to cultivate ties between Europe and the United States and to maintain stability no longer worked as they should. The crisis was structural, with no immediate resolution in sight, and challenged the foundations of Western capitalism. Politicians increasingly turned to national solutions as a way out of the economic and political crises. Attempts at world economic conferences to achieve even a minimum of coordination have produced no results.

The view is gaining ground in Western Europe, and especially in West Germany, that the American government, first under Carter and now even more so under Reagan, is endeavoring to reassert and reestablish its authority whatever the economic and political consequences for Western Europe. This is demonstrated in the crassest form by the disregard shown to the customs of consultation and in the order to withhold from Western European firms the technical know-how for building the Soviet gas pipeline.

The line between economics and politics has become blurred in this struggle between national economies. A new dimension has emerged, as in the attempt to link the stationing of the new American medium-range missiles to the embargo against Western Europe (officially against the Soviet Union).

Thus the security interests of the United States are taking on global dimensions that will be unacceptable for Western Europe.

The linkage doctrine, first formulated during the Carter administration and resolutely pursued by Reagan, which makes progress in relations with the USSR dependent on Soviet good behavior in the rest of the world, reflects hegemonic ambitions

Introduction xxiii

that are totally inappropriate to a bipolar or multipolar world.

Current U.S. policy toward the Soviet Union and Western Europe is reflected particularly acutely in German-American relations.

The change has, indeed, been considerable. As recently as 1977 it was Federal Chancellor Schmidt who discovered the "Eurostrategic gap" on the occasion of the stationing of SS 20 missiles and the impending SALT II agreement. For a long time the American government did not want to hear about bridging this gap. But when the Carter administration turned to get-tough policies,[23] demands for modern U.S. military hardware, particularly land-based medium-range weapons, rose. Initially Schmidt demanded sea-based missiles, but soon the Federal government found itself caught between U.S. demands and the opposition, embodied by the peace movement. Helmut Schmidt had hoped to influence the SALT negotiations with his call to close the "missile gap" and hence prevent the United States' disengagement from Europe, or at least make that disengagement more difficult. Instead the contrary has occurred: the closing of the missile gap has produced a growing anti-Americanism, and the security and economic interests of the United States and Western Europe have begun in fact to diverge.

However, there is also the point that the Federal Republic can more easily make military and political than economic concessions to the United States, since secure foreign trade is an essential ingredient of the "German model." It must therefore be maintained even at the price of sharpening conflicts with the leading power. The new American policy under Reagan has shaken the "German model" at its foundations, and the United States has put more pressure on the Federal Republic than on any of the other alliance partners to give in to a political and economic "division of labor" worldwide, the structure of which is to be determined by the United States global commitments. This means, first and foremost, largely abandoning détente, even though the Federal Republic has reaped the most benefits from it, and indeed its very existence is contingent on the continuation of détente.

The need to salvage at least the fabric of détente, an absolute economic necessity for West Germany but by no means the prelude to political dependence on the Soviet Union as the Reagan administration claims, explains why more and more West German politicians and even elements in the power elite have come not only to reject "modernization" but also to see the danger that a sharper confrontation could lead to a new armaments spiral and an arms economy. This in turn could mark the beginning of a "militarization" of the standoff between the blocs. Thus even respected SPD politicians like Oskar Lafontaine reject the notion of "balance" as absurd,[24] and even generals in the Bundeswehr, whose opinions can hardly be lightly dismissed, are against any impending conventional arms buildup (see General Krause's articles in this volume).

These fears of "militarization" and a new nuclear and conventional arms spiral, and of the threat they pose to stability in both blocks, have given the peace movement in West Germany and Western Europe a mass basis over night. As a logical corollary, critical circles within the ranks of the Social Democrats (now out of power and in opposition) are finally realizing, if much too late, that other alternative military strategies must be sought within the alliance (see the articles by Krause, Bahr, Trempnau, and Buro).

The peace movement, following the logic of the times, has in turn been groping its way toward addressing in a programmatic way broader social issues, ecological concerns, and the hegemonic pretensions of the superpowers.

At the other pole, the neoconservative counterfront—which now has a parliamentary majority as a result of the FDP switch in allegiance and has seized the reins of government through a no-confidence vote on Helmut Schmidt—regards the current debate as the greatest challenge to society today. Even the development of a worldwide peace and antiarmaments movement —e.g., the freeze campaign in the United States, which according to surveys has 70 percent of the population behind it— has made little impression on the conservative elite in West Germany, at least judging from their polemics.

If the political and economic crisis in West Germany continues to worsen at the current pace to the point of destabilizing parliamentary institutions, West German society could be split along its seams. The "alienation," for instance, between West Germany and the United States has already reached such proportions that there appears little likelihood that a new pro-American consensus could be fashioned. The American reader should therefore not be misled by the change of governments in Bonn. It is not a sign of a new, long-term conservative balance of power in government. While it is not very likely but hardly inconceivable that the CDU/CSU might obtain an absolute majority in the next Bundestag elections, over the long term, conservative circles may expect to see so great a transformation of values among their ranks with regard to both social and security policy that it will force them and their government to undertake a thorough rethinking of their positions. Since they have adopted an unequivocal position on the alliance question, one might expect signs of rapid disintegration to appear in their ranks on this issue in particular.

Willy Brandt perhaps described the actual political situation most clearly on the occasion of the Hesse regional elections in early October 1982 (in which the FDP failed to obtain the 5 percent of the vote necessary to be seated in the regional legislature, and the CDU failed to obtain an absolute majority) when he said that there was a majority to the *left* of the SPD/FDP government in Bonn. This majority has not yet been able to establish a consistent and coherent position, and for the time being it leads a fragmentary existence in the Green Party and Social Democracy. It may thus take several years for it to arrive at a common position.

All in all, however, the consensus between the various groupings is greater than within the conservative camp itself. Furthermore, it is not unimportant that after sixteen years of bearing the responsibilities of government, the Social Democrats have been able to close ranks and show a resolute front in their new role as opposition party, so that the current supposed majority on the left may well become an even greater majority in the foreseeable future. The present conservative government may therefore yet prove to be the transitory phenomenon that even Franz Josef Strauss has described it to be, albeit from a quite different standpoint than ours.

A policy for Europe and a policy for Germany

Just as in the past, a pro-American position entails not only accepting certain U.S. demands but also adopting the essential elements of the American model. That model has enjoyed undisputed sway since the founding of the Federal Republic in the mid-'50s and has created the broad consensus that served as the basis for stability and prosperity.

Today the opposition front derives its strength from the fact that the legitimacy and effectiveness of the model are steadily waning even as it entails ever increasing social costs. The United States' two-pronged strategy of militarization of bloc confrontation and austerity is being questioned as an effective response to the crisis, giving a structural and social dimension to the dispute between the Federal Republic and the United States. And that dimension will also persist, even with a change of government in West Germany; the mass base of conservative forces is itself not so immune to the bacillus of anti-Americanism.

But this anti-Americanism—as embodied in the peace movement which burst on the scene literally without forewarning—is not in the least a pro-Soviet position nor does it even tend that way; on the contrary, the drift toward disintegration is more profound and dramatic in Eastern than in Western Europe. The events in Poland, the liberalization in Hungary, Romania's independent foreign policy, the official reform efforts in the GDR, and the ossification in Czechoslovakia are examples. The dream of a Finlandization of Eastern Europe is today quite realistic (see Ulrich Albrecht's article). The common security problem of Eastern and Western Europe is more and more acquiring a political complexion. The undermining of détente by the United States and the Soviet Union (Afghanistan, Poland, etc.) represents a futile attempt to prevent the "Europeanization of Europe," which, however, is not the creation overnight of a new community of Eastern and Western European nations but rather a long and difficult process of social and political transformation.

This also explains why the development of alternative security strategies, to which more and more public figures and intellectuals are devoting thought,[25] can also be expected to encounter major obstacles, however. The project of a nuclear-free zone

Introduction xxvii

from Poland to Portugal[26] entails a wealth of both strategic and political imponderables feared by no one so much as by the superpowers themselves, who are mustering all their forces against it and will do everything, even in concert, to entrench their notion of "stability." This is evident in the dilemma of the discussion on nuclear-free zones in northern and southeastern Europe. The idea is tremendously attractive to large segments of the Eastern and Western European population, despite its antisuperpower overtones.

The concept has been denounced, overhastily, as a pro-Soviet idea in the Federal Republic, despite the fact that there is little evidence that the Soviet Union is really so eager to create a new security arrangement in Europe. Indeed, the idea of a nuclear-free Europe evokes the specter of Europe as a "third force" that would have more real political significance than in the '50s and give the Eurocommunist and socialist-social democratic parties a basis for a new historical offensive. But the Soviet Union fears nothing so much as this, in view of the structural and material impact it could have on Eastern Europe. The tendency that would emerge in those countries would not be antisocialist but, on the contrary, would be directed toward the democratization and socialization of production and society in general. And the germ could even spread to the Soviet Union! Not today, not tomorrow, but it would still be a definite risk.

It is thus in the clear interests of the Soviet Union and its parties and institutions in Eastern Europe to restrict the Western European and worldwide peace movements to the missile issue. Ideas of demilitarization, neutrality, and nonalignment of the Federal Republic (or of a reunified Germany) and Europe are even more remote from reality. But even these visions[27] have a certain dynamic to them. They could be the catalysts for the crystallization of a new "German" or "European" identity.

Less remote from reality, but just as complex for the Federal Republic and Western Europe as regards the effort to establish a new independent identity, are the arguments that take up de Gaulle's old dream of a "Europeanization of Europe" and at the same time seek to revive the notion of a European defense community to lessen the dependence of European security on the United States (see Bloemer's article in this volume, for ex-

ample). Although at first glance these various positions seem to diverge, they basically have one point in common: they all accept the logic of the bloc system (Bahr, Gaus, Bloemer), while others consciously contain elements that are incompatible with the status quo. The idea of a "Europeanization of Europe" bridges the two positions, and the physical bridge here is a peace movement extending over both blocs. Indeed, the first underpinnings of such a project have already been forged:
- meetings of East and West German authors;
- the Palme Report, compiled jointly by Eastern and Western European politicians and scholars;
- the peace marches to Eastern Europe;
- the disarmament debates in the UN;
- ideas about a nuclear-free Europe, the "Europeanization of Europe";
- Solidarity in Poland and the GDR "peace movement."[28]

The historical alternatives being debated at this juncture in Europe cannot be so radically suppressed as were the disengagement projects in the late '50s. Social Democracy and the trade unions will support these ideas. Some go back to the '50s, although the terms and the context are more complex and more varied. The forces of resistance in Europe against a new, updated version of bloc confrontation and cold war are much more powerful and have a quality about them that embraces the whole of European society.

Berlin, October 1982

NOTES

1. For a fundamental comment on this point, see H. K. Rupp, *Aussenparlamentarische Opposition in der Ära Adenauer. Der Kampf gegen die Atombewaffnung in den fünfziger Jahren*, Cologne, 1970; and K. A. Otto, *Vom Ostermarsch zum APO. Geschichte der ausserparlamentarischen Opposition in der Bundesrepublik 1960-1970*. Frankfurt on Main and New York, 1977. On political developments in the '50s, see H. K. Rupp, *Politische Geschichte der Bundesrepublik Deutschland*, Stuttgart, Berlin, Cologne, and Mainz, 1978; and Arnulf Baring, *Aussenpolitik in Adenauers Kanzlerdemokratie*, Munich, 1969.

2. For more details, see H. W. Schmollinger, and P. Müller, *Zwischen-*

bilanz. 10 Jahre sozialliberale Politik 1969-1979. Anspruch und Wirklichkeit, Hannover, 1980; Arnulf Baring, *Machtwechsel, Die Ära Brandt-Scheel*, Stuttgart, 1982; Hans-Adolf Jacobsen, et al., eds. *Drei Jahrzehnte Aussenpolitik der DDR. Bestimmungsfaktoren, Instrumente, Aktionsfelder*, Munich and Vienna, 1979 (translated in part as *GDR Foreign Policy*, M. E. Sharpe, 1982).

3. This is demonstrated in a number of areas:
● The U.S. balance of trade, which always showed high surpluses after the war, showed a deficit in 1970 for the first time in ninety years.
● The terms of trade, one of the important indicators of a country's competitiveness (relative level of export prices compared to import prices), fell to 63 in 1977, compared to 100 for the base year 1962.
● The balance of trade in technologically advanced goods is still very positive, but a nonnegligible decline in U.S. trade in high technology exports was observable. On this point, see O. T. Bayard, *Trends in U.S. Trade: 1960-1979*, U.S. Department of Labor, Office of Foreign Economic Research, Bureau of International Labor Affairs, Washington, D.C., July 1980; and *Twenty-Fourth Annual Report of the President of the United States on the Trade Agreements Program*, Washington, D.C., 1979.

4. "Modernization" (*Nachrüstung*)—the purport of the NATO decision of December 12, 1979, to improve Eurostrategic nuclear weapons with Pershing II and cruise missiles. The NATO commitment also entails providing for the control of such weapons, a qualification necessary to obtain the agreement of some of the smaller members of the alliance. It is therefore also referred to as the NATO double decision or two-track decision.

In contrast to the NATO double decision, the SPD double decision clearly stresses arms control negotiations with the aim of avoiding the stationing of the new weapons. In the FRG the SPD and NATO double decisions are usually regarded as equivalent. This is absolutely not the case. The stationing of new American long-range missiles is also referred to as "modernization" of the alliance, although it would seem to be more on the order of a Cuba crisis in reverse: the Soviet Union is thereby threatened with weapons that could strike its very heartland. These weapons thus have a strategic function, whereas the corresponding Soviet weapons systems cannot threaten the territory of the United States.

On these points see the articles by Günter Gaus, Herbert Ammon and Peter Brandt, Ulrich Albrecht, and the Committee for Basic Rights.

5. For details on the debate in the '50s and '60s, see F. Erler, *Ein Volk sucht seine Sicherheit. Bemerkungen zur deutschen Sicherheitspolitik*, Frankfurt, 1961; Helmut Schmidt, *Verteidigung oder Vergeltung. Ein deutscher Beitrag zum strategischen Problem der NATO*, Stuttgart, 1961; *Gesamtdarstellungen*, Uwe Nerlich, ed., *Abrüstungs- und Entspannungspolitik zwischen Sicherheitsbefriedigung und Friedenssicherung. Zur Aussenpolitik der BRD 1955-1973*; Lothar Wilker, *Die Sicherheitspolitik der SPD 1956-1966. Zwischen Wiedervereinigungs- und Bündnisorientierung*, Bonn-Bad Godesberg, 1977.

6. F. Erler, "Sicherheit und deutsche Einheit II," *SPD-Pressedienst*, April 4, 1955, p. 2.

7. Fritz Erler, "Was ist kollektive Sicherheit?" *Neuer Vorwärts*, October 15, 1954, p. 4.

8. Ibid.

9. Press report of the SPD Bundestag minority of May 23, 1957.

10. Important documents on Soviet policy on the German question are: Soviet outline of a peace treaty with Germany of March 10, 1952; Molotov's proposals in February-April 1954; as well as the note of the Soviet government of November 27, 1958, to the three Western powers on an agreement on a new free-city status for West Berlin (the Berlin Ultimatum); and the note to the FRG, the GDR, and the three Western powers of January 10, 1959, calling for a peace conference, with a draft of a peace treaty with the two German countries. They are published in *Wiedervereinigung und Sicherheit Deutschlands. Eine dokumentarische Diskussionsgrundlage*, edited by Dr. Heinrich von Siegler, Bonn, Vienna, and Zurich, 1963.

11. See Fritz Erler, "Möglichkeiten einer Politik des Disengagements," *Die Neue Gesellschaft*, 1958, no. 5, 437.

12. We use the term "disengagement" to refer to the withdrawal of troops by two neighboring countries or alliances and the creation of militarily free regions. Disengagement is also used to refer to a general military downgrading and the creation of nuclearly downgraded or free areas (nuclear-free zones).

13. For details, see Eugene Hinterhoff, *Disengagement*, London, 1959; Michael Howard, *Disengagement in Europe*, London, 1959; Charles Planck, *Sicherheit in Europa. Die Vorschlage für Rüstungsbeschränkung und Abrüstung 1955-1965*, Munich, 1968.

14. The Chairman of the Labour Party spoke on "The Art of Coexistence" at the Harvard University "Godkin Lectures." See *Manchester Guardian*, February 5, 1957; it also appeared as a book, *The Challenge of Co-Existence*, London, 1957.

Gaitskell's ideas were essentially:

1) gradual withdrawal of all foreign troops from Poland, Hungary, Czechoslovakia, and East and West Germany;

2) the reunification of Germany on the basis of free elections;

3) a neutral European security pact, guaranteeing the territorial integrity of the countries in the neutral zone, to be backed up by the United States, France, and Great Britain;

4) If the Soviet Union were to insist, the Federal Republic would withdraw from NATO, and at the same time the GDR, Hungary, Poland, and Czechoslovakia would withdraw from the Warsaw Pact.

Denis Healey defended similar positions which, however, concentrated more on the military significance of this plan. Neither, however, called for a withdrawal of American troops from Europe. They were to remain in Belgium, Holland, France, and Great Britain. George Kennan also defended similar positions at this time.

15. The proposal by the Polish foreign minister was limited to a nuclear-free zone in Central Europe, excluding all other questions (reunification, withdrawal of allied troops, etc.).

16. See the press report edited by the SPD Press Office, no. 89/58, February 19, 1958.

17. See the articles by Ulrich Albrecht and Günter Gaus in this volume. However, in the meantime a number of regional party officials and leading personalities in the SPD have spoken out in favor of nuclear-free zones in central Europe.

18. On this point see Dieter S. Lutz and Annemarie Grosse-Jütte, eds., *Neutralität eine Alternative? Zur Militär- und Sicherheitspolitik neutraler Staaten in Europa*, Baden-Baden, 1982, p. 9.

19. Palme Report, "Bericht der Unabhängigen Kommission für Abrüstung und Sicherheit," *Common Security*, Berlin, 1982, p. 199.

20. On the most important current scholarly criticism of NATO military doctrine of "flexible response," see K. Peter Stratmann, *NATO-Strategie in der Krise? Militärische Optionen von NATO und Warschauer Pakt in Mitteleuropa*, Baden-Baden, 1981.

21. Text of a speech before the German Society for Foreign Policy, *Frankfurter Allgemeine Zeitung*, December 8, 1981.

22. See Note 3, and on the recent discussion and evaluations in the Federal Republic, Ernst-Otto Czempiel, ed., *Amerikanische Aussenpolitik im Wandel. Von der Entspannungspolitik Nixons zur Konfrontation unter Reagan*, Stuttgart, Berlin, Cologne, and Mainz, 1982.

23. On the course of the modernization debate, see, for example, Klass G. de Vries, "Responding to the SS20: An Alternative Approach," *Survival*, June 21, 1979; Gert Krell, "Plädoyer für Rüstungskontrolle. Zur Kontroverse um die Nachrüstung," in Gert Krell and H. J. Schmidt, *Rüstungswettlauf in Europa*, Frankfurt, in press; as well as the article by Stephan Tiedtke in this volume.

24. Oskar Lafontaine, lord mayor of Saarbrücken of the SPD, one of the most important critics of Federal Chancellor Helmut Schmidt. The text of Lafontaine's memorandum is in *Frankfurter Rundschau*, February 23, 1982.

25. The most important basic document for all arguments on alternative military defense is the comprehensive scientific study by the research team of Carl Friedrich von Weizsäcker at the Starnberger Institute: Carl Freidrich von Weizsäcker, ed., *Kriegsfolgen und Kriegsverhütung*, Munich, 1971. See also Carl Friedrich von Weizsäcker, *Wege in die Gefahr. Eine Studie über Wirtschaft, Gesellschaft und Kriegsverhütung*, Munich and Vienna, 1976, and Horst Afheldt, *Verteidigung und Frieden. Politik mit militärischen Mitteln*, Munich and Vienna, 1976. Also, the new very strategically oriented book by the Committee for Basic Rights and Democracy, eds., *Frieden mit anderen Waffen. Fünf Vorschläge zu einer alternativen Sicherheitspolitik*, Reinbek, 1981 (extracts in the present volume).

26. The appeal for a nuclear-free Europe came from the Russell Peace Foundation in Nottingham, Great Britain, in 1980. It is based on the fundamental ideas from the '50s and '60s and quickly became one of the most influential international Western European appeals. The European movement sees itself as cutting across the blocs, and this appeal has been widely well received in Eastern Europe. It presents the political platform of the Western European Eurocommunist, socialist, and social democratic parties in alliance with large sections of the independent peace movement. This appeal served as the basis for the First European Peace Conference in Brussels, July 2-4, 1982. The Second European Peace Conference will take place on May 7-15, 1983, in Berlin.

27. Robert Havemann's letter to Leonid Brezhnev on the occasion of his visit to the Federal Republic in December 1981 was the first "all-German peace initiative." This letter was signed by almost all distinguished persons in the West German peace movement, as well as by 200 church and non-

church members of an independent peace movement in the GDR. The appeal itself appeared in six daily newspapers, covering several pages at the time of Brezhnev's visit, and called for the withdrawal of all allied troops from the Federal Republic and the GDR and a demilitarized status and neutrality for both parts of Germany.

28. The trade union movement in Poland is by no means dead after the military coup of December 13, 1981; rather, a new form of "dual power," consisting of an independent movement and the Communist Party—military rule, holds sway. Unlike the situation in Hungary in 1956 or Czechoslovakia in 1968, there will be no defeat in Poland extending over many years. If anything, the tide has only temporarily been stemmed. On the other hand, in the GDR an independent peace movement has emerged which, although it is not in opposition to the system in the traditional sense, nonetheless has broad support within the Evangelical Church. This movement has been able to hold major meetings with up to 7,000 participants in the last few months. See *Friedensbewegung in der DDR*, edited by Wolfgang Büscher et al., Hattingen, 1982; Klaus Ehring and Martin Dallwitz, *Schwerter zu Pflugscharen. Friedensbewegung in der DDR*, Reinbek, 1982. A central political document from his movement is the Berlin Appeal, written by the Reverend Reiner Eppelmann and Robert Havemann in January-February 1982. The appeal calls for a peace treaty for both parts of Germany and a social peace corps in the GDR. See also *Atomwaffenfreies Europa, Diskussions- und Informationsbulletin*, no. 1 and no. 2, 1982, which include interviews with Eppelmann and Havemann and reports on the GDR peace movement; for complete texts of all statements from East and West, see *Berliner Begegnungen zur Friedensförderung. Protokolle des Schriftstellertreffens am 13-14. Dez. 1981*, Darmstadt and Neuwiedt, 1982; and Bernd Eisenfeld, *Kriegsdienstverweigerung in der DDR—ein Friedensdienst? Geneis. Befragung. Analyse. Dokuments*, Frankfurt, 1978.

PART I
THE SOVIET THREAT — Is It Real?

Introduction

The four articles in this section are a selection on the security debate in the Federal Republic. The arguments of Brigadier General Christian Krause are a journalistic version of his research project at the Friedrich Ebert Foundation on "Conventional Balance of Forces in Europe" (published in May 1982). This project was a product of the "Study Group on Security and Disarmament in the Research Institute of the Friedrich Ebert Foundation" and hence has played an especially important role in the discussion among the SPD leadership. General Krause concludes that "there is no discernible need to offset the conventional superiority of the Warsaw Pact with nuclear weapons nor to undertake a drastic buildup in NATO's conventional arms. If NATO were to build up its nuclear arms or add chemical weapons to create a military balance, self-deterrence would also be considerably heightened."

It is clear that the arguments in Krause's article will be the basis for the security debate among SPD and FDP forces in the Federal Republic over the next decade. We have put it at the beginning of this volume because it poses the question of the reality of the threat to the Federal Republic in Western Europe in clear terms and draws conclusions of far-ranging importance.

The second article, by Stephan Tiedtke entitled "The Unfathomable Arms Modification," gives a detailed analysis of the arguments for and against stationing the new nuclear medium-range weapons in the Federal Republic and Western Europe. Tiedtke reaffirms German ties to the United States, unlike many other critics of NATO policy. He sees a positive side to the bond between the Federal Republic and the United States (troop presence, political and economic interests) because it tends to deter America from pursuing a security policy that would endanger the stability of Western Europe. Nonetheless, Tiedtke stresses the dangers of "modernization." His argument is balanced, closely reasoned, and informative.

The article by Ekkehart Krippendorff and Michael Lucas is analytical and takes an emphatically "anti-American" position; it demonstrates the systematic connection between security questions and the economic competition between Western Europe or the Federal Republic and the United States. It also sees a direct relationship between the boycott of the natural gas pipeline deal and the stationing of new nuclear weapons. There are of course a number of problems attendant on an analysis that argues in such global terms. Nonetheless Krippendorff and Lucas embody in direct and sharply critical form the continuation of the anti-American critique from the '60s and '70s (the Vietnam generation).

The fourth essay in this section, again by Stephan Tiedtke, gives a concise historical analysis of the development and the crises of the Warsaw Pact: the uprising in Hungary in 1956, the break in Soviet-Chinese relations in 1960-61 with its backlash on Europe, and the crisis in Czechoslovakia in 1968. Tiedtke omits treatment of the events in Poland since their structural consequences for the rest of Eastern Europe cannot yet be discerned. What clearly emerges, however, is that it would be wrong to consider the Eastern bloc homogeneous. The contradictions in the Warsaw Pact system are, despite Soviet political and economic hegemony, replete with unknowns; and Tiedtke makes clear the difference between the strategically important countries (GDR, Poland, and Czechoslovakia) and the less important southern flank (Romania, Hungary, and Bulgaria). It is all the more significant that 1961 (the Berlin Wall), 1968 (Czechoslovakia), and 1980 (Poland) revealed deep crises in the strategic center of Eastern Europe. How the Soviet Union will deal with the crisis in Poland and others that may occur in the future cannot as yet be foreseen.

Rudolf Steinke

CHAPTER 1

WHAT IS A MILITARY THREAT? AN ANALYSIS OF AN AMBIGUOUS CONCEPT

Christian Krause

There are two extreme views on whether the Warsaw Pact constitutes a military threat to Europe. One argues that in fact the military superiority of the Warsaw Pact represents a threat to Europe; consequently NATO must step up its armament effort. At the other pole it is claimed that the military threat is a pathological fantasy; unilateral disarmament is both possible and necessary.

The question of a threat is not merely academic. A threat has certain necessary implications with regard to political action which are all the more severe the greater the threat is deemed to be. We will mention only a few of those consequences here. Thus, for example, the willingness to increase armaments grows despite empty state coffers and declining numbers of draft-age young people each year, i.e., greater sacrifices are demanded for armaments to the detriment of other state priorities. In foreign policy the fear generated by the threat bolsters bloc discipline. National interests are subordinated to alliance defense priorities. In like measure the fruits of détente with the East are called into question. The exigencies of domestic and foreign policy often take precedence over psychological effects, however important they might be. In the public mind a military threat is frequently equated with a national emergency. The appeal to primitive nationalistic instincts strengthens conservative forces and obstructs rational political decisions. We would do well to remember that the decline of the Weimar Republic and Hitler's rise to power were furthered by constant allusions by conservative circles to the defenselessness of the state against external enemies. Such consequences should be a warning against frivolous use of the notion of a military threat. Before using it, one should carefully examine what this concept means.

Threat and the risk of war

In German usage "to threaten" is an acute act. On one side stands the threatening party who demands something, and on the other side is the threatened party, who must decide under pressure whether he will give in to the demand or resist. A military threat is therefore usually equated with the risk of war. For instance, in a brochure published by the Federal government we read: "The superiority of one side over the other entails the risk of vulnerability to political extortion or even an attack."

On the other hand, leading Western politicians deny any relationship between a military threat and the risk of war in Europe. Here are just three representative statements. In 1972 President Nixon said to the American Congress that he regarded a major war in Europe as unlikely in the foreseeable future. In March of 1979 Helmut Schmidt declared before the German Bundestag that Europe was the most secure continent in the entire world despite the buildup of massive military potential. Most recently, on Ash Wednesday of this year Franz Josef Strauss said, to the astonishment of his audience, that as long as the Western alliance functioned, the risk of war in Europe was nil. All these politicians assume that the existence of a huge weapons arsenal in Europe makes any war an act of senseless destruction in which there would be neither victor nor vanquished. But if the threat and the risk of war have nothing to do with one another, what is a military threat?

Threat as a variable in military planning

The term "military threat" comes from the United States. It has been used there for decades as a ploy to justify budget demands for the American forces stationed in Europe. Threat is equated with the existence of the powerful military forces of the Warsaw Pact, which supposedly must be matched by equivalent Western forces.

This ploy has also been taken up by the Federal Republic. The numbers of tanks, aircraft, missiles, ships, and divisions are totted up with an accountant's precision in the White Books of the Federal government, and the numerical advantages of the Warsaw Pact are called a military threat. Then from this threat is deduced the need to provide the Bundeswehr with more funds to enhance and modernize its defense potential.

There are major methodological flaws in the quantitative comparisons of military forces in the White Books. The figures for the armed forces of the Warsaw Pact represent no empirically testable reality; they are and have always been merely estimates and computer calculations by Western intelligence services. There is evidence that in cases of doubt, those figures are chosen which cast NATO in a dimmer light. This is called the "worst-case argument."

Military strength is compared solely in terms of what is countable and measurable. Qualitative features like the training and morale of the soldiers or the quality of arms are left out of account. If one includes French combat forces in NATO (and they could after all be committed together with NATO forces given France's likely consent), then NATO is in fact numerically superior to the Warsaw Pact in Central Europe. The time when a comparison is made also plays a role. The peacetime size of the Bundeswehr is 595,000 men, but the wartime strength is 1.2 million. But in comparing forces the size of the peacetime army is invariably used. Another element of uncertainty lies in the fact that the function of the forces being compared is not considered. While the defender might have fewer tanks than the aggressor, this is no sign of inferiority, for a tank is an element of movement, i.e., attack, while defense is based on firepower. A numerical comparison of divisions is especially questionable, since Warsaw Pact divisions are much weaker than NATO divisions. Division for division, then, Eastern strength is exaggerated and Western strength is underrated.

These flaws make a comparison of military power a poor standard for planning our own armed forces. It incites fears and prompts extra spending, but it sets no realistic planning targets. Rather than compare figures, it would be more reasonable to think in terms of the mission of the military, i.e., to ask what the armed forces are suppsoed to do. The issue then is primarily the military mission of the Bundeswehr as part of NATO, and how defense is to be accomplished. Hence the strength of the aggressor is only indirectly relevant. To construe the results of a comparison of the respective strength of military forces in Europe, which are in fact in many respects debatable, as evidence of a threat seems to be more than questionable. Especially in Germany, where a military threat is equated with the risk of falling under communist rule, the term should be used only when a risk is implied as well. It would seem to be high time, therefore, to strike the word "threat" from the vocabulary of armed forces planning. The term "military potential" would be more accurate.

What in fact is a military threat?

A threat can come only from some person or force that is actually superior, and whose superiority is acknowledged by the threatened party. If the latter prepares for defense in the belief that the threat can be resisted, either war breaks out, with unforeseeable consequences for both sides, or the threatening party has to back down.

To be able to mount the threat of war, a number of conditions must be met. First, a country must be militarily capable of waging war; then there must be the resolve to assume the risk of war; and finally, concrete preparations for war must be undertaken to back up the threat.

The military capacity to wage a war entails more than merely possessing superior potential. The range of responses available to the victim of the attack must also be taken into account. Furthermore, one must also consider the consequences of war for one's own country, and here geostrategic, economic, and many other factors play a role. For example, geostrategically the United States and the Soviet Union are in quite different situations. The United States has no military adversary worthy of consideration on its continent. For the United States war is something that happens abroad and nothing more. But the Soviet Union must always face the possibility of war on several fronts, with its own territory exposed to the effects of enemy weapons.

The resolve to assume the risk of war depends on political motives. The higher the risk assumed, the more solid the political motives must be. The risk of a war in Europe cannot be compared with the risk assumed by the Soviets when they invaded Afghanistan because in Europe nuclear escalation of a conflict cannot be ruled out. Military superiority would not be sufficient grounds for starting a war in Europe. It would be wrong, then, to equate military imbalances with a threat. If, for example, there were strong political reasons, i.e., if one's own existence were at stake, even a country that was militarily inferior could threaten war.

In traditional threat analyses the question of war preparations to back up a threat is usually dealt with only marginally. Major military movements or maneuvers are considered sufficient to elicit the requisite respect from the object of the threat. But they are not enough. As long as NATO is in place, any war in Europe could escalate into a world war. Thus a threat not accompanied by extensive war preparations on the part of the Soviet Union must remain without effect; either it is not meant seriously, or it is based on a miscalculation.

We will now examine the specific situation of the Warsaw Pact in terms of our three criteria—the ability to wage war, the resolve to assume the risk of war, and the preparations for war.

The ability of the Soviet Union to wage a war

The 1970 White Book of the Federal government contains the sentence: "The capacities of an adversary are to be determined from the relationship of its potential to one's own." Let us begin, therefore, with a comparison of potentials. According to the data in the White Book for 1975-76, the NATO countries have about 200 million more inhabitants than the Warsaw Pact nations. The gross social product of the NATO countries is twice that of the Warsaw Pact nations. From other Western sources we find that NATO is about on a par with the Warsaw Pact in conventional armed forces and is superior to them in nuclear warheads. A long-term analysis shows that the NATO countries spend on average about twice as much for armaments as the Warsaw Pact countries. The West has a considerable technological advantage as well. The conclusion to be drawn from this comparison is that NATO's resources are much vaster than those of the Warsaw Pact. Hence the military potential is at the least equivalent in the two cases. As regards the capacity to wage a war, NATO is in a much better position than the Warsaw Pact. This was also confirmed by Franz Josef Strauss in his previously mentioned speech, in which he says, "We are far stronger than the entire communist world."

But the comparison is still not complete. NATO is only one part of the U.S. network of alliances against the Soviet Union. By 1979 the United States had concluded almost 100 bilateral treaties with other countries, and many of them contained military clauses concerning, for example, arms and training aid, flyover rights, interservice support, and bases. The American network of alliances is worldwide: it embraces both the Pacific and the Atlantic and extends into the Indian Ocean. All the industrial nations of the noncommunist world, including Japan, are a part of it. Moreover, U.S. security interests (within certain limits) parallel those of China.

The Western network of alliances controls the sea lanes, and hence a large portion of the world's raw materials and fuels as well. In case of war the Soviet Union, for all practical purposes, must stand alone, if one disregards its handful of weak European allies. Should the Soviet Union attack in Europe, it will always face the risk of a world war. In assessing the Soviet Union's capacity to wage war, therefore, it is not sufficient to think only of Europe. And worldwide the West enjoys overwhelming superiority.

But is the Warsaw Pact superior in conventional arms even in Europe, as we so often hear? First, we must be clear that NATO has enough conventional arms in central Europe to form a solid defensive front from the Baltic to the Alps and, moreover, to hold sufficient operational reserves in combat readiness. In addi-

What Is a Military Threat?

tion, its long-range weapons can paralyze the transportation system in Europe, so that the Warsaw Pact could send in only a very limited number of reinforcements. Thus the NATO defense option is ensured.

If the Warsaw Pact wanted to attack NATO in Europe, it would have to put together superior forces. But it must be added that numerical superiority is not in itself a guarantee that a military attack will be successful. Given the right conditions, an intact defense front can repulse an aggressor even though the latter may be many times stronger. The Warsaw Pact has about ninety-five divisions ready for offense in Europe; sixty of them are Soviet divisions, and the rest belong to the satellite nations. About thirty of the Soviet divisions are stationed in the European satellite countries as occupation forces. The other thirty are stationed in the Western military territories of the Soviet Union. Only a third of the Polish, Czech, and Hungarian divisions are ready for peacetime deployment. The rest must be brought up to their full strength by call-ups. Hence at most sixty Soviet divisions can be regarded as ready for combat. The Warsaw Pact can concentrate sufficient forces in central Europe for an attack only if thirty divisions are brought from the western Soviet Union and the divisions of the satellite countries are mobilized. Without these measures the military potential of the Warsaw Pact is not sufficient for an attack on NATO.

However, the thirty divisions in the western military regions of the Soviet Union are, at the same time, the key military reserves for the entire Soviet Union. If these troops are tied down in Europe, the Soviets have less freedom to act vis-à-vis China and Southeast Asia. If the Soviet leadership should lose control of these forces, either partly or wholly, the military risk entailed would be high. Whether the thirty divisions of the satellite countries can still be considered an offensive potential after the events in Poland is also a serious question.

It is clearly an exaggeration, therefore, to regard the superiority of the Warsaw Pact in Europe in conventional arms as a hard and fast fact. In peacetime it does not actually exist; it would first have to be created through measures that would have serious economic and military consequences for the Soviet sphere of influence.

Moreover, geostrategic weaknesses also detract from the Soviet Union's capacity to wage war. We have already mentioned the possibility of a war on several fronts. Another weak point is the continental nature of the Soviet Union. It has only limited ice-free access to the high seas. Its capacity for a naval war is thus limited. Although it could disrupt Western maritime traffic, it would not be able itself to gain control of the seas. Furthermore vast areas of the Soviet Union are vulnerable to conventional air attacks from American bases or from carrier fleets. But the Soviet Union would have no possibility of attacking American territory from the air. The use of chemical weapons, for instance, would therefore be difficult for the USSR.

These few points alone should suffice to cast some doubts on the Soviet Union's capacity to wage war. As long as NATO and the other members of the Western network of alliances stand solidly together and maintain suitable armed forces, the Soviet Union must in any case reckon with high risk.

What risk of war can the Soviet Union assume?

In speaking about the risk of war for the Soviet Union, we must distinguish between two categories of war. First, there are wars in which the United States is involved directly, and then there are other wars that occur in gray areas of the world, e.g., in places where the respective interests of the world powers are only ambiguously defined. Europe falls in the first category. The spheres of interest are clearly demarcated, and American troops are present.

The Soviet Union has previously used force only when no direct confrontation with the United States was expected. The Cuban crisis was the only exception to this rule. But the Cuban experience made an impression on the Soviet leadership that should remain with them for a long time. If the Soviets hold back, it is because they realize that a clash with the United States at some central point could lead to an exchange of nuclear strikes and perhaps their own extinction.

All claims up to now that the Soviet Union believes that it could wage a nuclear war and win have been revealed as either

What Is a Military Threat?

absurd misunderstandings or propaganda. What the United States knows, the Soviet Union knows as well. It knows, for instance, that the short-term advantages that might be gained through a surprise nuclear first strike would be nullified by the counter-attacks that followed. It can be reliably demonstrated that the Soviet leadership fully appreciates this.

We assume that the Soviet leaders consider the continued existence of the Soviet state and communist society to be their highest priority. They will therefore avoid any risk that jeopardizes these valued ends. The claim that Moscow wants to spread world revolution by force of arms in total disregard of the well-being of the Soviet state is wholly without foundation. In the purges of the '30s Stalin neutralized or liquidated all important advocates of the position that world revolution had priority, and since then no communist leader in the Soviet Union has ever again expounded this view.

In the present power constellation within the USSR and the world at large it is difficult to imagine Soviet aggression against NATO. The change in faces that will take place with the impending leadership succession in the Kremlin might bring modifications in foreign policy, but even a new front line of leaders could not overcome Soviet isolation in the world and thus its inferiority; Soviet willingness to assume the risk of war in Europe should hence remain slight.

What war preparations would the Soviet Union have to make?

An attack on Europe would require preparations on three levels. The first and lowest of them is military preparations within Europe, such as mobilization of combat forces in the satellite countries and an offensive deployment of troops. Threat analyses are usually concerned exclusively with this level.

The next level would entail war preparations within the Soviet Union itself. They would be, for example, steps to switch the economy over to wartime production, the organization of civil defense, and military preparations for a worldwide war on the land, on the sea, and in the air. But there would also be the need to secure, both politically and militarily, a base of operations in the combat zone, i.e., geographically the territory of Poland, Czechoslovakia, and the GDR. Furthermore the Soviet Union would have to inform its allies overseas, such as Cuba and other countries, of its plans and ensure their defense. Finally, the support, or at very least the forebearance, of neutral countries like India that have maintained good relations with the Soviet Union would have to be obtained. This level would also touch the trading and fishing fleets of the Eastern countries, which would have to be ordered back to port promptly so as not to be confiscated by the Western powers.

The third and highest level is the strategic. In the first place, the strategic second-strike capacity of the Soviet Union, which lies in its missile submarines, would have to be assured. Because of the Soviet Union's unfavorable geostrategic position, these ships are concentrated in only three harbors that could be blockaded or destroyed by the West if war broke out. These ships would thus have had to put out to sea even before the start of hostilities. But this in turn would provoke countermeasures from the United States and would escalate the conflict to a higher level from the very outset.

The evacuation of people from densely populated to rural areas is another step that would be entailed at this strategic level. According to present plans the people themselves would have to dig underground shelters for protection against nuclear attacks, since there are neither sufficient quarters nor shelters in the countryside.

Many of the preparatory measures at all three levels could be maintained only for a limited time. Either the West would soon have to yield, or the Soviet Union would have to back down. Thus during a threat phase the Soviet Union would be under the pressure of time as well. This impairs the chances for achieving the goals of the threat. If, however, the USSR were to forgo thorough preparations for a major war, a counterthreat from the West could force it to back down prematurely, with considerable loss of prestige. On the other hand, a poker-type threat in which both sides bluff is inconceivable between two world powers that have the nuclear capacity to destroy one another many times over; the stakes would be too high.

To sum up, the fact is that the potential of the Soviet Union and its allies to wage war is clearly inferior to the West's. It remains at least an open question whether the Warsaw Pact could muster even regional superiority in conventional arms in Europe. Even if it could, it clearly could not exploit such superiority militarily without great risk. Finally, its unfavorable geostrategic position is a weighty negative factor for the Soviet Union. A decision to act would have fateful implications for the USSR, since it would be placing its very existence on the line. The preparations that would be necessary to make a military threat creditable would be so extensive for the Soviet Union and its allies that a threat would be feasible only if the USSR had resolved to enter into the ultimate clash with the West. However, the political motives for such a conflict are lacking.

Conclusions

It was our purpose in this analysis to show that the idea of a military threat has been used deliberately or unconsciously to evoke unfounded responses. Neither military aggression nor the exertion of pressure on NATO in Europe is likely A more probable scenario is that the Soviet Union would get itself into difficulties in Europe, e.g., through events like those in Poland, that will impel it to react erroneously. The West must counter such erroneous reactions firmly but also with respect for vital Soviet interests. The NATO concept of security and détente should prove a better instrument here than a unilateral display of military strength.

On the other hand, unilateral disarmament of the Federal Republic would probably entail severe disruptions in the status quo; the two military alliances are, after all, the most important forces for order in Europe.

But it must be asked whether the countries of Western Europe, and especially the Federal Republic, are not militarily "oversecure." Much that we assume to be the national interest in obtaining more security is after all based on the idea that we are threatened and that we must protect ourselves against extortion or aggression. If this notion is revised—and to encourage doing so was one of the purposes of our study—new perspectives for security policy would be opened.

CHAPTER
2

THE UNFATHOMABLE ARMS MODERNIZATION
Stephan Tiedtke

Analyses of Soviet military policy time and again are faced with the problem of deciphering the true motives of Soviet weapons decisions, since the official reasons given are usually unsatisfactory if not downright misleading. In the West the Soviet bureaucracy is repeatedly accused, not without reason, of being extremely restrictive in the information it provides about its military policy, thereby making arms control much more difficult. This reproach boomerangs, however, with regard to the proposed Western arms "modernization."[1] The chances of bringing the nuclear arms race in Europe under control can be reliably assessed only if the interests that lie behind "modernization" are laid bare (this applies, of course, equally to the reasons for the vehement Soviet resistance to "modernization"). What, then, are the military-stragetic interests of the Soviet Union vis-à-vis Western Europe?

The search for a rational basis for "modernization" first entails penetrating the logic of deterrence, which of course does not mean that deterrence as a system must be accepted. Doubtful notions of balance and exaggerated perceptions of the threat posed by the SS 20 missile merely obscure the inherent danger and the motives of "modernization." If the modernization debate is not to remain wide of its mark, it must venture boldly into the labyrinth of deterrence and military strategy. We intend to do just this. To prevent any misunderstandings, let us make clear from the outset that it is not our purpose here to develop an alternative to "modernization" in the guise of arms control or a peace policy. If, however, our criticisms are couched in military terms, it is in the conviction that the critics of "modernization" must develop an understanding of military matters; otherwise they will hardly be able to persuade their opponents. Furthermore, alternatives to "modernization" can have credibility only if their security implications have been thoroughly thought out. As long as we have no alternative to deterrence, a critical public, demanding arms control, disarmament, or even only military détente, must be able to evaluate the armaments decisions of both blocs from at least two perspectives:

First, do these decisions destabilize deterrence, which as a system is fragile enough anyway, by increasing the risk of war; i.e., do they engender less rather than more security?

Second, will they make future efforts to bring about arms control more difficult? Granted, these are not questions that point the way directly to peace without arms, just as doubts about the reliability and safety of nuclear power plants and the resistance to various construction projects have been unable to shake the nuclear power industry worldwide. Let us first take a look at the traditional arguments for "modernization."

 Is "modernization" a response to the SS 20?

Neither the Pershing II nor cruise missile is a suitable weapon against the Soviet SS 20; their range is too short. However, even if all potential SS 20 firing sites were within striking range of the Pershing II, they could still avoid destruction because they are mobile. Thus the SS 20 cannot be the direct reason for "modernization." Once the SS 20 and modern replacement weapons have been decided on and introduced, however, any arms decision can be legitimated ex post facto by reference to the opponent's decisions. In the West the SS 20 heightens the vulnerability of land-based medium-range weapons, which of course had to be modernized even without the SS 20 to keep deterrence stable. The Pershing II is vulnerable and thus enhances the temptation of a preemptive strike in the case of crisis. It thus undermines the stability of the deterrence system.[2] However, it seems doubtful whether the mobility of the modernization system will indeed create the desired stability within the small space of the Federal Republic, with its high population density.[3] The opposite seems rather to be the case: Soviet military planning for crisis contingencies would necessarily have to aim at knocking out the Pershing II, which is, after all, a first-strike weapon, before it could be employed against Soviet territory; the weapon suited for this is the SS 20.

What is the balance of power in strategic arms in Europe?

Quantitative demonstrations of Soviet strategic superiority in Europe, like, for instance, the one-page table in the latest White Book from the Federal government, are intended to legitimate "modernization" and back up demands for Soviet limitations. Peace researchers have aptly criticized this obvious manipulation by the institutional experts of the West German government and permanently shook the foundations of this sort of legitimation of "modernization."[4] But in their endeavors to present a more accurate picture of the strategic balance of power in Europe, a number of critics of "modernization" have made the same systematic error as those who support it; hence they wind up down a path where the dangers of "modernization" simply are not to be found. Both sides convey the impression that strategic weapons in Europe can be weighed meaningfully against one another in isolation from other nuclear weapons, and that a strategic conflict between the two superpowers in Europe could take place on a level somewhere between the tactical and strategic. But the engagement of even a part of NATO's strategic weapons in Europe, namely, the sea-launched missiles aimed at Soviet territory, would probably mean an all-out nuclear war. This is to say nothing of the Soviet deterrence doctrine, the aim of which is to avoid a limited nuclear war in Europe, which would certainly become a European strategic war (more on this later). A comparison of forces can be meaningful only if it includes nuclear systems at all combat levels and the combat potential of all nations that could be drawn into an East-West conflict (thus also the Chinese).

In reality NATO's interest in "modernization" has nothing to do with achieving a balance in numbers with the Soviet potential in Europe. The numerical balance of forces will have been scarcely changed even after "modernization." For every Pershing II, one American Pershing IA will be withdrawn; and in terms of the number of warheads, the SS 20 potential aimed at Western Europe exceeds the number of cruise missiles deployed. This means that in the future, the numerical balance of power in European strategic arms will evolve rather to the detriment than in favor of the West.

Why did the Soviet Union introduce the SS 20?

The Soviet bureaucracy has left its critics just as much in the dark about the reasons that led to the introduction of the SS 20 as does NATO with regard to "modernization." The following reasons perhaps had something to do with the Soviet Union's decision to develop and introduce the SS 20:

a. *Conflict with China*: by the end of the '50s (the Ussuri incident) the Soviet leadership probably became certain of the inevitability of a nuclear arms race with China. Foreign policy considerations, however, have imposed restraints on the Soviet Union (unlike China) in this race. The SALT agreements, seen by the Soviets as a preparatory phase for further agreements on strategic nuclear potential, block, at least ultimately, the Soviet option of threatening China with strategic weapons. To compensate for this a solution had to be sought in medium-range systems, which are no threat to the United States and accordingly are not subject to the SALT limitations. The nuclear arms race with China required a modernization of the Soviet medium-range potential, which was based on obsolete missiles of the SS 4 and SS 5 types (introduced in 1961-64). The pressure taken off Soviet strategic potential by the introduction of the SS 20 (the first SS 20s were deployed against China) was all the more necessary since the United States no longer included the contingency of an American-Chinese conflict in its armed forces planning in the late '70s, and its strategic systems are now aimed exclusively at the Soviet Union.

b. The technological trend: Virtually no military expert would dispute that the SS 4 and SS 5 are technologically obsolete in terms of the logic of deterrence and that Soviet medium-range missiles must thus be modernized. The fruit of this modernization, the SS 20, makes optimal use of the technological resources the Soviet Union has developed in the strategic arms race (multiple warheads and precise aim), if we leave unasked the question of the extent to which it is opportune to deploy this arms technology against Western Europe.

c. Neutralizing differences in interests within the bureaucracy: The internal logic of technological development is hardly a sufficient explanation of why the Soviet Union has deployed the SS 20 against Western Europe. It has been assumed that this was the result of a compromise between different interest groups within the Soviet leadership. The wishes of its military notwithstanding, the USSR did manage to get the forward-based nuclear potential of NATO (FBS) included in the agreements, although the Soviet Union feels just as threatened by it as by American strategic missiles. The Soviet military, so goes the argument, demanded and got a modernization of medium-range missiles in compensation.

d. Reasons of military strategy: The Soviets justify the modernization of their European strategic potential by referring to "MIRV-ed" American Poseidon missiles, some of which were placed under the NATO Supreme Command as medium-range weapons in 1970. This seems plausible, since the Poseidon missiles, even though they are said to be not overly precise, reduce the survivability and hence the deterrent effect of the SS 4 and SS 5.

In NATO the modernization of its medium-range system is also explained by the fact that the capacity of Western bombers to penetrate the enemy's defenses to attack bases and communication lines in the rear has considerably declined. Only missiles, it is said, can reliably do this job.[5] Soviet military planners could also adopt this argument: the capacity of Soviet bombers to penetrate the European hinterlands of NATO has been considerably reduced. However, why NATO needs the Pershing IIs as a replacement for bombers when the Pershing IIs are a first-strike weapons, and why sea-based medium-range or cruise missiles are not sufficient remains unanswered.

It would be a threat to NATO if the Soviet Union were able to achieve with the SS 20s a first-strike capability against the nuclear weapons in Western Europe. The Soviet Union's purpose, it is alleged, with such a capacity is to create a *fait accompli* in Western Europe that would keep the United States out of a battle for Western Europe that was already lost.[6] However, all the risk that the Soviet Union would thereby be assuming does not jibe with this scenario. First, the Soviet Union cannot rule out the possibility that the sea-based medium-range missiles under NATO would not be fired in response. Second, France and Great Britain, the nuclear powers directly concerned, which will have about 1,000 sea-based nuclear warheads by the early '90s, could hardly forgo a reprisal strike.

The strategic disparities between NATO and the Warsaw Pact

The military standoff between the United States and Western Europe on the one hand and the Soviet Union on the other is marked by strategic differences that have far-reaching implications for deterrence. Unlike the United States, which is threatened "only" by the Soviet nuclear potential, the Soviet Union is threatened from two quarters (disregarding for the moment the Chinese): namely, by American strategic missiles and bombers and by the nuclear weapons deployed in Europe. In terms of deterrence the Soviet Union finds itself put in an extremely unfavorable position by this double threat. In both Soviet and American eyes, the function of the American nuclear potential in Western Europe is to enable the United States to limit nuclear war in Europe. The Soviet Union thus must cope with an almost insoluble problem: if as they see it, the United States were to start or threaten a limited nuclear war in Europe, the Soviet Union would have only one choice: either to join in, which would mean accepting that its territory, in contrast to the American continent, would be drawn into the nuclear conflict as well, or to escalate the conflict to an all-out worldwide cataclysm, thereby running the risk of its own annihilation.[7] Since neither alternative is acceptable to the Soviet Union, the one possibility left in this dilemma is to maintain the deterrent effect of its military potential at such a high level that a war in Europe would become an unthinkable risk for the United States. Given this interest, if it is to remain creditable, Soviet deterrence strategy must include total strategic nuclear potential in its calculations even in a European conflict.

Two conclusions for the modernization discussion can be drawn from the strategic disparity in Europe: first, the Soviet Union must regard the respective nuclear potentials of the Western nations as a unit. The fears about the threat posed by the Soviet medium-range potential repeatedly voiced by Western Europeans are in the Soviets' judgment unfounded, since they disregard the global nuclear context. Second, then, negotiations on strategic weapons in Europe can be successful only if they are carried out within the framework of, and at the same time as, the SALT negotiations. This global strategic context of the Soviet missile buildup has been taken into account in the SALT negotiations to the extent that the United States has at least implicitly assured the Soviet Union that the "agreed global strategical balance of forces would not be violated by American changes in forward-based systems."[8] But this is precisely what "modernization" is all about.[9]

Can NATO tolerate Soviet strategic superiority in Europe?

It should be clear from our argument that numerical comparisons of forces that stay at the level of nuclear confrontation make little sense, especially considering the course a nuclear war would probably take. Nevertheless the stability of the deterrence system, with its various stages of escalation from a conventional war to engagement of the strategic potential of the two nuclear superpowers, requires such point-by-point comparisons of forces —not, of course, in terms of a quantitative balance sheet of respective potentials but in terms of the credibility of military options, particularly deterrence options. The goal of the Soviet strategic arms buildup in Europe is to deter the United States from waging a limited nuclear war in Europe. The means is the threat of escalating a European war to American territory. It is also in the interests of Western Europeans to prevent a nuclear war in Europe. Since, therefore, the Americans are prepared if necessary to escalate a European war into an all-out nuclear war as part of their deterrence policy, the respective interests of Western Europe and the Soviet Union converge, however different the rationale on one point here, namely, the existential interests of the United States that would be served by its entry into a Europan conflict.[10] A result of this "common" interest is that both sides, as part of the logic of deterrence, must deem the nuclear superiority—strategic arms included—of the Soviet Union in Europe a necessity.

Such superiority is in line not only with the basic thinking of the Western flexible-response strategy but also with Western European interests: NATO inferiority at levels short of strategic arms constitutes an instrumental constraint on escalating to intercontinental warheads.[11] If conventional or nuclear parity exists, the risk of a regionalization of a European nuclear war, that is, the risk that the United States will stay out of a European war, is automatically increased. For the Soviet Union parity is a token of American capacity, and in the event, American readiness, to risk a regional nuclear war in Europe.

From the NATO standpoint, of course, Western inferiority in medium-range missiles must never become so great as to give the Soviet Union an undisputed upper hand in escalation. That would mean that if the Soviets were to attack Western Europe, NATO would no longer be able to deter them with its medium-range potential but would have to directly threaten reprisal with U.S. strategic systems—not a very credible alternative considering the vulnerability of American territory.[12]

The U.S. interest in nuclear disengagement from the European theater

Since Soviet nuclear attack on American territory has become a credible possibility (since the '50s), and the American nuclear threat to the Soviet Union has to that extent become implausible, it must lie in U.S. national interests to prevent nuclear endangerment to American territory should a conflict break out in Europe. But should the United States succeed wholly and completely in ruling out this possibility, it would mean the end of NATO in its present form (France withdrew from NATO in 1966 because de Gaulle believed France could no longer rely on the guarantee of American nuclear protection). For this reason American strategy in the alliance is aimed at forestalling a nuclear threat to U.S. territory as long as possible in the event of a European war. However, Western Europeans have exactly the opposite interests: to limit destruction the United States should enter the fray as early as possible and threaten the use of its tactical and then its strategic nuclear weapons if the Soviet Union does not promptly halt its aggression. NATO has had to live with these contradictory interests for more than twenty years. Alliance decisions that could affect military strategy must, if this divergence of interests is not to split NATO at the seams, be susceptible of an interpretation such that Western Europeans and Americans could both feel their interests were safeguarded, i.e., they must be ambivalent. This also applies to the modernization decision. The United States could see that its interests in disengagement are ensured in the fact that the land-based missiles in Europe are clearly distinguishable from the United States' global strategic potential. Their use makes a Soviet retaliatory strike against American territory less likely than if the sea-based medium-range missiles (which represent a floating link between the traditional nuclear weapons in Western Europe and the United States' strategic potential) were used instead. On their account, Western Europeans could argue that an American missile strike from Europe against the Soviet Union would, in Soviet eyes, be a strategic attack. Theo Sommer put this Western European hope quite trenchantly: "As if this trick with a second domicile would really deceive the Soviets as to the true identity of the launcher."[13]

Does the Soviet Union care whether a missile attack originated in the United States or in Western Europe?

If the United States, as Theo Sommer suggests, were really so clearly placing its own existence on the line with the new weapons, it would hardly have agreed to "modernization." That this is not so clear becomes evident if we consider what the Pershing II missiles mean for the Soviet Union in terms of deterrence policy: the United States has 108 launch ramps for the Pershing II, designed for strikes at military targets in the Soviet Union.

Can the Soviet Union respond to the use of this limited potential with all-out nuclear war and thus risk its own extinction, especially if losses among the Soviet population are to be minimized? Must it not rather interpret the use of the Pershing IIs as a signal from the United States that it wants to prevent a nuclear war of annihilation? The Pershing II has driven the Soviet Union into a corner, for it now faces the dilemma of a decision that both superpowers want to avoid—starting an unlimited nuclear war.

In a certain sense the United States has thereby gained the upper hand in escalation at the level directly prior to the engagement of strategic nuclear arms. Calculations of this sort may seem unrealistic and dangerous, and indeed they are; however, they fit neatly into Western deterrence doctrine, which regards a systematic escalation, interrupted by "pauses" (to resolve the conflict), up to an all-out nuclear war as quite thinkable. Following this logic, the Soviet Union would have only one recourse—which, however, would be devastating for the Federal Republic—namely, to knock out the Pershing IIs before they could be launched. The scenario of an American missile attack from American territory or from submarines makes graphically clear that the question asked earlier must be answered with an emphatic no: for the Soviet Union it would be an unequivocal signal that the United States had begun an unlimited nuclear war.

Is there a difference for the Soviet Union between forward-based nuclear systems and the new weapons?

The weapons entailed in the "modernization" decision by no means represent the first time that the Soviet Union has had to face a nuclear threat by NATO from Western European territory. Before the Cuban crisis the Thor missiles in England and Italy and the Jupiter missiles in Turkey were aimed at targets in the Soviet Union, and even today fighter bombers can reach the Soviet Union with nuclear weapons from Western Europe.

Has "modernization" therefore changed anything for the Soviet Union as regards deterrence policy? The U.S. interest contained in its phasing out the Thor and Jupiter missiles[14] is a graphic illustration of the difference between the forward-based systems (FBS) and new weapons; moreover, as part of the flexible-response strategy, it reflects American interest in not permitting a nuclear war in Europe to escalate to American or Soviet territory; or if it does, then only in a later stage of the conflict. The phasing out of these missiles was intended to convince the Soviet Union of U.S. readiness to engage in a limited nuclear war inasmuch as it shifted the United States' strategic threat to Soviet territory away from Western Europe. Although the logic of its deterrence policy makes it impossible for the Soviet Union to accept a limited war in Europe, relief from having to decide between the options described above was in the interests of Soviet security. The nuclear weapons that remained in Western Europe and the system that was later introduced either would not be able to reach the Soviet Union (Pershing I) or were not expressly intended for use solely against Soviet territory but also against targets in Eastern Europe, the doorstep to the Soviet Union. With the flexible-response strategy the Soviet Union could assume that nuclear weapons would not be used against Soviet territory until a later stage of the conflict, if at all. In contrast, the modernization weapons are intended expressly for use against Soviet territory and hence represent a return to the status before the Cuban crisis.

Why "modernization"?

Let us now return to our original question. What are the reasons for again threatening Soviet territory with medium-range missiles from Western Europe; why has NATO returned to the status before Cuba?

However much certain advocates of "modernization" would like us to believe so, it is hardly to be assumed that the United States is again prepared to allow a European conflict, if one should occur, to put its territory in greater peril. U.S. policy toward Western Europe and unambiguous statements by American politicians[15] are evidence against such a readiness. One point at least seems certain: use of the Pershing IIs makes a Soviet retaliatory strike against American territory less likely than would be the case if the sea-based Poseidon missiles were brought into play. This means that the U.S. strategic capacity to escalate in Europe has become more credible. This might seem to be desirable for Western Europeans as well, both in view of the divergence of interests between Europe and the United States—which makes the problem all the more real—and by the very logic of deterrence. If the U.S. nuclear guarantee of Western European security can extend "only" so far as the threshold of a strategic exchange of nuclear strikes, which would include both U.S. and Soviet territories, it should then be in the deterrence interests of the Western Europeans to guarantee escalation up to just this point.

Even then some doubt will of course remain whether in fact the United States will be prepared to accept the risk of the Soviet Union seeing the firing of Pershing II missiles as the overture to a strategic nuclear war. However, because the system is stationed in Western Europe, pressure for the United States to launch them is relatively high. Seen in this way, "modernization" is the logical consequence of reduced American nuclear protection for Western Europe. But what does this mean for the stability of deterrence?

The price of a creditable American guarantee of protection below the strategic threshold is greater instability for the deterrence system as a whole. The logical response of the Soviet Union to "modernization" as far as deterrence is concerned would be to station equivalent medium-range systems in Cuba to make up for the strategic structural disadvantage vis-à-vis the United States and to attain a state of "equal security" (the Soviet term for balance) with the United States. The failure of this attempt in 1962 is of course hardly an encouragement to venture this risk again. Thus basically the only military option open to the Soviet Union is a response to the Pershing II missiles, i.e., to destroy them before they can be launched.

To escape from the dilemma of having to begin an unlimited nuclear war against its own interests as a response to Pershing II, and moreover, since the Pershing II is a first-strike weapon, the Soviet Union may feel it has no choice but to undertake this preemptive strike against Western Europe. An arms decision, however, which in the case of conflict forces the opponent to try a preemptive use of nuclear weapons can hardly be seen as contributing to the stability of the deterrence system.[16]

In view of such risks, why have the Western Europeans and the United States agreed to "modernization"? The hope that the Soviet Union will not assume the risk entailed by a preemptive strike is just as unfounded as the American hope that the Soviet Union will not respond to the use of the Pershing II by a strike against the United States. The heightened Western readiness to accept this risk can only be explained in terms of the changes in American military strategy, as codified in the Presidential Directive 59. The goal of this "new" strategy is not only the capacity to wage a limited nuclear war in Europe (that has been the aim for some time) but above all, with its counterforce option (offensive attacks against enemy military installations), to meet the contingency of a limited strategic nuclear war against the Soviet Union. The upshot of this is that in addition to their deterrence function, these U.S. strategic arms take on an increasingly independent warfare function. This also applies to the strategic arms in Europe. As first-strike weapons, precision cruise missiles, which are all but impossible for the enemy to stop, and the Pershing II, just as precise, fit perfectly into this concept of strategic war.

The United States is attempting to widen its scope for action vis-à-vis the Soviet Union with its "new" military strategy, since parity at the strategic level, so goes the argument, has condemned the United States to immobility against expansive Soviet foreign policy. In 1974 the then American secretary of defense, Schlesinger, formulated this program in so many words in his comment that the American president must not allow the mantle of world leadership to slip from his shoulders.[17] For reasons of domestic politics, however, strategic arms will be accepted in the United States as arms for warfare and as instruments of policy only if the American populace can at the same time be assured that the devastating consequences of a strategic nuclear war will be thereby reduced. This is just what the counterforce strategy (the attempt to knock out a large part of the Soviet strategic system, with what survives being concentrated on military targets in the United States) hopes to provide. The price for this, of course, is that this strategy, with its attempt to spare a greater part of the American population, increases the likelihood of war. If the American counterforce strategy were consonant with Western European security interests, the consent of Western Europeans to "modernization" would make good military sense; but the "advantages" of an American strategy aimed at sparing the greater part of the U.S. population is of no benefit to Western Europe, especially the Federal Republic. On the contrary, the greater risk of war means a heightened threat to its population.

Now let us sum up what we have said in four points:

1. The Western European consent to "modernization" is militarily defensible insofar as it draws the consequences from a nonexistent U.S. readiness to escalate a regional European conflict to the intercontinental level. The American guarantee of nuclear protection is made more credible by "modernization," although only up to the threshold of engagement of its strategic arms system.

2. The United States is ready to take this step (which also has its risk for America), since the modernization weapons fit into the American counterforce strategy concept. Without "modernization" a vacuum would be created for strategy in geopolitically important Europe. As the use of the new European counterforces against targets in the Soviet Union need not mean the prologue to an unlimited nuclear war of annihilation, they represent a new stage of escalation prior to a strategic nuclear war.

3. The Soviet Union cannot accept this strategic option of strategic arms in Europe because of its geostrategic disadvantage vis-à-vis the United States. It can be expected that should conflict break out, the Soviet Union will see itself forced to take the step, heavy with risks for it too, of a preemptive strike to

destroy the modernization system; the result, of course, would be that the countries involved, with Federal Republic of Germany heading the list, would cease to exist. This means, then, that the greater risk of war entailed by the American strategy falls primarily on Western Europe, where the "advantage" of the U.S. strategy, namely, that of sparing the greater part of the American population, shows its obverse side.

4. The willingness of the Western Europeans to assume this risk can no longer be justified militarily, even in terms of Soviet arms decisions; its justification must rather be sought in the politics of Western European-U.S. relations.

Should Western Europe disengage itself militarily from the United States?

If modernization heightens the risk of war, and as a consequence of its being bound to the overall design of U.S. military policy, Western Europe is forced into a tougher confrontational course vis-à-vis the Soviet Union, and thus an intensification of the arms race, Western Europeans must indeed ask whether the trans-Atlantic military partnership is still consonant with their military security interests.

The idea of Western Europe as an "island of the blessed" between the superpowers is an absurd response to this dilemma. Indeed, should a nuclear war break out between the United States and the Soviet Union, Western Europe would be drawn into this conflict disengaged from the United States or not. But if so, then it must be in Western Europe's vital interests not to separate itself militarily from the United States but rather to do its utmost to influence U.S. military policy (this is just what American critics of the military policies of the Reagan administration are hoping for, inasmuch as they see no possibility for them to influence the government's course in the United States at this time).

This must not be construed as a vote in favor of the existing structures of NATO but rather as a plea for an equal partnership between the United States and Western Europe, especially in European security matters. As long as no military détente has been reached to defuse the confrontation between the blocs, military disengagement from the United States would lead to a conventional and nuclear arms buildup in Western Europe the outcome of which cannot be assessed.[18] Surely this cannot be the Soviet aim, however incessantly its propaganda calls for a dissolution of the military blocs. Under present strategic conditions the Soviet Union, as we have shown, continues to be interested in keeping the United States as intimately engaged as possible in the European theater, so that should it come to a war in Europe, the United States would be forced to put its own national existence on the line.

Ultimately, only those making the decisions can confirm whether our interpretation of the military and deterrent motives of "modernization" is correct, barring logical errors. Since they have linked the modernization decision to a commitment to arms control talks in the coming years—before the modernization systems have been installed—they will, one hopes, be forced by an increasingly critical public to make their modernization decision more creditable than they have done so far or to abandon it.

NOTES

1. To mention just a few references: A. Mechtersheimer, " 'Modernisierung' gegen Sicherheit. Zur Stationierung amerikanischer Mittelstreckenraketen in der Bundesrepublik Deutschland," in Studiengruppe Militärpolitik, *Aufrüsten, um abzurüsten?*, rororo aktuell 4717, Reinbek bei Hamburg, 1980, pp. 54-66; D. S. Lutz, "Wieviel Vernichtung (skapazität) ist genug? Ein Worst-Case-Szenario gegen Westeuropa," ibid., pp. 78-94; A.-A. Guha, *Der Tod in der Grauzone*, Fischer TB 4217, Frankfurt, 1980.
2. See M. Leitenberg, "Die taktischen Nuklearwaffen grosser Reichweite der NATO und WVO," in Studiengruppe Militärpolitik, pp. 34 ff.
3. See G. Wettig, "Die Sowjetunion und die eurostrategische Problematic," in *PVS*, 1980, no. 4, p. 355.
4. See D. S. Lutz, "Das militärische Kräfteverhältnis bei dem euronuklearen Waffensystem," in *DGF-Jahrbuch 1979-80, Zur Entspannungspolitik in Europa*, Baden-Baden, Nomos-Verlag, 1980, pp. 357-400; E. Müller, " 'Nach'-Rüstung und Rüstungswettlauf," in *Argumente 3*, Tübingen, Verein für Friedenspädagodik, 1980.
5. L. Ruehl, "Der Beschluss der NATO zur Einführung nuklearer Mittelstrecken-waffen," in *Europa-Archiv*, 1980, no. 4, pp. 101-16.
6. See G. Wetting, p. 350.

7. Ibid., p. 347; for more on the Soviet Union's strategic arms control, see S. Tiedtke, *Rüstungskontrolle aus sowjetischer Sicht. Die Rahmenbedingungen der sowjetischen MBFR-Politik*, Frankfurt on Main, Campus-Verlag, 1980.

8. Ibid., p. 348.

9. This gives rise to the question whether rearmament might not have been conceived of as a means to intensify American pressure for the resumption of SALT II negotiations.

10. In accordance with the realization that each side sees itself only as the victim of aggression; the means of engagement, however, differ: the Western Europeans rely primarily on exerting influence on the decisions of the American president, while the Soviet Union relies on the use of specific weapons systems and military options.

11. See A. Mechtersheimer, "Weder Abschreckung noch Verteidigung. Zur militärischen Funktion der Bundeswehr damals und heute," in *Friedensanalysen*, 14, Frankfurt on Main, Edition Suhrkamp 1056, NF 56, 1981, p. 244.

12. On the concept of escalation dominance, see K.-Peter Stratmann, *NATO-Strategie in der Krise*, Baden-Baden, Nomos-Verlag, 1981, p. 14.

13. Theo Sommer, "Weltuntergang als Notlösung," in *Die Zeit*, March 9, 1979.

14. The American intercontinental missiles made this phasing out possible; until they came onto the scene the United States had to rely on FBS to mount a nuclear threat to the Soviet Union on a broad front.

15. In September 1979 Henry Kissinger underscored this point quite clearly at a meeting in Brussels.

16. See G. Wettig, p. 356.

17. Quoted in A. Mechtersheimer, p. 248.

18. Destabilization of deterrence necessarily leads to intensification of the arms race.

CHAPTER
3

"ONE DAY WE AMERICANS WILL HAVE TO CONSIDER THE DESTRUCTION OF EUROPE"

Ekkehart Krippendorff and Michael Lucas

The unofficial premises of the Pershing II

In the public discussion on the NATO decision of December 1979 to deploy the new American middle-range missiles in Western Europe too little was said about the point that these weapons, aimed at the Soviet Union, must be seen in a more global rather than a merely European context. To be sure, the official justification for stationing Pershing II and cruise missiles insists that they are intended as a deterrent to a conventional or nuclear attack from the Soviet Union or the Warsaw Pact nations. Yet there also exists a broad consensus, even among observers with rather conservative leanings, that an unprovoked war of aggression against Western Europe can be all but ruled out. Nonetheless both superpowers leave room in various game plans for the contingency of a limited nuclear war in central Europe. If we extend the horizon of potential conflicts beyond Europe, then the preparations for war currently taking place mostly on German soil begin to make sense. Indeed, the possible scenario for a conflict leading to a nuclear war has its origins in the Third World, which since World War II, the loss of China, and especially since the early sixties, with their innumerable military actions, has provided the setting for a third world war. In his article "Countdown to Nuclear War," Daniel Ellsberg pointed this out:

> Limited nuclear war against countries that do not have nuclear weapons has never for one year been unthinkable over the last 35 years to

the leaders of our country. They have secretly been prepared to think about, plan for, and carry out threats of nuclear strikes against such countries in virtually every term of every administration since 1945—Korea, China, Laos, Vietnam. Since these countries have allied to the Soviet Union it has been necessary to prepare for the possibility of response—even nuclear response—by the Soviets. One could pretty well approximate the range of contingencies that have had some reality in the minds of the planners who are designing our nuclear strategy by saying they involve the possibility of nuclear responses by the Soviets to nuclear initiatives by the United States or by U.S. allies . . .

—and indeed, a first strike in the Third World against adversaries who do not have nuclear weapons. To this extent the American insistence on stationing the new middle-range missiles (and the neutron bomb as well) does have to do with the protection of Western Europe, presuming a more aggressive military engagement of the United States in the Third World to regain lost territories. In other words, Western Europe must be armed for a limited nuclear war so that the United States can pursue its rollback strategy vis-à-vis Soviet influence and Soviet (or Cuban) presence (as in Africa), including the use of nuclear weapons, if need be, in the Third World without the danger of a Soviet strike "from the "rear" in Europe. It must be borne in mind that this is not a new strategy first developed under Reagan but in fact dates back at least to the second half of Carter's presidency. It was set out in detail in Document PD 59, which caused a justifiable stir when it appeared. The United States had to break the state of military paralysis in which it had been languishing since the Vietnam War. Furthermore, there were to be no more Vietnams, in the sense of the militarily and politically frustrating predicament of not being able to use its nuclear potential: a "second Vietnam," i.e., an American withdrawal and a military defeat, rather patchily concealed at that, would never happen again. American engagement would also have the nuclear option available if necessary. Even under Carter, who was unquestionably more scrupulous in military questions, Secretary of Defense Brown threatened the possible unilateral use of nuclear weapons in the Middle East to protect "Western interests" (February 1980).

Whatever the case, this scenario of U.S. blackmail of a third country with ties to the Soviet Union is by no means farfetched and unrealistic. It must be remembered that this was exactly the situation in the 1962 Cuban missile crisis, when nuclear war almost happened as a result of a consciously calculated risk. At that time the United States threatened a nuclear first strike if the Soviet Union did not withdraw its missiles from Cuba; Khrushchev backed down.

Those "thirteen days" when the world stood on the brink of a nuclear war are celebrated as a victory of the United States' and Kennedy's strategic composure. The Soviet Union firmly resolved not to let this happen a second time, and its massive nuclear arms buildup dates from October 1962. We can be reasonably sure that the present Soviet general staff, much better armed with nuclear weapons, will not "blink first" the next time (just after the crisis Robert Kennedy said, "We stood eyeball to eyeball, and the other guys blinked first"). A possible scenario in 1981 might be a U.S. ultimatum on withdrawal of Cuban troops from Angola and the Soviets from Afghanistan, backed up by nuclear force—the demand itself has already been made.

The internal purpose of the European missiles and the discussion of strategy

The NATO decision to station missiles in Europe, made under Carter we might point out, assumes a further dimension seen in this context: as the risk grows of Western Europe's being drawn into a local nuclear war in the Third World started by the United States, Israel, or an Arab power to provide rear-guard support against the Soviet Union, Western Europe itself becomes more and more vulnerable to extortionist demands made by the United States. This applies especially to the Federal Republic of Germany, which is the most exposed part of Western Europe. American diplomats and politicians stated this openly, if on a smaller scale, in 1979 and 1980 with regard to West Berlin: this isolated city, the Eastern bloc's open wound, had once been solicitously maintained by subsidies as a challenge to the German Democratic Republic; now, however, its function in American strategy took a 180-degree turn. The Federal Republic was placed forthwith on notice in questions of armaments policy as well, with allusions, no longer veiled, to the (American) Allies' military defense function in Berlin. The city was used as leverage against the Federal Republic, for after all, it could be "let go." The American nuclear presence on West German territory is thus becoming a vital threat, if it has not done so already. However, whereas in the past the exchange of nuclear strikes in theoretical strategic game plans had also included American targets, whether purely military or cities, today's contingency planning assumes the "controllability" of limited nuclear strikes, restricted, at least in a first phase of the conflict, to Western Europe, i.e., in the first instance, the territory of the Federal Republic. The European missiles make just such a war possible; they would keep combat operations, that is, nuclear devastation, away from U.S. territory because in the strategic pipe dreams of the United States, a Soviet nuclear counterstrike would be directed wholly against targets in Western Europe. This would give the two superpowers time for a stock-taking pause to decide whether to launch direct attacks and destroy one another as well. The way has been cleared for Western Europe and the territory of the Federal Republic to serve as a theater for nuclear war if one should break out. The credibility of U.S. deterrence is thereby vindicated, since, so reason American military strategists, the Soviet Union would not take seriously a deterrence policy or the threat of nuclear war that put a country's own cities on the line at the risk of their destruction.

These modest reflections on strategy must also be seen in the light of the political and economic competition currently going on between the United States and Western Europe, particularly the Federal Republic. "Among themselves," so to speak, American NATO officers draw the ultimate consequences with a mixture of cynicism and historical realism. In 1980 the Supreme Commander of the French nuclear forces, Admiral Antoine Sanguinetti, reported on some of his obviously close acquaintances among his American professional colleagues: "When I was serving in NATO, now more than twenty years ago, I was struck time and again by the arguments of some American officers. They would declare to me quite openly: 'Look, I'm convinced that one day we Americans will have to ponder the destruction of Europe. You are, after all, by far our keenest competitor.' And that is true. Russia is still a negligible quantity. Its gross product is just about half of the Europeans'. Europe is by far the leading trading power. If the United States is now undergoing a crisis, if the economies of the West have problems, it can only benefit the American economy if Europe is destroyed" (quoted in *Die Neue*, March 20, 1980).

Call it what you will—diseased thinking, pathological science fiction—the fact remains that in international "security policy," these or other less explicitly economic interests are first quite candidly and soberly translated into terms of the nuclear destruction of central Europe and Germany, and weapons systems and military strategy are then planned with this in mind. We could repress this whole situation as a nightmare and imagine that things could never go so far, that at the last minute the "voice of reason" in responsible statesmen will prevent such a catastrophe. However, the past gives us no evidence of this "voice of reason" to support such a—psychologically plausible—attitude. On the contrary, if we can learn anything from history, it is the lack of reason in *raisons d'état*, and that the logic of *raisons d'état* has started wars, not prevented them. The historian George F. Kennan, a trustworthy observer with considerable experience of his own and by no means inclined to dramatize, writes (1980): "I know of no point in modern history at which such a collapse of political communication and such a triumph of unrestrained military mistrust as in current Soviet-American relations has not ultimately led to armed conflict."

Differences within the alliance over détente

But even if things did not go so far, the "renewal of the Cold War" by the United States, i.e., the strategy of confrontation with the Soviet Union, has a direct "European dimension" in that it is intended to put the damper on European-Soviet, and especially West German-Soviet, détente. Although détente is also in American interests, it has been more an offensive challenge to the Soviet Union (as was demonstrated under Carter), with a view toward weakening its political leadership (e.g., the human rights campaign), than a policy giving priority to the easing of military and economic tensions. However, the related American hopes with regard to Soviet and Eastern European markets have not been fulfilled. For Western Europe and the Federal Republic, on the other hand, détente has paid off economically. Since 1980 Western Europe has had a greater economic interest in the Soviet market than has the United States, despite resumed U.S. wheat deliveries. The Federal Republic has become the most important trading partner in the Eastern bloc. In chemical products West Germany accounts for 50 percent of Common Market trade with the East and 35 percent of the trade of all OECD countries with the CMEA. A deterioration of East-West relations would thus hit Western Europe harder than the United States. From the standpoint of European-American competition and rivalry, the United States even has an economic interest in subverting détente, as beneficial as it has been to Western Europe.

This clash of European and American interests has also been evident in their different reactions to Polish events since the summer of 1980. The United States repeatedly sounded the alarm and acted as if the troops of the Warsaw Pact had already invaded Poland, making détente a dead issue once and for all. The credits given by American banks to Poland, totaling billions of dollars, were used by the U.S. government to influence Poland's economic course.

In contrast, spokesmen of Western European governments took careful pains to stress continually that the Soviet Union would not intervene militarily in Poland. They are now granting credits (with the Federal Republic heading the list) to stabilize the Polish situation, so that the discontent of the Polish working class, revolutionary at core, does not lead to a radical change in regime. (To this extent European right-wing politicians like Franz Josef Strauss, are correct in their charge that the Federal Government is deliberately and consciously strengthening the old repressive regime against the workers, although Strauss, like some of the members of the Reagan government, would just as soon see a Soviet invasion, so that he could better and more militantly pursue a confrontation with the Soviet Union.) In March

"The Destruction of Europe"

1981 a member of the American National Security Council (NSC), the Harvard historian and Russian expert in the Reagan government, Richard Pipes, made a highly revealing comment about what one segment of the inner circle of the present administration thought about its own *"Ostpolitik."* (The American government took this incident so seriously that it issued an immediate denial in telegrams to all American embassies, saying that it was the personal opinion of Professor Pipes and not the view or attitude of American policy.) Pipes said that over the long run the Soviet Union had basically only one choice, namely, between a fundamental reform within or a change of regime in the direction of Western parliamentary constitutional system, i.e., to become "Westernized" and permit capital production relations or to face war. In Pipes's opinion, in any case, American strategy should ultimately be to force the present-day Soviet Union to face this alternative, i.e., to extend the John Foster Dulles rollback strategy far beyond the Polish-Soviet border.

The natural gas deal

Economically the conflict of European and American interests is reflected with graphic clarity in the West German-Soviet project for a 5,000-kilometer pipeline to deliver Soviet natural gas from Siberia to Western Europe. It is the biggest East-West deal ever negotiated and is a major part of the new Soviet five-year plan. The total cost of this enormous construction project would amount to 20 billion DM; by the mid '80s the Soviet Union would annually deliver 40 billion cubic meters of natural gas to Western Europe, 12 billion to the Federal Republic and the rest to France, Belgium, Holland, Austria, and Italy. This giant project would be financed by fourteen West German banks. The Soviet interest lies in tapping its own energy sources with the aid of Western European and West German capital and Western technology so as to meet its own energy demands and those of the CMEA members, and in acquiring hard currency from the oil and natural gas transactions with the West. The United States, on the other hand, is engaged in major diplomatic efforts in West Germany and Western Europe to prevent this gas deal from coming off. The reasons are quite revealing in the context of American foreign policy: the gas deal would bring the Soviet Union and Western Europe economically and thus politically closer together and thereby weaken American influence. In addition, the deal represents an economic defeat for American firms, and it would create a precedent for excluding American firms from similar deals in the future. For the Federal Republic, however, closer economic relations with the Soviet Union and the CMEA countries are not only important economically, they are also a means for extricating itself from its one-sided dependence on the United States and its new Cold War strategy. Dependence on the energy sources of the Middle East (still largely under American control) would be diminished, and new market opportunities for Western European and West German industry might also be created.

It is in this context that one must see, for example, the urgent efforts of the West German government to dissuade the United States from its hard-line anti-Soviet course and prod it into arms negotiations. This is just what Federal Chancellor Schmidt was not able to do, aside from a few rhetorical concessions, on his first visit to Reagan in May 1981; consequently the Chancellor at present sees no other alternative than to bend to American pressure and adopt the whole of U.S. military logic with regard to stationing missiles. The American objective—to strike a powerful blow to the West German-Soviet rapprochement policy, to put it in check, if not completely to revise it— seems to be bearing its first fruits: in July 1980, on his visit to Moscow, Schmidt was still regarded and treated as a friend and sympathetic partner in détente. In May 1981, after his return from the United States and his defense speech on the need for a further buildup and missile bases, the latest word in Moscow from official quarters was suddenly that Schmidt was in the worst tradition of German militarism and neo-Hitlerian tendencies. "Not too long ago this man was still for détente, defended SALT 2, and loudly proclaimed his desire for neighborly relatins with the Soviet Union. Now he can only speak of the Soviet Union as an enemy power, as a threat, with which one can only negotiate with a stone in one's hand" (TASS, May 28, 1981). In addition to the attempt to roll back Soviet influence in Europe through the politics of arms, American interest in a more hardline anticommunist strategy is also dictated by the goal of draining Western European support from Latin American reform movements (such as the El Salvador Liberation Front), which threaten U.S. hegemony in its own hemisphere. The most serious European opponent of the United States in this domain at present is the Socialist International, which received a bracing long-term boost with the victory of the French left in May and June of 1981. One must therefore expect that the United States, allied with the anti-left-wing French bourgeoisie, will attempt to generate all sorts of problems for Mitterrand's France and make his government's socialist-reformist experiment fail.

Missiles and austerity programs

The American strategy for the '80s is not the outward manifestation of some sort of particularly aggressive malevolence or the blindness of a few political figures like Reagan, Haig, and Weinberger, who are indeed cold warriors. There is something more fundamental behind it. Reagan's presidency presumably marks a new turn, something more than just one of the many presidential and party changes that we have become accustomed to seeing in the United States since the days of Roosevelt.

The election of an outspokenly right-wing candidate does not necessarily mean that there was positive agreement on Reagan's program among the electorate; it was primarily a vote against Carter's presidency. Carter marked the end of the American tradition of social assistance and the modern welfare state as it has developed in the United States since Roosevelt's New Deal.

In the economic strategy of "military Keynesianism," which has dominated postwar growth in the United States from the very beginning, rising arms expenditures and rising expenditures for welfare programs went hand in hand. Both kinds of government spending boosted demand and economic growth—an effect which the market alone could not have achieved to any satisfactory degree. Social measures like unemployment compensation, pensions, food stamps, etc., also had the advantage of forestalling opposition to military spending that grew every year.

As long as the economy expanded, whether on its own or by dint of an inflationary fiscal policy detrimental to the world economy, increasing government spending for "guns and butter" was a thoroughly practicable and feasible strategy. The severe economic crisis of the '70s, which brought unemployment, inflation, and stagnation coupled with international competition, made it impossible any longer for the United States to maintain at the same time a strategy of arms expansion and government welfare programs. A choice had to be made between the two, and Reagan has opted for military spending. With the slogan "taking government out of business and off the backs of Americans," the Reagan government announced its attempt to resuscitate ailing industry with tax relief and concessions on environmental and labor protection (which cost too much). In effect, Reagan's program aims at a major rechanneling of capital flows away from the public sector into the private sector. The new policy does not herald a return to the old days of laissez faire—this is no longer possible in the modern world—but rather has quite deliberately set its sights on deflation. The government intends to cut social spending through radical tax reductions at the same time as the arms budget is being increased by no less than 26 percent for the coming year. The share of social spending on the social product is already only half as large as in the Federal Republic and in France. It is not surprising, therefore, that cuts in social spending in the name of the "Greatness of America" are making many people fear social unrest in the near future. What is more, liberal and conservative economists alike agree that inflation will grow rather than decline because of the arms spending planned. It is not only the poor, the unemployed, and the other groups of welfare recipients who are affected by the policies of the Reagan government. The immense growth in the arms budget and the rechanneling of government spending from the civilian to the military sector will certainly stimulate the economy, but only to a very limited extent. The arms industry has, after all, become a very capital-intensive sector of the economy. Therefore, although the new generation of strategic weapons, like the MX missiles and nuclear submarines, will devour fantastic sums, they will have no significant influence on restoring full employment or on the competitiveness of industry, which thus will continue to lag behind Europe and Japan.

The fact that the NATO allies are being coerced into stepping up their military spending is thus not merely a sign of the political and economic decline of the United States and the expression of plans to reduce the American share in the armed defense of Europe, but also a means to put a strain on Europe's economy and to divest it of its unfair competitive advantage (so at least it is hoped in the Reagan camp), an advantage from which West Germany, where defense spending is comparatively small, especially benefits. In a word, the Europeans, and the Federal Republic in particular, are to be forced to adopt American economic policy, which is based on an arms buildup that in the present crisis necessarily entails cuts in the social budget and wage reductions, all in defense of "freedom and competitiveness." The drastic austerity measures that have now been undertaken in West Germany, at the same time as the call to increase defense spending is growing louder, appear to confirm that Reagan can successfully foist his military economic policy on us as well.

CHAPTER
4

MILITARY DÉTENTE AND DIFFERENCES ON MILITARY POLICY WITHIN THE WARSAW PACT

Stephan Tiedtke

Traditionally little attention has been paid in the West to relations between the members of the Warsaw Pact with regard to military policy. The Vienna negotiations on troop and arms reduction in central Europe evidently could alter nothing in this respect, although the security interests of the junior partners in the alliance, namely, Poland, the GDR, and Czechoslovakia, were touched on in particular by the Eastern European negotiators.

How can we explain this lack of interest, especially when we consider the close attention paid by Eastern European journalists and scholars to questions of military policy within NATO? One factor, undoubtedly, is the extremely unsatisfactory access to first-hand information; this in itself reduces the incentive to devote much attention to the matter. The Eastern European bureaucracies do not publicly air their controversies over military policy and give as little detailed information as possible on the ways in which they cooperate. It is only in exceptional cases that signs of conflict over military cooperation can be gleaned from the sources, and even then the shroud of secrecy remains essentially intact. Since 1964 Romania has steadily, if with varying intensity, sought to extract itself from the constraints of military cooperation, and in its efforts to achieve some measure of independence has relied on the international public; yet it too shrinks from violating the common principle of releasing minimal information on the disputed questions of cooperation in military policy and the weapons industry.[1]

Yet we should not overestimate the importance of the restrictive information policy of the Eastern European bureaucracies in seeking to explain this failure by scholars. Although the Soviet bureaucracy is just as reticent in releasing information on its military policy, a vast amount of literature is nonetheless available. Clearly some fundamental political assessments of the importance of military cooperation have made excessive concern with it seem unnecessary. In contrast to analyses of economic relations within the CMEA, on military matters the system of Eastern European states continues to be seen as a monolith in which the interests of the Soviet bureaucracy prevail as a matter of principle. The result is that to Western observers, military cooperation in Eastern Europe that is of relevance to the East-West conflict is as good as nonexistent; there is only Soviet military policy, and the Soviet Union's Warsaw Pact allies must take a back seat to it. The Soviet bureaucracy's mistrust of its allies thus makes it necessary to control military policy; a corrollary, of course, is that allied military potential must be kept low. What is more, détente has done little to shake this cast of mind: the growing military threat from the East constantly conjured up in recent days is backed up almost exclusively with statistics on the Soviet army; the potential of the Soviet Union's allies is wholly disregarded.

Of course, there are a number of real factors in military policy that would seem to support the view that the Soviet Union has almost a free hand with the Warsaw Pact:

• The standardization of the equipment of the Eastern European armies, with the Soviet model usually setting the tone, has come quite a long way compared with NATO.

• The key military positions within the Warsaw Pact are still firmly in the hands of Soviet officers.

• The proportion of Soviet troops among the forces stationed in central Europe is about twice as high as the proportion of American army troops in Western Europe.

In assessing to what extent these factors serve to entrench the Soviet dominance in military policy in Eastern Europe there is always the danger of assuming that the conflict structures in the Western alliance apply to the Eastern European alliance as well. For instance, unlike the situation in NATO, the standardization of equipment in the Warsaw Pact is not hampered by the competition of national capitals so characteristic of intrasystem relations between the Western industrial nations. While it is true that conflicts within NATO could even result in a withdrawal from the alliance's political organizations, in central Europe the lines of conflict are drawn more tightly owing to the direct social and military confrontation with the opposing system and the web of interlocking multilateral economic relationships. There is some tolerance for conflict within the Warsaw Pact depending on the region (Albania and Romania), but on the whole the permissible margins are comparatively narrow. A state apparatus based on a uniform social organization and the same socio-economic foundations considerably restrict the potential for conflict among Pact members. However, the coordination of interests among the state bureaucracies, possible in principle, is hampered by the fact that in formulating their alliance policy, these national bureaucracies must consider the contradictions within their social systems. The extent to which these contradictions are considered also depends on the extent to which the interests of the other bureaucracies will be affected by them. Management of internal social conflict reaches its limit when social changes within the national domain of one bureaucracy jeopardize the authority of the other bureaucracies in their own backyards.

The limited conflict potential and the indicators of military policy listed above both seem to point to Soviet hegemony within the alliance; they must not, however, be interpreted too rashly as signs of a monolithic military policy. The historical setting within which Western analyses of economic relations among the Eastern European countries have taken place is in itself reason for reflection. The West first began to take notice of the national economies and trade conditions within the CMEA when economic pressures in the West stimulated interest in cooperation with Eastern Europe. In the interest of military détente in Europe, therefore, ought we not analyze just as carefully the national military policies[2] and conditions for military cooperation within the Warsaw Pact? This acknowledged, there are then the more complex questions concerning the internal social conditions of cooperation within each Warsaw Pact nation, to what extent planning of the alliance's military strategy shapes this cooperation, and how military strategy and internal conditions affect the size of the military burden shared by the junior partners. If problems within the alliance are not resolved unilaterally by the Soviet bureaucracy—and we assume this to be the case—then we must also investigate the ways in which conflicts between the ruling bureaucracies are solved. Space does not permit us to examine here the full range of differing national interests within the alliance nor the share of each nation in collective arms expenditures; we shall therefore limit our discussion to the alliance and security policies of the GDR and Romania, since within the Warsaw Pact they are at opposite poles as regards foreign policy.

The relevance of our study for détente lies in its implications for Western policy attitudes toward Eastern Europe. An incorrect assessment of the security policy situation within the Warsaw Pact, or the notion that the Soviet Union can do or not do as it wishes as regards military cooperation, necessarily leads to unrealistic Western efforts to promote military détente, especially when they entail substantial "alterations" in military security policy. The futile efforts to isolate the GDR in Eastern Europe, as sometimes attempted by the West, demonstrate that the interests of the individual Warsaw Pact nations cannot simply be dismissed. For Western military détente policy this means that the military and security interests of the smaller Warsaw Pact nations, which are by no means congruent, must be given due consideration within, of course, the larger framework of the Eastern European alliance.

Internal social conditions for military cooperation

The degree of military cooperation in Eastern Europe depends in the first instance on the intensity of military and political confrontation between East and West. Internal social factors as well, however, such as the stability of the social system in the Pact nations, the loyalty of the armies, and the economic means available for providing the military apparatus with such resources as seem necessary also play an important role. A brief retrospective glance at the history of the Warsaw Pact will make this clearer.

The first break in Warsaw Pact history took place one year after its founding. The Hungarian uprising of 1956, the result of internal political repression and economic problems, led to the exclusion of the Hungarian army as an ally of any importance in the following years; accordingly, military cooperation in the southern regions of the Warsaw Pact stagnated. Moreover, the "collapse" of the Hungarian army during the uprising confronted the allied bureaucracies with the task of having to step up ideological efforts within their respective armies, at the expense, as it happened, of technological training and thus military cooperation among the alliance armies.

In the northern region of the Warsaw Pact, which is of more importance for security policy, the Soviet Union and its allies had to face the difficult problem of solidifying the social and political order in the GDR to the extent that it could participate in military cooperation. Indeed, as long as the GDR remained out of the picture, military cooperation at the boundary of the East-West conflict would remain ineffective. The construction of the Berlin Wall in August 1961 created the essential conditions for this. The expansion of the East German National Volksarmee (NVA), which hinged on the introduction of compulsory military service, could then be started and the East German army drawn into the military bloc. Accordingly, the beginning of intensive military cooperation between the northern nations of the Warsaw Pact, the GDR, Czechoslovakia, Poland, and the Soviet Union, dates from 1961. The increased military role accruing to the smaller Pact nations as a result of this cooperation is reflected in the multilateral maneuvers and the improved equipment of the alliance armies.[3] For the Soviet Union this has meant that it is now no longer able to dismiss out of hand the military contribution of its junior allies, especially the three to the north, and that indeed it has even become partly dependent on them.

These changed conditions in military cooperation came to bear in the Czech conflict of 1968-69. Benefiting from the increased military roles of the smaller allies and the social and political changes that took place in Czechoslovakia during the

"Prague Spring," the Czech military called for a review of the consultation process within the alliance, demonstrated a greater independence of mind in thinking on military strategy and military policy, and was no longer disposed to tolerate the informal channels of the Soviet Secret Police into the Czech army.[4] Although the reforms decided on by the Political Advisory Committee (PAC), the highest body in the Warsaw Pact, for the alliance organization in March 1969 in Budapest were not the direct result of the Czech criticism, that criticism did reflect the general dissatisfaction with traditional structures that had led to the reforms in the first place. The fruit of the March PAC meeting was a complicated system of compromises that belie the view that Soviet interests prevail unconditionally. The decision to establish three new institutions—the Committee for the Coordination of Military Technology, the Military Council of the Combined Chiefs of Staff, and the Committee of Defense Ministers—gave the junior allies a greater say in military planning. At the same time, however, military integration, of interest especially to the GDR and the Soviet Union, was pushed ahead. This change in the way the dominant power regarded its junior partners in pursuing its military policy is also reflected in the Soviet eagerness to bring the Czech army back into the process of military integration as quickly as possible after the invasion of Czechoslovakia. Whereas in the '50s and '60s the loyalty of the army, buttressed by ideological training, privileges offered to the officers, and allocations of vast resources to the military apparatus, was the keystone of military policy of the Pact nations, by the end of the '70s this long-established priority no longer seemed to apply without restriction. Ceausescu's refusal to increase his defense budget, as his allies demanded at the PAC meeting in November 1978, was a sign of the emergence of a broader interpretation of national security. In a rejoinder to the alarmist views of his alliance partners on the heightened military threat, Ceausescu stated: "We are all, I should think, clear that any additional expenditure of national resources for arms purposes is only possible at the expense of the funds available for development and to raise the material and intellectual living standards of the people."[5] Ceausescu justified his refusal to assume additional expenditures for the arms sector in terms of the international situation. However, he also said, "The combat and defense readiness of our entire nation will be enhanced the more we develop our nation's economy, and the greater success we have in implementing the program worked out by the Eleventh Party Congress for strengthening the productive forces and raising the standard of living and prosperity of our people."[6] Unilateral steps like Romania's refusal to increase its defense spending are usually regarded by the Warsaw Pact allies as undermining this common defense and are so criticized. In this the Warsaw Pact differs in no way from NATO. However, in the case of Romania's refusal, the vehemence of the reactions was surprising; indeed, they bear no comparison with the criticism which the Warsaw Pact allies have otherwise made of Romania's go-it-alone military policy. The Romanian decision fits in with the general trend toward a shift of priorities (a recurrent topic of discussion in the Soviet Union as well) from the heavy industry sector (arms industry) to the consumer goods industry. It quite plausibly is taken by the allied bureaucracies as a social and political provocation that could destabilize their social systems.[7] Memories of efforts during the Prague Spring to cut the Czech defense budget because of the tense economic situation are probably still fresh in the minds of the alliance partners.[8]

This brief historical survey shows a high level of dependence everywhere of the degree of military cooperation on domestic conditions in the smaller Warsaw Pact nations,[9] with the important difference, of course, that initially, military and security interests as dictated by the Soviet bureaucracy shaped efforts to achieve social stability, whereas since the beginnings of détente, domestic social problems appear to be having a growing influence on the stance of the smaller Warsaw Pact nations on military policy. However, this has not been a continuous process that has involved all the smaller nations to the same degree. Differences in the degree to which each nation is affected by the military confrontation in Europe restrict or widen each country's margin for maneuver in setting military policy.

Differences in the military contributions of the smaller countries

Despite the view that there is a monolithic military bloc in Eastern Europe, the Romanian bureaucracy has been able largely to pull out of it. Its foreign and military policies, seen as a kind of Gaullism, are usually contrasted to the alliance politics of the GDR, which tries to conform to Soviet military policy and plays the role of guardian of alliance interests. These two positions describe the margin (a margin, by the way, not unlike that existing within NATO) for decision-making in military policy within the Warsaw Pact at present.[10] Since due consideration of national and military interests in the East is essential for a realistic Western policy of détente, one can ask how this discrepancy can be explained in terms of alliance politics and security. For example, is the rigid position of the GDR bureaucracy merely the outward expression of its repressive social policy, or might not the special security and alliance interests of the GDR be behind it?

The margin for maneuver in military policy by a smaller Warsaw Pact member is essentially determined by the importance of its armed forces in the common defense. The more important its armed forces and its territory for common defense, the narrower is the range of action permitted it in military policy. This situation can be illustrated by the example of the United Armed Forces, which are comparable to the integrated armed forces of NATO.[11]

The preeminent military importance of the United Armed Forces over other military units in Eastern Europe is underscored in an article in the Soviet army newspaper *Krasnaia zvezda* [Red Star]: "The establishment of the United Armed Forces increased the defense potential of the socialist countries immeasurably because the best-trained units, i.e., those in the highest state of military preparedness, have been detailed to the United Armed Forces."[12]

Since the United Armed Forces have critical combat tasks to perform in the case of a military conflict, the number of units which a Warsaw Pact nation places under the Joint Chiefs of Staff tells us something about the relative importance of that country in the military security system of Eastern Europe. However, on the other hand, the margin for decision-making in military policy with regard to these units is limited by their being part of the United Armed Forces, and this in turn means a narrowing of a country's margin for action in military policy. Since the equipment of the United Armed Forces is broadly standardized, the organizational structure of the units the same, and training coordinated, the bureaucracies that place the majority of their troops under the Joint Chiefs of Staff no longer have a free hand with these troops, in contrast to those countries which furnish only a small number of troops or none at all. This difference is most clearly evident in the example of the GDR and Romania.

The military and political standoff between the blocs is the most intense at the seam in central Europe. The best equipped and best trained troops of the Warsaw Pact are accordingly stationed there, and furthermore, the East German Volksarmee has largely been incorporated into the United Armed Forces. Even if this limited GDR control over the Volksarmee—and for reasons peculiar to the German question there was no other alternative—the GDR nonetheless had a broad interest in integrating its army into military cooperation. The incorporation of the GDR and its army into the Eastern European defense system and the United Armed Forces made the political integration of the GDR into the Eastern European system of nations indispensable; it opened the way to the GDR's equal status as a state with its alliance partners.

Romania, on the periphery of the Warsaw Pact and hence less important in military strategy, evidently places no troops under the command of the Joint Chiefs of Staff. When the Warsaw Pact entered into a new phase of increased military cooperation in the mid- '60s, the first signs of Romania's efforts to achieve independence in military policy became evident. In 1968 the Romanian army was reorganized to wage a defensive people's war with no direct support from the alliance partners. The Romanian leadership embarked on this new course for reasons of foreign and social policy, but it was militarily possible only because the Romanian armed forces did not have to meet the demands of the United Armed Forces.

The three northern Warsaw Pact nations, on the other hand, cannot pursue such an independent military policy; the experiences during the Prague Spring demonstrated as much. Withdrawal of Czechoslovakia from the Warsaw Pact was out of the question in 1968, but both the Soviet Union and Czechoslovakia's northern allies evidently had second thoughts whether the Czech leadership would remain willing in the future to press ahead with military integration, or whether it might not attempt to avoid the demands of integration by reducing the Czech defense budget.

The effects that military integration might be expected to have on the arms budget, and hence on the social costs of armament, might be presumed to have been the most important factor in the decision of the Romanian leadership to pursue an independent military policy. Membership in the United Armed Forces permits no differences in the equipment of its constituent armies that would be broad enough to jeopardize the operational unity of the United Armed Forces. In concrete terms this means first of all alliance constraints on the procurement of weapons and gear. Romania is immune to such constraints. And it tries to stay free of them, and of possible Soviet pressure through stoppage of deliveries, by building up its own armaments industry, which has now gone so far as the joint development and production of a fighter plane with Yugoslavia, which is not a member of the alliance.

The Soviet divisions in central Europe, which have the technically most advanced equipment, set the standard for the procurement of weapons and gear for the smaller Warsaw Pact nations and their units in the United Armed Forces. However, for various reasons the technical level of the smaller armies in the alliance cannot be expected to fully meet the level of the Soviet army: the Soviet Union's alliance partners cannot place undue burdens on their budgets for the procurement of expensive new gear; they must keep such spending within more or less socially justifiable limits. On the other hand, the Soviet Union has no interest in equippping its allies unconditionally with its latest weapons systems. The absorption of advanced technical manufacturing methods and of suitably trained personnel, neither of which are present in sufficient quantities in the Soviet Union, in the production of the most advanced weapons places limits on the Soviet Union's delivery potential.[13] In addition, the Soviet Union must also take into account the effects of its weapons deliveries on armament dynamics in central Europe. The delivery of the most advanced Soviet weapons to the Near East and not to the European allies would seem to be a case in point.

How has the equipment of the armies of the three northern Warsaw Pact nations evolved over time? In the first half of the '60s there was an armaments buildup in the armies of the smaller Warsaw Pact nations that considerably reduced the technology gap compared with Soviet troops. Since then, however, it has widened again as a consequence of quantitative and qualitative changes in Soviet troops in central Europe. The November 1978 decision of the alliance partners to step up their armaments efforts[14] was clearly aimed at improving the equipment of the alliance armies. The seriousness of the gap in armaments between the Soviet divisions and the armed forces of the northern Warsaw pact nations is made clear by two examples:

• In the East German Volksarmee the type T-54/55 tank was the predominant model; according to the data in *Military Balance* there are only 600 obsolete T-34 tanks left in the East German armed forces, but it is evidently not clear whether they are still with the troops, stockpiled,[15] or have been junked.[16] Contrary to earlier reports, the modern T-62 does not exist in the Volksarmee.[17] On the other hand, Soviet divisions in the GDR have the T-62 as standard equipment and evidently already have T-72s as well. And the armed forces have moved apart quantitatively as well. In the Soviet divisions in central Europe there has been an increase of about a third in the number of tanks. In contrast, according to *Military Balance*, the number of tanks in the Czech armed forces has remained constant since 1971, aside from a few minor fluctuations.[18]

• Another example is the equipment of the air forces. The Polish air force still has the MIG-15 fighter, which was in use in the Korean War; there are ample numbers of the MIG-17s, but the most modern interceptor fighter in the Polish armed forces is the MIG-21.[19] In contrast, the Soviet air force in central Europe has the modern MIG-23 interceptor.

What is the military relevance of these differences in equipment? The armaments buildup in the Soviet armed forces in central Europe during the past ten years has served to enhance the mobility and fire power of the ground troops. Together with a revision in operational warfare, this is a response to technological developments that have clearly favored defensive combat with conventional weapons.[20] The U.S. Undersecretary of Defense for Research and Technology, W. J. Perry, sums up the technological advance on the field of combat as follows: "If a target is visible it can be destroyed. This capacity, together with improved reconnaissance over the field of combat, will in my opinion revolutionize modern war. As long as the enemy moves, his equipment gives off heat, or it is recognizable by radar contrast against the surface background, he can be defeated."[21]

To reduce the vulnerability of their armed forces, the smaller Warsaw Pact nations feel themselves compelled to adopt the Soviet improvements, at least in part. An armaments buildup, at least in the northern three Warsaw Pact nations, may therefore be expected in the upcoming years.[22] The appearance of the T-72 in the anniversary parade of the National Volksarmee on October 6 in East Berlin might be the first confirmation of this.[23]

The military strategy of the Warsaw Pact

Romania's go-it-alone military policy has remained a unique case in the Warsaw Pact. That it was possible at all is on the one hand attributable to the fact that what Romania could contribute to military integration was felt to be dispensable; on the other hand, however, the Romanian leadership clearly had an interest in disengaging Romania's military security from that of the northern nations of the Warsaw Pact. The reasons for this lie in the military strategy of the Warsaw Pact, which is based solely and exclusively on a central European conflict and assumes that such a conflict will not be contained but will escalate into an all-out nuclear war. From the standpoint of the northern Pact nations, this is an optimal military strategy, especially because in their context the Soviet guarantee of nuclear protection enjoys a high degree of creditability. But what interest can a country like Romania have in a strategy that may indeed make deterrence creditable for central Europe, but that when it fails draws Romanian territory into the conflict? Unlike its northern allies, Romania would probably be interested in a Warsaw Pact strategy which, like NATO's flexible response, leaves a limited conflict in central Europe as a strategic possibility.

However, the divergent security interests do not end with Romania but in fact constitute a general problem between the north and the south in the Warsaw Pact. Regional security alliances, in which greater consideration is given to divergent military security interests, have often been discussed in Eastern Europe. When the Warsaw Pact was being formed, there were throughts of restricting the alliance to Czechoslovakia, the GDR, Poland, and the Soviet Union, i.e., what was later to be called "the Northern Triangle."[24] For the southern part of the Warsaw Pact, in 1971 Bulgaria proposed a "pactlike security agreement" that would go beyond the borders of the system to embrace the six Balkan countries.[25] Romania has been pursuing this goal since 1957 with its proposal to create a "zone of peace" in the Balkans.[26] However, so far no concrete steps even remotely comparable with the level of integration of the northern triangle have been taken toward the formation of a southern subregion. The logic of Romania's alliance policy should, however, make good sense for the Bulgarian and Hungarian leadership. Hungary did not seem prepared to step up its armaments efforts in 1978.[27] A widening of the gap between the north and the south in the Warsaw Pact can also be expected over an MBFR agreement. The northern pact countries, which are all in MBFR strike range, and the Western European countries also affected by an MBFR agreement would form a zone that militarily would have a special status spelled out in an agreement between the two systems.

Implications for the West's arms control policy

The range of differences over military policy among the Warsaw Pact nations that we have described, however incompletely, here refutes the notion of a monolithic military policy in Eastern Europe. This conclusion is not unimportant for the process of military détente in Europe, for it seems unlikely that differences in military policy will not, and indeed have not already, led to controversies with regard to joint military détente policy. Once again, the examples of the GDR and Romania can serve as an illustration.

As long as the Warsaw Pact has existed, the political and military leadership of the GDR has consistently and continuously advocated further military integration—and not only for reasons of its own military security. Ever since the GDR achieved equal status within the Eastern European system, it has been pushing for military integration on the quite plausible assumption that the higher the level of integration in military cooperation, the easier it would be to prevent uncoordinated steps being taken toward arms limitation and détente in Eastern Europe. The GDR would after all have to be the first among the smaller Warsaw Pact nations to fear the implications of such steps for its own security. However, it has not merely pushed the material process of integration through, for example, more consultations and joint maneuvers; it has also tried to block disintegrative tendencies in the ideological domain. In proclaiming military as well as economic integration to be socialist[28]—in contradiction, we might add, to the text of the Warsaw Pact, which is mute on this point—the GDR bureaucracy restricts its own political control over decisions bearing on military cooperation. The GDR bureaucracy's firm adherence to the principle that the socialist states must maintain superiority over NATO even in the era of political détente, and moreover at a time when this requirement has long since been given up in the Soviet Union, is along the same lines. In this way the GDR leadership pointed up its reservations with regard to the position that a balance of forces was prerequisite to military détente in Europe and voted against any flexibility whatsoever in the Eastern European two-pillar doctrine.[a]

The security fears that lie behind the GDR's espousal of military integration are not shared by the Romanian bureaucracy. On the contrary, their alliance policy, which is aimed against integration, has implications for détente that would be unacceptable to its ally, the GDR. This again came to the surface in November 1978. Five days after a PAC declaration argued for

---

a. The Warsaw Pact two-pillar doctrine couples (1) peaceful coexistence with (2) the necessity of maintaining military superiority or at least equivalence. This differs from the Khrushchev disarmament program of the fifties and early sixties (reduction of troups by one-third to 1.2 million). Khrushchev also advocated a calculated minimal deterrence doctrine for nuclear arms.—R.S. and M.V.

stepped-up efforts toward an arms buildup in the light of "decisions" and "actions" of NATO aimed at "giving the NATO states military superiority over the socialist countries and other countries of the world,"[29] Ceausescu described a quite different picture of the military threat: ". . . it is our firm conviction that far from safeguarding independence, security, and peace, the military pacts do nothing but maintain the state of tension. It is our view that the means at our disposal, i.e., of both the Warsaw Pact, NATO, and other countries, are far more than what is required."[30]

Ceausescu was presumably thinking more of Romania's special military geographical situation than of the military standoff in central Europe, as indeed can be discerned from his passing comment that countries such as Greece and Turkey are also not "busy building up their armaments."[31]

However, in the northern Warsaw Pact countries, integration has reached a point that makes the call for a dissolution of the military bloc (which after all is implicit in the Romanian statement) seem illusory. Nor does the system of bilateral agreements change anything, despite conjectures by Western critics that they could replace the alliance organization. This is a fiction. It is hard to imagine how the level of integration of the Warsaw Pact could be maintained by bilateral agreements if no multilateral institution existed.

However, even if the breakup of the military blocs cannot be the goal of current military détente, it must nonetheless be realized that military cohesion in the northern part of the Warsaw Pact, which after all sets the tone in the Vienna negotiations, shapes military détente policy in the Warsaw Pact nations. Just as NATO and, especially, the Federal Republic of Germany begin from the assumption that the Federal Republic's ties to NATO must not be weakened by a European arms control agreement, it is a principle in the Warsaw Pact as well that an MBFR agreement must not loosen the GDR's ties to the Warsaw Pact. The hope that military détente will bring about a diversification of national security interests among the northern Warsaw Pact nations is just as unrealistic as similar efforts by the Warsaw Pact nations with regard to the Federal Republic of Germany. Rather, each side should make it a principle to accept the alliance framework within which the other side fashions its military détente policy and limit itself merely to plumbing the range of compromise and flexibility it can allow itself for an arms control agreement. The sociopolitical system at the basis of cooperation plays an important role here; for the present state of military détente, however, the different principles guiding the military strategies of the two alliances, which are the most general expression of the collective need for military security, are more decisive. The strategic unity of the Eastern European alliance, at least in its northern sector, is to a greater degree given, by dint of the fact that the alliance leader is a European power, than is the case in NATO, which must always consider the possibility that the United States will disengage itself from Western Europe.

NOTES

1. The Czechoslovak General V. Prchlik was brought to trial in 1971 for his informative critique of military cooperation in the alliance, which he gave in a press conference in July 1968; see the indictment against General Prchlik in R. Crusius and others, eds., *CSSR, Fünf Jahre "Normalisierung" (Dokumentation)*, Hamburg, 1973, pp. 236 ff.
2. If one disregards the GDR, there are no detailed and comprehensive studies of the military apparatus and military policies of the smaller Warsaw Pact nations.
3. On this point see S. Tiedtke, *Die Warschauer Vertragsorganisation*, Munich and Vienna, 1978, pp. 68 ff.
4. Ibid., pp. 83 ff.
5. Speech by the General Secretary of the Romanian Communist Party and President of the Socialist Republic of Romania, N. Ceausescu, before the Plenary Session of the Central Committee of the Romanian Communist Party on November 19, 1978, in *Europa Archiv*, 1979, no. 1, p. D31.
6. Ibid.
7. D. Bender backs up this assumption with reference to the statements by Eastern European diplomats in the *Herald Tribune*, November 30, 1978, p. 4.
8. On this point see Tiedtke, p. 89.
9. The Soviet alliance policy can also not be separated from socioeconomic trends in the Soviet Union; see the case study J. Tiedtke and S. Tiedtke, "Auswirkungen innenpolitischer Probleme der Sowjetunion auf die Entwicklung der Warschauer Vertrags-Organisation," in Egbert Jahn, ed., *Sozioökonomische Bedingungen der sowjetischen Aussenpolitik*, Frankfurt, 1975, pp. 141-92.

10. So far NATO has not yet had to deal with the total withdrawal of one of its members from the alliance; in the Warsaw Pact this occurred in 1968 when Albania withdrew.

11. The United Armed Forces were created pursuant to Article 5 of the Warsaw Pact, in which the parties to the Pact agreed to "create a unified command for those of its armed forces which in accordance with an agreement between the parties would be placed at the disposal of that command, functioning on the basis of jointly established principles." Cited in B. Meissner, ed., *Der Warschauer Pakt, Dokumentensammlung*, Cologne, 1962, p. 99.

12. *Krasnaia zvezda*, March 26, 1971.

13. On this point see M. Checinski, "The Costs of Armament Production and the Profitability of Armament Export in Comecon Countries," in *Ost-Europa-Wirtschaft*, 1975, no. 2, p. 123.

14. See the declaration of the Central Committee of the CPSU, the Presidium of the Supreme Soviet, and the Council of Ministers of the Soviet Union of November 29, 1978, on the PAC meeting in *Europa-Archiv*, 1979, no. 1, p. D33, and Ceausescu's speech of November 29, 1978 (Note 5).

15. *Military Balance 1976-77*, p. 13, and *1978-79*, p. 14.

16. F. Wiener, *Die Armeen der Warschauerpaktstaaten*, Munich, 1974, p. 42.

17. *Military Balance* and Wiener.

18. In 1966 Czechoslovakia had 3,200 tanks, and in 1978 over 3,400; according to data from *Military Balance. 1966-67*, p. 6, and *Military Balance 1978-79*, p. 14.

19. *Military Balance 1977-78*, p. 15.

20. For more on this see S. Tiedtke, *Rüstungskontrolle aus sowjetischer Sicht, Die Rahmenbedingungen der sowjetischen MBFR-Politik*, Frankfurt on Main, 1980, pp. 54 ff.

21. W. J. Perry, "Die Stärkung der NATO durch die Technologie," in *Europäische Wehrkunde*, 1978, no. 3, p. 110.

22. On this point see Ph. A. Karber, "The Impact of New Conventional Technologies on Military Doctrine and Organisation in the Warsaw Pact," in *New Conventional Weapons and East-West Security*, part 1, The International Institute for Strategic Studies, Adelphi Paper 144, London, 1978, p. 31.

23. *Frankfurter Allgemeine Zeitung*, October 8, 1979, p. 3.

24. See the speech by O. Grotewohl at the "Conference of European Countries to Safeguard Peace and Security in Europe," in December 1954, in *Dokumente zum Warschauer Vertrag (1954-1961)*, East Berlin, 1962, vol. 2, pp. 14 ff.

25. *Frankfurter Rundschau*, April 23, 1971.

26. See F. S. Larrabee, "Europäische Sicherheit und Sicherheitsprobleme auf dem Balkan," in *Osteuropa*, 1974, no. 3, pp. 172 ff.

27. See 95/2, U.S. Congress, JEC, Subcommittee on Priorities and Economy in Government, *Hearings: Allocation of Resources in the Soviet Union and China—1978*, part 4, *Soviet Union*, Washington, 1978, p. 172.

28. See H. Brunner, "Der proletarische Internationalismus—Grundzug der Erziehung der Armeeangehörigen zur sozialistischen Waffenbruderschaft," in *Militärgeschichte*, 1974, no. 4, p. 409.

29. Declaration of the members of the Warsaw Pact, adopted at the meeting of the Political Advisory Committee on November 22, 1978, in Moscow, in *Europa-Archiv*, 1979, no. 1, p. D17.
30. Ceausescu, p. D30.
31. Ibid., p. D31.

PART II
THE "GERMAN QUESTION" AND EUROPEAN SECURITY

Introduction

For many, a discussion of European security policy runs the risk of degenerating into a debate about military hardware; the numerous "equilibrium analyses" by NATO must shoulder a good portion of the blame for this. One of the great merits of détente is that it has restored the link between security and politics. Thus the essay by General Christian Krause in Part I provides a global strategic perspective on security policy, while the articles by Egon Bahr, Günter Gaus, Peter Brandt and Herbert Ammon, and Ulrich Albrecht focus on the political and geopolitical aspects. All the authors come from West Berlin, and all the essays were either written or presented there. This is no accident; Berlin continues to be the sore point of East-West relations.

Two distinct positions stand in clear contrast to one another in this section; Dr. Peter Brandt, historian and son of SPD Chairman Willy Brandt, and his co-author Herbert Ammon hark back to the positions of the '50s, which they see as containing elements crucial for keeping the peace in Europe. A vehement debate arose in the peace movement on this position, which has considerable support from the "Alternative List," the new radical democratic and environmentalist party represented in the Berlin parliament for a year now (7.2 percent of the votes). Brandt and Ammon assume that a link between the two German states extending even to the institutional level (the formation of a "German Community") would be of major significance for defusing the stand-off between the two blocs in Europe;

however, the aim is not the annexation of the GDR by the FRG, or vice versa, but rather a new type of state, a kind of confederation. Many in the present West German peace movement would see these views as a threat to peace, for the dream of a confederation or even a reunification of the two German states would in their view be destabilizing.

The position of Egon Bahr is diametrically opposed to that of Brandt and Ammon. He starts out unconditionally from the present mutually acknowledged status quo, as established in the early '70s by the agreements between the allies, between the FRG and GDR, and between the FRG and Poland. Bahr would reject any speculation on the possibility for reunification in the historically foreseeable future. In his latest book he formulates his position unmistakably: "Germany can only become an object of our thoughts again when the division of Europe is a thing of the past" (*Was wird aus den Deutschen? Fragen und Antworten*, Reinbek, 1982, p. 29). Bahr has often been maligned as a "traitor to the country" by the extreme right-wing press in the Federal Republic. It was especially hard for him to gain insight into actual political power relations, but only in this way was he able to become a protagonist of European détente and of a reconciliation with Poland and the Soviet Union. When he speaks in the first person in his analysis of the treaties and agreements that have come into being since the '70s, he has every right to do so: he has devoted the whole of his person and a long period of his political and personal life to reconciliation between the European nations.

The speech by Günter Gaus is of central importance. He places a considerable portion of the blame for the stagnation in German-German relations on the FRG government. Even in the '70s he was often an inexorable critic of any prevarication in pushing ahead with détente; he spoke out vehemently against unwarranted imputations and characterizations that cast the Soviet Union and Eastern Europe in the role of the enemy. In his speech he clearly spells out the responsibility of the Federal Republic with regard to developments in Poland. Many, overhastily, might see Gaus as "Moscow's man." Nothing could be further from the truth. But he does see the political limits and possibilities of détente, as well as the risks of destabilization

Part II: Introduction 67

posed by conflicts within Eastern Europe. His proposal for a nuclear-free zone, on the joint initiative of both German states, is thus a concrete contribution supporting the process of democratization in Poland and Eastern Europe. If the grip of party and state on the peoples of Eastern Europe is ever to loosen, the security problem of the Soviet Union must be solved once and for all. Gaus sees the consequences for Germany of Europe's division and, unlike Brandt and Ammon, clearly rejects any dreams of reunification. But he also sees the need and the opportunities for a new national identity.

The argument by Professor Ulrich Albrecht is not unknown in official circles in Eastern Europe. He assumes that the security problem of the Soviet Union is the key to European security. For him the present situation, in particular, represents a growing threat to Soviet security, for the crisis in Eastern Europe has become permanent. However, Soviet policies will have to take a radical turn to bring about or even make possible fundamental changes in the relationship between the party and the people. So far such a turn has been lacking. The Finlandization of Eastern Europe may be a horror to some, since it would in fact mean that the "enemy," as conjured up by anticommunism, would lose all substance. But for Europe it would be a chance to develop its own identity and create the preconditions for a new and lasting European peace.

Rudolf Steinke

CHAPTER
5

BEARING RESPONSIBILITY FOR GERMANY: TWENTY YEARS OF THE WALL— TEN YEARS OF THE FOUR-POWER AGREEMENT

Egon Bahr

Twenty years of the Wall—ten years of the Four-Power Agreement: not merely a coincidence of dates but the signposts of a political evolution with its own internal logic; a true occasion for reflection, I felt. A letter was waiting on my return from vacation, informing me that the topic "Bearing Responsibility for Germany" had been selected for this address. From such a perspective the thoughts and recollections evoked by these two dates, ten and twenty years ago respectively, fell into place in a rather unexpected way. Later, in the midst of working on the present talk, we received news that the American president had given the go-ahead to the production of the neutron bomb. Our experiences from those times fit well with the changes that have come about in the present situation; but we could also well ask what implications such changes might have for today and the times ahead.

I. Each of us here today has his own personal memories of that sunny Sunday of August 13, 1961.[a] What our eyes were forced to witness defied all belief. The sense of bitter indignation we felt, compounded by our sense of powerlessness, is still present as if it were yesterday.

The bewildered, pain-wracked faces of innocent people remain engraved in our memories as sober reminders, beyond even

---

a. Egon Bahr is speaking from his own direct political experience. At the time the Wall was built he was director of the Berlin Press and Information Office and a close colleague and advisor of Willy Brandt—R.S. and M.V.

the tears of joy experienced when the first border passes put people in one another's arms once again. The Wall is no pretty sight, neither then nor now. The rush of feelings was staggering: anxiety over how many hours it would be before the first patrols of the three powers would show at least that they were there; worry about the incomprehension in Washington, Paris, London, and Bonn; realization of the full magnitude of what was taking place; the seventy hours needed to convey a measured protest to Moscow; the joy at the sight of the American vice-president at the head of an American unit in Berlin in a show of friendship and solidarity, someone quicker to come across the ocean than Adenauer was to cross the Rhine; the contemptible routines into which official Bonn again withdrew in the midst of the Bundestag election campaign. And when it all was over, the Wall was still standing, in all its stark, cruel, and commanding reality. The Berlin Senate had to protect its citizens, and not least the students who in their understandable outrage wanted to blow the monster to bits faster than it could be rebuilt.

The Wall was there. It was time to think. It was no secret that the "stream of emigrants" constituted a serious drain for the Soviet zone regime and had touched a vital nerve. Blockading the Soviet sector of Berlin from the rest of the Soviet zone and the imposition of checks at the sector borders to control traffic, hitherto free, were conceivable possibilities. The repeated urgings of the governing mayor that a four-power conference of foreign ministers be convened to discuss the looming crisis came to nought in Bonn. Negotiations would, it was hoped, prevent unilateral action. The same argument is with us today, namely, that negotiations will prevent a unilateral stationing of Soviet missiles, with the difference, of course, that this time Bonn is also party to the urging.

The Americans, Russians, French, and English were hurt by the Wall; the pain was borne by Germans alone, on both sides. But even this became clear to us only later, which is to say quite generally that Germans on this side of the Wall had no advice to give at all for specific actions, only for demonstrations. No German could rattle sabers with the Allies: their rights were safeguarded, if somewhat cramped, and to defend a right that would jeopardize peace was, of course, and rightfully so, out of the question.

Bearing Responsibility for Germany

The solution of the German problem is not worth a war; that was the opinion then, and that is the opinion now, although to this very day there are still some who behave as if they believe that the East could be constrained to yield or retreat through pressure and the show of force. In those days the advocates of a politics of power were in office in Bonn. To be sure, power politics have not been able in the interim to prevent the Soviet Union from becoming a superpower, with atomic or hydrogen bombs, with Sputniks and long- and medium-range missiles. But the West, as we know, remained militarily superior. But even then the risk was excessive. Those who today take up the cause of a politics of power must give heed: remember 1961. The risks have not diminished since then.

In the autumn of that year events came to a head on Friedrichstrasse: American and Soviet tanks facing one another at 150 meters: neither side wanted to shoot, nor did either dare, so they drew back. Power politics showed how truly weak it was.

In Berlin Khrushchev had the geographical situation in his favor, and his victory with the Wall may have seduced him into risking challenging America in Cuba a year later. Cuba, outside Soviet territory, was to host medium-range missiles that could strike a powerful blow to American targets without warning and with no possibility of interception: the American response was equal to the challenge. Both sides peered into the abyss and recoiled; the risk was too great. It was safer for both sides to disengage their medium-range missiles. The Soviets withdrew from Cuba, and the Americans from Turkey and Italy. We should not have to go through this experience again, when a threat of force cannot be followed through; for in 1981, no less than in 1961, the other side is too strong to warrant the risk, and the size of the missiles, whether small or medium, does not change the picture one iota. Since then both sides have become even stronger. Their weapons systems are more precise and more limitable in their effects. The West maintains its advantage in technical precision but is unable to make use of it. The world has become too dangerous a place for us to allow ourselves the luxury of another confrontation, only once more to recoil from the abyss in the realization that cooperation and accord are surer means to a lasting peace than an armaments buildup without limit.

It was not only the politics of power that collapsed in 1961; some internal political illusions also evaporated, at first unnoticed. That the greatest hope of postwar Germany had been dashed once and for all was obvious. The Union Parties (CDU/CSU) had hoped that consolidation of the West into a single camp and rearmament would necessarily lead to reunification; and the SPD, while not sharing this hope, at least entertained it as a possibility. This was now a dead issue. The second watchword—"No peace without unity"—became hollow as well. The principle continued to be defended, but it had lost its credibility. I will not go into all the ins and outs of the internal political discussion as regards the price the Union Parties are still having to pay today for finding it so difficult to discard old illusions.

Many friends of the CDU/CSU Youth will scarcely understand today what happened then: the great Adenauer, armed with an absolute majority and with Strauss as minister of defense, should have shown how such a situation had to be handled, how the Soviets and the SED had to be dealt with, and how to follow up grandiloquent phrases with appropriate deeds. After all, the Adenauer regime had the responsibility for Germany and, indeed, even claimed to be the sole bearer of that responsibility.

What actually happened was nothing to speak of. However, those who reproach us today for the hopes that the *Ostpolitik* has left unrequited and for the dead at the Wall must take a look at the Wall themselves and ask themselves what steps were taken toward achieving German unification between 1949 and 1966, even if the unity desired did not come about.[b]

Thus the Senate was condemned to face the realities of the situation; if, indeed, the firmness of statements, the genuineness

---

b. This passage can only be understood in the context of the current domestic political dispute between the SPD-FDP *Ostpolitik* and the negative attitude of the conservative opposition. The Adenauer regime had rejected any "recognition" of the Pankow regime (e.g., the GDR) and thought any solution of the "German question" had to be based on an agreement among the allies. After the Soviets rejected reunification with neutral status once and for all, however, this position reached a dead end. The call for reunification, together with total integration into the Western alliance system, became an empty slogan. The SPD-FDP *Ostpolitik* that followed marked the first step toward a rapprochment between the two German states which might, it was hoped, one day lead to a new link between the two—R.S. and M.V.

Bearing Responsibility for Germany

of feelings, the justness of the demands, and the sheer power of the demonstrations had been the deciding factors, the Wall would have long since ceased to exist. An attempt had to be made to create holes in the Wall, and to do so the Berlin Senate had to speak with those who had and still have the power to issue and to refuse passes. They did not sit in Bonn, nor in Washington, nor in Moscow, nor even in Pankow, but in East Berlin.[c]

It would require a separate chapter, written with an accomplished satirical pen, to describe how difficult it was to replace the label "zone regime" with the neutral phrase "the other side," and so to agree on that famous formula permitting disagreement on the names of official positions and places.

Later the terms "phenomenon" and the "so-called GDR" would be used, and the dreadful Wall became a reference point even for the terminology of internal German affairs. One could recognize them from their words: the empty phrases having little to do with Berlin, which Senator Blüm[d] piped on August 14, 1961, so pleasant-sounding and barren, so pluckily noncommital, were the self-indulgence of Bonn's politics then and later. What was one to think when Helmut Kohl,[e] asked about his own personal recollection of August 13, answered: "When I heard the news about the Wall on the radio ... ," when in fact on neither the thirteenth nor the fourteenth of August did the word "Wall" occur in any news broadcast. How pleasant, on the other hand, was Richard von Weizsäcker and his speech as the governing mayor,[f] which I shall come back to later.

    c. Pankow was the original seat of government of the GDR. It was later moved to East Berlin. The expression "Pankow regime" continued to be used, however—R.S. and M.V.

    d. Senator Norbert Blüm, born in 1935, was a tool and die maker with Opel and later an editor and activist in the Christian (Catholic) labor movement. Federal director of the Christian Democrat workers organization from 1968 to 1975, he has been a member of the Bundestag since 1972. Senator for Labor and Social Services in Berlin since May 1981, he has been Federal Minister for Labor and Social Services since October 1982 in the newly formed Kohl conservative-liberal coalition government—R.S. and M.V.

    e. Helmut Kohl is chairman of the CDU and newly elected Federal Chancellor in Bonn succeeding Helmut Schmidt—R.S. and M. V.

    f. Richard von Weizsäcker is currently the mayor of Berlin. He was one of the advocates of the SPD-FDP government's Eastern agreements, but did not vote for them because of internal disputes within the CDU/CSU —R.S. and M.V.

In those days we left the rights of the Allies alone in our Senate affairs; and therefore we were not obstructed, although we were watched attentively, pickily even, and this applied even more to Bonn. But experience showed that Berliners had to look after their own interests, and so we did. Translated into other terms, responsibility for Germany had to be borne by Germans themselves.

The assumption of full responsibility for Germany: that is ultimately the bedrock of our policy, which we were compelled to develop and see through against all the charges and accusations after the Wall was built. Later it became the basis for what came to be known as *Ostpolitik*. The extent of this responsibility for Germany is also the central problem of our present situation.

II. To comprehend in tangible terms what the Four-Power Agreement achieved, we must remember the situation at the outset. The Friendship Treaty[g] between the Soviet Union and the GDR declared that Berlin would be regarded as an independent political entity that legally was a part of the GDR, even though it was still occupied by foreign powers, and it had a social system different from that of the GDR. When the Western powers pointed out that they had approved the establishment of closer contacts between Berlin and the Federal Republic and that these ties would continue to be maintained, insofar as this did not infringe on Allied rights, the Soviet Union responded that the Western powers were thereby undermining the foundations for the continued presence of their occupation forces in West Berlin.

In April 1965 the GDR announced that participants in the planned Plenary Session of the German Bundestag would be prohibited transit. Civilian traffic to and from Berlin was temporarily brought to a complete halt, and no protest was of any help.

---

g. The Friendship Treaty is an extension of the "Treaty on Relations between the German Democratic Republic and the Union of Soviet Socialist Republics" of September 20, 1955. The Friendship Treaty of June 12, 1964 (the treaty on "Friendship, Mutual Assistance, and Cooperation") extends beyond the year 2000; it commits the GDR to providing troops to assist the Soviet Union, and the Soviet Union to stationing troops on the territory of the GDR even after dissolution of the Warsaw Pact, whose existence is tied to the existence of NATO—R.S. and M.V.

In March 1968 the GDR issued a prohibition of entry and transit to members of the Nationale Partei Deutschlands (NPD).[h] In April the prohibition was extended to ministers and leading officials of the Federal government, and again neither protests by the Western powers nor resolutions from the Bundestag helped. In June the GDR introduced compulsory passports and visas and imposed fees on both merchandise and people. But Bonn and the three powers accepted these dispositions, and the Federal government offered financial compensation to offset the new fees—truly a case of services tendered with nothing offered in return.

In February 1969 in Berlin, President Nixon declared with good reason that the situation was not satisfactory and should be regarded by all as a call to action. On the suggestion of Foreign Minister Brandt, official feelers were sent out by the three powers in Moscow, and Gromyko responded by declaring his readiness to discuss the prevention of complications over West Berlin with the "wartime Allies"; the Germans were not asked.

We wished here only to make clear how far apart the various sides were from one another, and which side's vital interests later prevailed. At that time no one believed that the Soviet Union would assume its own responsibility; that civilian traffic to and from Berlin would flow free and unhindered; that everyone could participate in it; that there would be sealed trucks and trains; that there would be through trains in which travelers need only show identification; that fees would become a flat sum, and that in this way a legal foundation would be created for civilian German traffic; that the Soviet Union would accept the existence and potential growth of ties between West Berlin and the Federal Republic of Germany; that the Federal agencies would remain in Berlin, and that none of those employed there would have to leave the city. I can still hear Mr. Barzel's[i] con-

---

h. The NPD was a right-wing radical grouping to the right of the CDU-CSU. For a time in the '60s, owing to internal economic crises, it reached the 5 percent representation that is the minimum in regional elections; and it thus achieved some representation in regional governments. It never reached this minimum in Bundestag elections, however, and today is of no significance electorally—R.S. and M.V.

i. Rainer Barzel, born in 1924, member of the Bundestag since 1956, Federal Minister for the German Question from 1962 to 1963, Chairman cern lest the Federal Eagle would have to be taken down. Who at that time could imagine that the Soviet Union and its allies would be willing to accept the Federal Republic's taking over the limited representation of Berlin's interests abroad (already approved by the Allies), particularly the consular services, or the Federal passports, or the capacity to extend international treaties and agreements to apply to West Berlin, to represent West Berlin in international organizations and conferences, or to participate in international conferences and exhibitions in Berlin. But all this and even more took place for our sake, and we have become so used to good things that no one likes to recall the way things were in the past. Furthermore, much of what was later achieved had not even been demanded by the CDU/CSU at that time. They made things easier for themselves. They protested and demanded reunification through free elections. A demand most devoutly to be wished, but a political washout. If today a friend or two want total disarmament and a nuclear-free Europe, I have to say to them: most devoutly to be wished, but you make things too easy for yourselves; politically that is another washout. All or nothing. That is not a politics of responsibility, neither from the right nor the left.

What is interesting in the present context is that the feelers of the four powers did not initially bear fruit. Negotiations did not really get started until early 1971, when the Moscow agreement began to take shape, and the Germans were for the first time accepted as a partner whose vital interests in Berlin's welfare were taken just as seriously as was its readiness politically to draw a line through the past. We defended our interests there just as we had with the three powers. In the one case a partnership was the result; in the other we acquired or strengthened a friendship. No one except the Germans themselves was capable of deciding what we could or could not bear, and thus we encroached on the rights of no one else. Why should this be less so today, ten years later, when missiles are the issue? The same that applied to Berlin holds for missiles and neutron bombs as well. Bonn

---

of the CDU Bundestag minority faction 1964-73, during which time he instituted the constructive no-confidence vote against the Brand-Scheel government in 1972, which failed. Thereafter he more or less retreated from the leadership of the CDU. Since October 1982 he has once again assumed his old, although renamed, post as Federal Minister for Internal German Affairs in the Kohl government.

may not be the seat of sovereign power, but it is the seat of vital German interests.

Nothing of what has been accomplished would have been possible without the alliance; and for everything that has been done we have the will to cooperation and détente to thank. Nothing could be accomplished through armaments or pressure, and everything through the will to achieve a balance. Alone, the four powers were able to achieve nothing; German involvement was required in everything; none of what was done has harmed anyone in Europe, but all the agreements and accords have improved the situation for Europe and for everyone.

Before I draw any conclusions from this glance in retrospect, a few topical comments are in order.

III. We are criticized by the Soviet Union, and we are criticized by the Americans. The one says, "You've been living for twenty years with the SS 4s and SS 5s. Eash has a destructive force of one megaton, i.e., of fifty Hiroshima bombs. The SS 20 is more modern, smaller, and more precise; and suddenly the Germans get upset about medium-range missiles." The other says, "What do you have to say about the inhumanity of the new small weapons when you've lived with the inhumanity of the large dirty ones for more than twenty years?" That Moscow is so un-Christian as to reproach us for not having accustomed ourselves to evil is less suprising than when the same chords are struck in Washington. Unfortunately, the situation is not as funny as it seems when one side says that they have only the weapons of peace, while the other side says that they have only defensive weapons. All are lethal.

What we hear from the leading powers in East and West is the arrogance of power, and the arrogance of the victor lingers in the ear. We have learned what power means, and we have learned how to face realities as well. We have also learned to live with the balance of terror and have seen—even before August 13— the mighty powerless to solve problems. We have learned that taking small steps of cooperation is better than spouting inflated words about going it alone.

We have traveled the path of creating the space others already enjoyed through negotiations with Moscow. Since in fact we Germans were unable to get along with one another fraternally —whether we wanted to or not is another question—there was no other alterntive than to found a state. As the Federal Republic of Germany we have also helped the German Democratic Republic acquire weight in world politics. In the last twelve years the weight of the Federal Republic has grown both politically and economically, and responsibility has grown commensurately.

Responsibility has a twin sister: self-determination.

The year 1945 reduced German responsibility and German self-determination to approximately nil. Since then both have grown. Khrushchev made emphatically clear to Ambassador Krol that the responsibility for building the Wall was his; Ulbricht's shoulders were too narrow to bear it. The Germans were executors, extensions, movers, those who exhorted to both good and evil. The more willing Germans were to assume responsibility, the more say they had in determining things. Having a say in things and responsibility complement one another. Where was this known better than in Berlin, where the victors had become defenders, whose rights of primacy were commensurate with their responsibility, taking precedence even over greater German self-determination?

When the Americans and the Russians agreed to end the blockade and return to the situation beforehand, German rights were left unconsidered and unsettled. When the Wall was built as a concrete marker of the boundary between American and Soviet power in central Europe, it was the Germans who suffered. When we negotiated the Moscow Agreement and made clear that our relationship with Moscow could not improve if it were not accompanied by an improvement in Berlin, but that Berlin was not subject to negotiation, the four-power talks took place.

The Four-Power Agreeement is a thing of greatness; not only did it bring more security to the city and its people, it also marks that point in postwar history when the victors were no longer able to undertake any measures in the center of Europe that touched Germany without the two German states also participating. In his memoirs Henry Kissinger interestingly observes how difficult it was to determine who was actually conducting the complicated negotiations. A clever journalist at that time asked what would happen if the two German states did not come to an agreement on the transit accord. The answer was simple: "Then there would be no Four-Power Agreement." The four powers could do nothing without the Germans, and the Germans could do nothing without the four powers. Mutual dependence, a mutual say, and mutual responsibility. German self-determination and German responsibility grew likewise. And so it is today in Bonn and in East Berlin, in the two German states in 1981, when talk turns to missiles and nuclear weapons.

In this domain little has changed. The Germans are still the extensions, the movers, the proposers; but they do not want to be merely the executors. The responsibility of the four nuclear powers is as good as undivided. German self-determination is a zero quantity. This cannot and will not so remain. To place German demands above all else does not sit well in Europe, nor does it well become us either; and to place the interests of the nuclear powers over German interests does not sit well in Europe, nor of course in Germany.

Our answer to criticism from Moscow and Washington for choosing to discuss nuclear weapons now, whereas before we had nothing to say on the matter at all, is simply: "We were not asked when the race began." But with regard to its continuation or updating we must be asked. We are more aware of our self-determination, at least in the Federal Republic.

De Gaulle saw that sovereignty today ultimately consisted in possessing the ultimate and most extreme weapon, the atomic bomb. The command to use it places the very existence of a state on the line: it is understandable and logical, therefore, that no atomic power will share the responsibility for its use. Nor will this change because no nuclear power can make its own existence dependent on a decision shared with a nonnuclear power. When the American Secretary of Defense recently declared that "Even our closest ally cannot deprive the American government of the power to decide what is best for the American soldier stationed in Europe," this was not only the arrogance of power, it was also the awareness of an indivisible responsibility. And the tune is the same from Paris, London, and Moscow. The four powers acquired their rights of primacy over Germany before they had the power that made them the four nuclear powers that are of such importance to us.

When the question is asked in the United States whether we know what we are actually demanding when we expect that powerful and proud nation, with its overkill capacities, to place its own existence on the line as a surety for us, we can only say, "Yes, we know." We have always known it, from the time of the blockade, the first ultimatum against Berlin, the building of the Wall, down to this very day. The guarantee of a nation which bears the responsibility of a guardian power and a leader carries weight only if its readiness to put its own existence on the line as required remains credible. But the difference is that it is the United States which decides, not we. Moreover, its decision also decides our existence; we do not. A nation that has nuclear weapons also has the power of decision over its allies and their existence. The converse is not the case. It is therefore only consistent that no NATO strategy is an automatic process that unfolds of itself; the decision remains in the hands of the American president when and to what extent he will cross the threshold beyond which our own existence, and perhaps that of others as well, will be snuffed out. Here, too, German self-determination and responsibility end. Nor can we do without the protection of our alliance as long as the alliance in the East and its power are as they are. In Berlin this is known all too well. The two alliances guarantee stability in Europe and thus help to preserve the peace. The way to self-determination on the issue of nuclear weapons is barred to Germans both by treaties and out of our own convictions. We have learned what power and reality mean. But along the way from the Wall to the Four-Power Agreement and on to the Accord on Fundamentals, we have also learned that confrontation is frailer than cooperation. Politics is the art of finding a way out of the dead end of the never-ending arms race. And here begins the next chapter in the growth of German self-determination and responsibility.

When America decides what its interests call for, we must decide what ours need as well. In our alliance this must be reduced to a common denominator; otherwise the alliance begins to rot at its very core. Their leading power must not degrade the consent of their partners to a pro forma matter or a political cosmetic.

When Weinberger says that the United States decides what is best for American soldiers in Germany, legally he is right. But to translate this statement into hard realities, he would have to appeal to the troops agreement, and so turn the wheels of history back to a time when foreign command over the revised occupation statutes had become a part of the past, and we had acquired a limited self-determination that later was expanded politically. When the Federal government discreetly but unequivocally stated that it expected to be consulted about the stationing of neutron bombs on German soil, even with American troops, this meant that the friendship which has developed with the United States prohibits the invocation of the relics of the occupation statutes. I say this in Berlin in particular, where Americans and Germans have learned that a trustworthy friendship is more important than legal statutes.

Legally, the United States can bring neutron bombs to Berlin, about this there is no doubt; politically it could not get them so far. Here, too, again there is no doubt. Anyone these days who follows the arguments that are being made in favor of the neutron bomb, i.e., that it is best against high-powered conventional attacks, especially against tanks, and hence promotes the cause of peace, will see the flaw in this argument when he asks: why then no neutron bombs to Berlin? The political weight of this weapon is greater than its military importance.

Weinberger said ironically that opponents of the neutron bomb call it immoral; actually, the security of the democratic nations will be enhanced by this weapons system, he observed, and thus make discussions about moral questions possible. This argument is about as incontrovertible and conclusive as the question of how many divisions the Pope has. It is not this dimension but the military and political dimension that is today under discussion. Militarily the Bavarian prime minister was correct and consistent when he said that the Federal army should be equipped with the neutron bomb. If the neutron bomb was supposed to be effective against tanks, it should be stationed where tanks can come, and that is on the north German lowlands, where there are no American units. (Strauss agrees with the Soviet Union on this point, from which I want to conclude only that even Soviet arguments sometimes can be correct.) One can put the point even more harshly: no argument for the neutron bomb makes sense if it is not given to the Bundeswehr. This makes it more than clear what military and political persuasion the technical qualities of a weapon exercise, unless one simply says no and, rather than accept submission to a weapon, declares that "reason, interests, and political self-determination must carry the day."

Politically the Bavarian prime minister is behind the times; in nuclear matters the Adenauer prescription that we will acquire a greater say in things the more willing we are to go along no longer works. To demand the stationing of bombs the Americans do not have or have not yet required would, as I see it, not do justice to German interests nor to German responsibility for a cohesive alliance.

Our dilemma is that it is not we but others who make decisions about our vital concerns. Our hope derives from the fact that we Germans are not alone in this situation. We share it with all the nations of Europe that do not have atomic weapons. All nonnuclear nations have a common interest in not becoming hostages to be commanded about, yet at the same time securing the alliance's stability. They recognize that all nations have a common interest in peace, that the nuclear powers have other rights, and that hence the nonnuclear powers have other interests.

It would be no more than just for the nuclear powers to undertake certain commitments with regard to the nonnuclear powers, as in the Four-Power Agreement. This applies to the whole of Europe. But even if others do not want this, our increased self-determination and increased responsibility would enable us, the Federal Republic of Germany, to safeguard our own vital interests. Others will not do it for us.

From the Wall via the Four-Power Agreement down to the present day we have traced our responsibility for Germany. We shall bear this responsibility and serve it best if we see it in a European context, working together with all our neighbors, whose destiny is also our own.

CHAPTER
6

THE RELEVANCE OF THE GERMAN QUESTION FOR PEACE IN EUROPE

Herbert Ammon and Peter Brandt

In the following we will attempt to develop a political conception for the objective connection between the German question and the safeguarding of peace. We will pose the *German question* in radical terms, i.e., in terms of national sovereignty and the right to self-determination, basic principles of the democratic "left," which moreover are fundamental to any thought concerning equality and emancipation vis-à-vis the internal and external structures of authority and rule. Critical of both the systems currently "actually existing" on German soil, we stand firm on this doctrine, with its origins in the left; but as regards its realization, we give due account to the relatively stable power relations in both states and military alliances and to the unpredictably disruptive process of destabilization. In addition, let us bear in mind the principle of self-determination for the entire German nation, with particular application to the GDR, as set forth explicitly in the opening phase of the new *Ostpolitik*, from Willy Brandt's Erfurt Declaration to the "Letter on German Unity."[a] Erich Honecker's statements in February 1981 once

---

a. The Erfurt Theses, in 1970, represented an attempt by Willy Brandt in the early stages of détente to engage the cooperation of the GDR government, which was at that time obstructing the establishment of a new relationship between the two German states with its maximalist demands for immediate and full diplomatic recognition. The meeting in Erfurt provoked considerable attention, since it was the first meeting with a German Federal Chancellor on GDR territory. Initially, however, it brought about no progress in the talks and treaty negotiations. The Moscow negotiations were the first to yield results.
The "Letter on German Unity" refers to the letter appended to the 1972

again made clear that on the other side, the GDR also lays claim to the right of Germans to self-determination, if with a class-specific accent. We urge the need for a national democratic identity for all Germans, which in our opinion cannot be found in separate states, especially since each of the two German states is able to legitimate itself only by marking itself off from the other. Academic controversies aside, the term "nation" has for us a concrete historical and political content: the continued suffering of the people in both German states as a result of Nazi fascism calls for continuing political reflection and practical action leading to the abolition of this state of affairs. For the first time in the twentieth century, this task is consonant with the interests of our European neighbors; there are hopes for a state of peace that will transcend Europe's divided existence. The "national task" of Germans in both East and West, therefore, has to do not with the reciprocal relations to which they are ordained within their respective alliances, but with going beyond the status quo.

It is in this respect that we respond critically to the achievements of the SPD-FDP policy détente. By showing its internal contradictions we call into question the prevailing interpretation, which with the slogan "Peace before Unity" has elevated acceptance of the status quo to a maxim in the German question. We intend to show that this article of faith relates to an artificial contradiction that has already been rendered obsolete by the threat to peace in Europe.

"Balance" brings no security

East-West balance, the prescription for security that has served as the rationale for staking out West German policy on the German question firmly within the NATO alliance, makes that policy dependent on the climate of the East-West conflict.

Treaty on Basic Principles with the GDR. This letter, which has the force of a treaty, stresses that the conclusion of the treaty does not imply any recognition of the GDR by the FRG in terms of international law. It rather assumes that the German question is still open.—R.S. and M.V.

Every deterioration in the climate has a backlash effect on internal German politics. The events in Poland in the winter of 1981-82 demonstrated the consequences of this prescription. In the end the military-political balance that served as the theoretical basis for détente has repeatedly stabilized the partition of the world since Yalta. The right claimed by the Soviet superpower to intervene within its bloc has been respected by the West in every case: 1953, 1956, and 1968. The danger of an intervention, which the military coup in Poland has by no means quelled, is a consequence of the alliance structure imposed on the bloc by the Soviet Union. This danger would be reduced considerably if a zone of neutrality were to be created in central Europe from which Soviet troops had been withdrawn after a general demilitarization of that region as part of a genuine security system.

Conversely, the security doctrine that has become customary among Western Europeans, namely, that their own security is to be found only under the U.S. nuclear umbrella, constitutes the rationale for de facto dependence on the Americans. Adjurations that the Europeans must make clear their own interests to the superpowers are at best suited as evidence of the nonexistence of a secure European infrastructure; France's nationally self-centered security policy can serve as an example. Nor are such adjurations able, for example, to lessen the pressure exerted by the American leading power on the Federal Republic, the most powerful and, in the end, the only relevant NATO force to adhere loyally to the U.S. security model.

This model, which has led an unassailed existence in the Western Alliance, has an inner logic and an inner morality of its own. A criticism of the alliance security dogma must therefore proceed on both levels. Though we are unable here to undertake a detailed refutation of the security policy of the West German Federal government, we can at least indicate a few places where the logic appears flawed:

1. The deterrence doctrine prescribes a second-strike capability at each stage: the aggressor will be deterred from a surprise attack by an anticipated counterstrike. However, such a goal is achievable without "balance," with a second-strike capability at the lowest level.

2. The doctrine of flexible response purports to widen the margin of strategic action and avoid "unnecessary" escalation. However, in the above logic it necessarily leads to escalation if deterrence is to remain credible.

3. At each level of escalation there is a real and present danger that the dominant American power will withdraw from the system out of self-interest in its own survival. Conversely, the temptation to undertake a preventive strike is enhanced at each new stage in the arms race.

4. Even at the very lowest level of confrontation, the risk of nuclear suicide exists. In view of the assumed conventional superiority of the Warsaw Pact, NATO itself does not expect a conventional attack to be successfully repulsed. Even at this level, therefore, defense is to be undertaken with tactical nuclear weapons. In densely populated central Europe this means the annihilation of much of the German civilian population (on both sides of the border). However, the premises on which deterrence is based are undermined by this threat of nuclear suicide: they become implausible. A concept of defense that lacks its own military logic, since in the doubtful case it cannot perform its own security tasks, demolishes its own ethical claim.

The chances for bloc nonalliance in the light of the global interests of the superpowers

Consideration of an alternative to present policies concerning security, foreign affairs, and the German question calls for a brief treatment of the global position and power interests of the superpowers. We will confine ourselves to the following observations:

1. In the United States a leaning toward coexistence or détente, made necessary by the nuclear threat, has competed since the Kennedy era with a countertrend toward maintaining the conflict (below the crisis threshold) with redoubled effort.

2. U.S. and Soviet perceptions have undergone a change since the emergence of the Soviet-Chinese conflict. At the same time, the rules of the game have undergone appreciable changes with the entry of China, a developing nation, into the ranks of the world powers.

3. The focal point of the conflict has clearly shifted from Europe, i.e., essentially Germany, to countries of the Third World, especially the important raw materials areas. This means, however, that (a) the wait-and-see attitude that has prevailed on both sides since 1976 (Cuba's participation in the Soviet mission in Africa) is increasingly restricting the freedom of movement of the European allies; (b) the readiness to conduct regional surrogate wars and to undertake direct interventions has increased, and this in turn can cause the conflict to backlash onto Europe owing to alliance commitments.

Within the American consensus, which has never been seriously called into question among the power elite either before or since the Vietnam War, the issue is to find and use methods to maintain worldwide defense and to create a model American social system (the American dream). In domestic politics this issue is reflected ideologically in the rivalry between the conservatives and the liberals, while in foreign policy it is reflected in the dispute over the correct course to take in pursuit of the national interest. Underlying this dispute over ideas and methods is the common conviction of the superiority of American institutions and the capitalist system.

The succession of ruling groups that have passed across the scene in the postwar era have all taken the conflict with the Eastern superpower as a given, even in the period of détente. The problems concerning how to parry the global opponent, the Soviet Union, emerged clearly into the forefront in the interlude of the Carter government. Concepts in which geostrategic and military paradigms are allowed uncritically to prevail over political alternatives today dominate thinking in the Reagan government. The hardest stance toward the rival superpower is personified not only in Alexander Haig, the former NATO Supreme Commander, now Secretary of State, but in Reagan's intellectual following as well. Common to all of these new leading elite is the belief in the American mission in the world. This conviction, which means a greater readiness for confrontation with the Soviet Union around the world, carries more weight, as we see it, than Reagan's undiplomatic rhetoric at his inauguration.

In the context of global conflict, Europeans have been required to place themselves within the community of interests of the "Atlantic Community" (a term from Kennedy's "Grand Design") since the partition of Germany. The United States' chief ally, the Federal Republic of Germany, has no room to maneuver within this design. Because of its special political vulnerability (Berlin) and its military exposure, the FRG is doomed to support any U.S. action in global conflicts. This role alone dashed any hopes of achieving the national goal of overriding the German partition by bringing the opposing systems closer. The rival systems would have first to be brought round, however, and that is hardly to be expected. A realization, therefore, of West Germany's junior partner role in the alliance makes some rethinking necessary.

The risks and chances of a *nonaligned policy* depend essentially on how Soviet foreign policy is assessed. On this point our discussion must necessarily move to a more hypothetical level, as the power structures and major relations in the decision-making centers in Moscow are not as transparent as they are in the West. Controversies and divergent positions on most issues of domestic and foreign policy usually become discernible only after the fact, when the hawks are separated from the doves. But such speculation does not tell us much about actual Soviet strategy, for instance, with regard to Afghanistan, since it leaves unanswered the question whether the factions that form have their roots in fundamental differences of view about ends—namely, an expansionary imperialist policy or an imperialist defensive strategy—or whether they are merely a dispute over means.

We see the Soviet Union as a system in which respective elites in the bureaucratic apparatus of the party, the army, and the economic leadership compete to secure their rule by slowly but steadily satisfying more and more material needs, backed up by a massive suppressive appratus. The concept of totalitarianism no longer satisfactorily describes this system, at least for the present. Counter to the Western hypothesis of détente and convergence, the phase of waning repression coincided with the Khrushchev era, i.e., a transitional period from the Cold War to coexistence, while in the decade of détente between 1970 and 1980 in the Brezhnev era, the authoritarian and repressive features again became stronger. As regards the goals of Soviet foreign policy, views vary depending on the observer's situation and his assessment of the relevance of the ideology of world revolution.

Critics of the Soviet regime and Soviet emigrants assume an undiminished and massive ideological and political expansionism on the part of the Soviet superpower. While we do not want to make light of such positions, we draw other conclusions from the global policies of the two superpowers: these policies constrain Germans and ultimately all Europeans to retreat from bloc confrontation in the interests of self-preservation. Furthermore, we can only partly share the view that the aim of the Soviet Union is "world revolution," since, as its interventions in Africa and Asia have shown, this goal is not always applied on a global scale; moreover, the Soviet Union does not always have an unemcumbered hand in the governments of its allies. It would be a tragic mistake to lose sight of the decolonizing process and the social revolutionary situation in the Third World in evaluating the role of the Soviet Union's world politics.

The Soviet Union is today, like the United States, a superpower in distress. This circumstance, borne out in particular by the signs of dissolution in its Eastern European perimeter, seems to us to be more relevant than any discussions about a presumed love of peace or plans for world domination on the part of the Soviet leaders. As long as those forces do not fully gain the upper hand which, under the banner of a new nuclear "war communism," see the only way out to be total bloc confrontation, we must assume that the Soviet Union's superpower politics are on the whole calculable.

Under the trauma of the German invasion of 1941, the Soviet leaders kept alternatives open in their German policy for a long time after 1945 (perhaps even into the 1960s). Once the Cold War broke out into the open in 1947-48, the chance for establishing a joint suppressive rule over Germany was gone and with it the chance to freely bleed the country for reparations. Two possibilities then remained: essentially either the German danger could be neutralized by keeping the country divided, or the Federal Republic could be wrenched from its Western alliance by reaching an understanding with noncommunist German forces.

However, to accomplish this the GDR would have had to be

let loose from the Warsaw Pact, and the people's democracy form of government would have had to be discarded; that would have entailed high risks for the cohesion of the Eastern bloc. It cannot escape notice that the second alternative receded in the course of time and by the '60s and '70s was no longer seen as a serious prospect.

There are major counterarguments today to the duality we have assumed in the German policy of the USSR: does the Soviet Union, a nuclear power on a par with the United States in the 1980s, still find it necessary under certain conditions to think twice about those options so advantageous to us; do historical chances for an alternative Soviet German policy still exist? In the past history of German-Soviet relations, Soviet diplomacy has time and again demonstrated that it knows how to catch any balls that might be tossed its way.

We do not blindly insist that the second Soviet option we have assumed is real, although recurrent press statements indicate that the Soviet leadership still entertains some thoughts along these lines. However, the unconditional alignment of the Federal Republic with the West prohibits West German government from sounding out, even only at the discussion level, Soviet readiness to find a solution to the German question overall.

Soviet policy attentively registers signs of mutations in political consciousness and attempts to turn such changes to its own advantage. Denuclearization and bloc nonalignment of central Europe as an aim of the Federal Republic would fundamentally alter the entire political situation for all parties.

At this point the specter of Finlandization is usually invoked —initially with Yugoslavia as the model for the GDR and Sweden for the Federal Repuclic. The treaty clauses that restricted the Finns' margin of freedom date from the postwar period, historically an extremely unpropitious time for Finland. The sociopolitical and economic circumstances of this small nation in Scandinavia are wholly different from those of the two German states. The translation of military superiority into political sway also requires a readiness to assume a military risk. Under no illusions, we do not set the threshold of moral restraint from military action either higher or lower for the Soviet leadership than for the current American leaders. On the other hand, it is difficult to imagine a nuclear attack on a nonaligned Federal Republic literally over the territory of a nonaligned GDR if one assumes the aggressor would have "rational" predatory intentions of directly appropriating West German industrial capacity. Neither of the two nonaligned states would by any means acquiesce in a conventional attack on them, or on the Federal Republic, without putting up a defense; and their flexible mobile territorial defenses would make sure that it entailed a high risk for the aggressor.

One can assume that the overwhelming majority of the population in the GDR would be in favor of a withdrawal of Soviet divisons. Deliverance from the danger of intervention in any movement toward socioeconomic and political emancipation is probably the best that the East Germans can expect for the present. On the other hand, the Berlin Wall and the nature of the border between the two Germanies are more than an image problem for the GDR. On account of them the SED leadership still commands only a relatively narrow basis of legitimation among the population. Once the regime showed a greater flexibility and readiness for reform, this basis would be expanded to include those strata that so far have demonstrated only tacit loyalty. In addition, such a policy would accommodate the nationalist sentiments of the East German population in that it would recognize special political relations with the Federal Republic. Assuming, therefore, a relatively strong need for legitimation in the SED, a detailed model of overall German nonalignment and cooperation could, despite its inherent risks, find a positive response in the East German state party, with the exception of the neo-Stalinist faction and a group advocating annexation that might place a big bet on the crisis in the Federal Republic.

Changes in the military status quo

A precondition for the withdrawal of the two German states from their respective alliances would have to be the formation of a nuclear-free zone in central Europe. Efforts in East and West Europe to achieve nuclear disengagement would make it more difficult for the superpowers to nip any serious pan-

German initiative of this sort in the bud. To acquire the consent of the European nations and the superpowers for a withdrawal of the victors in World War II from the whole of Germany, this move would have to be combined with a conversion of the Bundeswehr, the West Germany army, and the Nationale Volksarmee, the East German army, to territorial defense.

At the same time, the foreign armed forces in all four sectors of Berlin would be reduced to a symbolic contingent. Even assuming a real threat to West Berlin, the troops stationed there have ultimately only symbolic value. Their withdrawal would improve the psychological preconditions for German peace policy without causing any serious disadvantages with regard to security in the context outlined here. Since an arms reconversion would increase rather than diminish military security against any potential aggressions, it could also be undertaken unilaterally. The same would apply to a proclaimed readiness to withdraw from the alliance system together with the other German state.

Changes in the political status quo

The formation of a "German community" binding the two German states together by treaty, with its seat in (East and West) Berlin, would be aimed for. A joint basis might be the realization that beyond the incompatibility of their respective social and state orders, the two German states have kindred and cultural points in common that have a history behind them, that a close collaboration is in consonance with the will of the populations in both German states, and that the maintenance of strict separation is a menace to peace, both outwardly and inwardly. Since there would be conflicting views concerning the structure of a newly unified Germany, only a confederative association would be possible at first. The mutual commitment to strive for unification only with the consent of the other state would mean a renunciation of forcible undermining of the other state but would not be a guarantee of its internal constitutional system.

An all-German council of deputies, consisting of representatives of both parliaments, and an all-German coordination office could be the organs of such a "German community"; the latter would be directed by two special appointees of the two heads of government and would coordinate practical collaboration.[b]

Both states would commit themselves to gradually removing all restrictions on the entry of citizens from the other state. The German community would stand in the stead of the "basic treaty" of 1972. It might require amendments of the two constitutions. A new agreement on the question of citizenship would also be possible within the community.

The status of West Berlin, which ultimately is simply untenable, would have to be redefined as an integral component of such a confederation. West Berliners would have to decide whether they want to enjoy their constitutional rights, still restricted today, as a state with special status within the Federal Republic or as an independent "free city." Commissions should be set up between the two Berlin city administrations for all matters requiring cooperation.

Initially, to give Germans freedom of movement in Berlin, the GDR might be allowed to participate in the monitoring of air traffic from and to West Berlin. (The GDR already exercises sovereign rights, albeit clearly restricted, in West Berlin through its visa office.) Over the middle term the GDR would then perhaps find the Wall dispensable. In return the GDR would have to agree not to take up legal proceedings against citizens of its state who temporarily stayed in West Berlin and to cease the criminal prosecution of former "fugitives from the republic."

Even before the Wall was dismantled, a number of facilities for visitor traffic are conceivable, such as the elimination of entry fees and the compulsory visa for West Berliners and a reduction of the age limit for East Berliners.

Changes in the economic status quo

Withdrawal from membership in the CMEA and the EEC respectively would not be required in the confederative option. Despite these integral ties to multinational economic blocs, special economic relations have long existed between the Federal

---

b. These transitional arrangements borrow quite clearly from the SPD Germany treaty of 1958-59 and the GDR and Soviet confederative plans entertained into the '60s.—R.S. and M.V.

Republic and the GDR (including the covert membership of East Germany in the EEC). These relations should first be established by treaty and then cultivated as a constituent part of the German community. As European cooperation between the CMEA and the EEC in general increased, a more intimate economic community between the Federal Republic and the GDR could perform a bridging or linking function (long a goal of Eastern politicians). Elements of the "German economic community," such as the GDR's membership in GATT and the convertibility of the GDR mark, would be compatible with the ideas considered so far.

For West Berlin, German economic cooperation is a vital issue. Fundamental questions would first crop up for the economic blocs and the economies of European nations other than Germany only when a total economic integration of the whole of Germany was achieved. Therefore we will not discuss this aspect of the question here.

Changes in the legal status quo

The two German states and the German community could conclude a peace treaty with the victorious nations of World War II after they had redefined their positions relative to one another and within Europe. German nonalignment, following the Austrian model, would have to be respected by the former wartime Allies, and any intervention in Germany explicitly renounced. Germany would recognize all borders, particularly the Oder-Neisse line, as permanent. The last Allied occupation rights ended with the Four-Power Agreement on Berlin. The victorious powers would have to declare their prior agreement to a potential reunification accepted by the two separate states.

Germany policy—a left-wing policy for peace in Europe

On the surface our reflections might seem to be wholly politics imposed from above: deliberations of leading politicians, negotiations between governments, agreements between states. Clearly, however, a disengagement of the two German states from the two blocs, i.e., from the hegemonic powers, would hardly be possible without a massive movement from below. The beginnings of such a movement may be discerned in the emerging all-German peace movement. The new German peace movement is in need of a goal such as has been prefigured, for example, in E. P. Thompson's pan-European campaign. But it also needs sober, realistic political goals to free it from the dilemma of involuntarily becoming the supporter of either of the power blocs. It requires responsive partners and allies within the political elites of both East and West Germany and must therefore relate to the aims of those most directly affected. Our discussion was meant to serve this purpose—hence the seeming onesidedness of our perspective.

The armament reconversion model we have advocated undoubtedly demands some rethinking within the peace movement, since it is incompatible with fundamentally pacifist positions. A military strategy modified along the lines we have sketched out would initially entail a severe financial strain, even if over the long run it would be cheaper. Above all, it would be linked to some defensive militarization of civilian life.

The one telling advantage of this model, however, lies in the fact that it allows the question of whether either of the superpowers is arming or operating offensively or defensively to remain safely open and permits the pursuit of an active and unambiguous peace policy without neglecting the security needs of the population.

The transition to a policy of bloc nonalignment would be tantamount to eliminating the latent civil war situation in Germany. It would mean a fundamental improvement in the political climate and create a juncture favorable to left-wing emancipatory politics.

In the fifties and sixties every success of the leading group in one German state strengthened its counterpart in the other state. The Adenauer wing of the CDU-CSU and the Ulbricht wing of the SED thus de facto pursued their politics in a spirit of conflicting mutuality. Nonalignment, armament reconversion, and the confederation of all Germany would make the way clear for the opposite mechanism to take effect. A reunification of Germany on an anti-imperialist basis would become a goal realizable from below.

Far from being a nationalist rebellion against Europe, every serious attempt to break up the confrontation of the blocs in Germany under the hegemony of the superpowers has ultimately had the effect of making "peace, democracy, and national autonomy in East and West a single interlocking issue" (E. P. Thompson).

The goal of a nuclear-free Europe would come into realizable proximity, and the danger of nuclear confrontation at the center would be eliminated. To the objection that the prospects for a unified or even just a tightly structured German confederation could not yet achieve a majority consensus among our neighbors, we offer the following consideration: the policy we have outlined here aims at a disengagement of the hegemonic powers in central Europe. It alone can guarantee true security against the permanent danger of their intervention into social and political processes of emancipation in Europe. Furthermore, it is interesting that the challenge levied at the superpower bloc structure in Europe has created a renewed awareness of the particular touchiness of the German situation, stemming from the interests of the peoples of Europe themselves. The Swedish disarmament expert Alva Myrdal has repeatedly referred to the unsolved German question as the key problem of European peace. One year after the Brussels NATO decision, she declared that she missed "incentives from the Germans" for a nuclear-free zone in central Europe, "since after all, it should lie mainly in their interests to have the two superpowers withdraw their nuclear weapons from the two German states." Why, she asked, is there no German politician "who says this openly, i.e., who in the first instance pursues a German policy and represents German interests instead of American or Soviet ones?"

CHAPTER

7

A PEACE POLICY FOR GERMANY
Günter Gaus

The current armaments issue between East and West is, I believe in its substance and methods not totally independent of the fact that a new government with a quite definite position has taken office in the United States. To say this does not mean that we have a kind of red monocle over our left eye, so to speak, which clouds our vision as to Moscow's share in the responsibility for the tension, dangerously close to belligerency, between the world's great military blocs.

Yet here in Germany the banal assertion that to adequately appreciate the forbidding situation one must also look into the intentions of our ally Ronald Reagan and his government's offices suffices for many Germans to be wrongly accused of harboring an irrational anti-Americanism. Of course, this anti-Americanism does exist, and its existence is no accident. However, whatever arguments we might present in its defense, as such it is just as dangerous as every other kind of irrationalism in politics. It must be resisted. More important at present, on the other hand, is not to lose sight of the fact that in the Federal Republic of Germany it can in no sense be said to exist as a movement with a following of millions. Millions are concerned, quite reasonably so, about peace. Anti-American they are not, but they have their doubts, not unfounded, whether American and German priorities are sufficiently in accord in the present situation. To reach such an accord without paying the price of our acquiescing to the status of a dependent partner—or jointly to work out a compromise that keeps the alliance intact even if full accord cannot be reached—is to understand alliance politics correctly.

But what, then, about the politicians and the media that denounce the not only inevitable but also necessary debates on this question as anti-American—what indeed can then be the conception of a Western alliance? If this anti-Americanism should some day become a reality, they will certainly have had a strong hand in creating it. Either the alliance whose policies they would have discussed publicly exclusively in conformist terms is based on servility and would not survive such self-exposure with the requisite stability, or the politicians and media that mouth the malicious, dangerous, and self-destructive word "anti-Americanism" know that they are lying; and then they would be lying because it served their particular party interests, namely, the advantages they presume will accrue to them from being able to drive the left-of-center political forces, particularly the Social Democrats, into a corner where at one time one could read: without fatherland.

French President Mitterrand has currently the dubious good fortune of being presented to us, who are denounced as being anti-American, as an exemplary armaments politician by these same politicians and their media. This has softened a bit, for the time being, the abhorrence of his nationalizations and his government coalition with the communists. It is credulously reported that Mitterrand would have no objections to the new American medium-range missiles on West German soil and is even willing to discuss the neutron bomb.

Of course, even those who recommend him to us as an example to be followed on this (and only this) point cannot wholly avoid the question of why he takes this position, even though it is expediently veiled in terms becoming their purpose. But even under this veil we find that Mitterrand and his followers are no anticommunist crusaders, such as one often encounters here in Germany and in the United States. The talk from Paris is about the West German bastion, France's conveniently situated, forward-based buffer. It is a quite old French national policy that Mitterrand did not develop, but which with a matter-of-factness worthy of envy he carries on. The motives of the French have little to do with NATO or the European Community.

Who could blame Mitterrand for looking after the interests of his country as he sees them? It is to his advantage that France's national policy at present accords more fully with American policy in the arms question than, say, in de Gaulle's time. Mitterrand's policy on this issue (and perhaps not only on this issue) may be shortsighted, but it is easier to justify from France's position as a nation undivided than a similar attitude would be here in divided Germany.

No words can be sharp enough against those who would hold up France's quite special attitude to our shame without straightforwardly acknowledging wherein lies the source of the difference in frame of mind—namely, the relative casualness of many French and the uneasiness of very many Germans. Do those who conceal or even suppress the reasons for this difference think that they can treat alarmed West Germans as idiots, or are they gambling on their impotent resignation? Or in the end, perhaps, might they themselves not be the ones who are deceived in their deception, unable any longer to perceive even so glaring a difference as that between the French and the German situations?

Those who read France's national arms policy as conformity to NATO cast anxious Germans unjustly in the role of fools by making their concern for their own country suspect as a kind of "nationalist neutralism." I will have something more to say on the matter of German neutralism later on. But we should be clear here and now what the current campaign against this purported West German nationalist neutralism demonstrates: it shows that for centuries little has changed in the way we Germans handle the national question. Even today we find ourselves once again seeing that the only version of national sentiment that is not suspect and not reviled among the public at large is the one that conforms to the dictates of the leading forces in our country. Any tune different from the one they whistle has in their ears, and according to their unimpeachable insinuations, nothing patriotic about it but is simply an obscenity.

The West German peace movement, which, to be sure, contains dangerous irrationalist elements, needs neither rubles nor a guiding light from Moscow. For many reasons, of which the Soviet SS 20 and the American Pershing missiles are but one, convictions, certitudes, and general understandings already decades old are being devalued and cast in radical doubt ever more frequently because they have proven to be spurious. The peace movement is only part of this process (which has shocked many —quite understandably so), the end of which is not yet in sight.

What notion of a commonweal, of life together in a democratic state can these politicians and journalists have who are more inclined to speak of communist infiltration and popular fronts (to use a totally nonpolemical and reserved term) than to concede that the reasons for all those people congregating in the Hofgarten in Bonn were, wrong or not, at least honest and their own? Don't they care at all about the implications of insinuating that hundreds of thousands had allowed themselves to be controlled by outside forces?[a]

And so once again, a minority, and this time not so small, is being excised from our body politic. The havoc that missiles can wreak does not begin where they are stationed. We Germans are bringing it on ourselves because we are ostracizing the forces swimming against the stream. If the arms buildup question should develop as I fear (and it easily could), that is, if rage and acrimony seize control of the peace movement demonstrators should they see their efforts come to nought, then in what ghetto are they to be confined—after all, that would only be consistent with the way they are already being raked over verbally. How high will the casualty rate among engaged youth be, how many can we still afford to have stigmatized as blind and dangerous outsiders without inflicting on state and society even more harm than is already evident?

The SPD has certainly seen times of greater strength in office than just now. But it has its feet planted firmly in its best traditions in its endeavors to maintain a dialogue with these engaged people who have reasons, some right, some wrong, to draw

a. On the occasion of the first major West German peace demonstration on October 10, 1981, in the Bonn Hofgarten, the conservative press accused the SPD of entering into a popular front with the Communists. More than fifty Bundestag deputies had declared their solidarity with this demonstration. The influence of the Communists was not insignificant, but it was by no means dominant. They were unable, for instance, to get even one speaker for the final proclamation and are still unrepresented in the official organizing committees of key peace demonstrations.—R.S. and M.V.

A Peace Policy for Germany

other conclusions from the present situation than those of the majority setting the tone in the country.

If it is still not too late for German Social Democrats to emerge from their spell of impotence, they will have some long and patient information work to do. It seems to me that to see through the often automatic mechanism of our political opinion-making industry ourselves and to enlighten others about them is a more necessary task for the success of Social Democratic détente policy than holding one missile forum[b] after the other, so that every member can become a Pershing expert. We are not only running the risk of dangerous prejudices assuming a dangerous control over us; the experts themselves are taking independent initiatives to hand out their expertise (against which as such there can be no objections) as policy. The havoc starts in our own minds.

Let me try to clarify what I see as determining our situation as West Germans living in a divided Germany in an alliance that is presently finding its very foundations called into question. There seem to me to be four overriding points to be considered:

● Afghanistan, especially as regards its effects on NATO, its altered internal and external circumstances;

● Poland, specifically to raise a basic question which for Europe makes the present year the most dangerous year since 1939;

● the political psychology of the United States under President Reagan, to sound out the chances for reaching a compromise, as befits the political situation, between the leading Western power and its European allies that goes deeper than the facile phrases of the NATO communiqué issued after the autumn meeting of the foreign and defense ministers; and finally,

● certain aspects of the world of political ideas, both those that have been long dominant in the Federal Republic of Germany, and those that are just now entering into people's consciousness, to help clarify the national question and the possibilities open to Germans living as a divided nation.

Our analysis is based on the realization that the current mod-

b. Gaus refers to the Peace Forum held by the SPD in 1981, to which it had invited almost all tendencies and major figures in the West German peace movement for a discussion. See also *Sicherheit contra Frieden? Ein Forum zur Friedensbewegung*, Berlin-Bonn, 1982.—R.S. and M.V.

ernization debate has in substance begun too late. We are discussing minimal or maximal armaments positions before we have gotten a clear idea of the political complexion of our own camp and the, in some cases quite different, intentions concerning arms that it has engendered, and finally, before we have weighed these intentions against one another insofar as is possible. We are proceeding as if NATO were a monolithic bloc, as indeed it may once have been (before de Gaulle). Today, in any event, from Washington to Athens, from The Hague to the Bonn Hofgarten, it is monolithic no more. This anyone can see: but we act as if there were still a congruence of interests which has remained unchanged since 1949 and a political cast of mind that is roughly the same for all partners, opposed by only a few groups that have gone astray or are controlled by outsiders.

Nothing jeopardizes NATO more than this as-if attitude. It has generated endless debates about missile deployments or no missile deployments on land or on sea, all before NATO is discussed at all—for the purpose of preserving it, I hasten to add. This self-jeopardy comes from the kind of humdrum thinking that goes on behind office doors, which equates the nations of NATO with the NATO Council of Ministers. But this no longer works. The public debate must begin at the beginning of the problem and not at the way-station marked by the double decision[c] of the Council of Ministers; in a word, the task at hand must be repoliticized.

Afghanistan—that is, the Soviet invasion of Afghanistan—marked at least temporarily a gain of position for the Soviet superpower against the North American superpower in an important part of Asia. It was not good for the West. But for NATO, i.e., for the governments and their official mood-makers, Afghanistan was a soft summer rain after a long drought. Red Army soldiers in Kabul: that was something that bore comment not only politically but also morally.

c. In its double decision after the NATO double-track decision (see Introduction, Note 4, p. xxix), the SPD laid unequivocal emphasis on negotiations aimed at making unnecessary the stationing of new American medium-range weapons in Europe. The decision was an internal party compromise that bound the Schmidt government to do its utmost to carry forward the negotiations between the superpowers. The peace movement equates the SPD double decision with the NATO double-track decision. —R.S. and M.V.

Many Western politicians quite publicly fancied Afghanistan would now allow them to defer the extremely difficult problem of how NATO, a regional European alliance, could be enlisted to uphold the transregional interests of NATO's leading power, the United States, or whether it might or even ought to be kept apart in that respect. This question, at first cloaked in moral indignation over Afghanistan, was practically nonexistent during the first two decades of the Atlantic pact. Over that entire period, although the Soviet Union had carved out for itself a few nuclear cudgels from the tree of life, it was still a second-class power at sea compared to the United States. Today this is no longer the case. The strength of the Soviet fleet testifies to this.

I would accuse no one of deliberate hypocrisy with regard to Afghanistan. But I do say that whether deliberately or not, the Soviet intervention in Afghanistan was used by the West to recast the basic problem of NATO today, i.e., whether in moral terms legitimate European regional interests were separable from the legitimate transregional interests of the United States. Some Western politicians and journalists, especially in West Germany, have of course gone even further: for them the question does not even exist. With their attitude of marching uncritically with the United States, they put themselves in the front lines of a worldwide ideological crusade that is rapidly gaining strength again, at least in the United States if not elsewhere.

The Western European countries of course also have vital interests beyond our continent and must give some thought to how they too can best be safeguarded; in some cases they are identical with American interests, and where that is so, it would be wise for the Western Europeans to coordinate policies with the United States. But the touch of moralism in some of our reactions to Afghanistan had little to do with this. It derives wholly from the illusion that Asian matters could provide just as compelling an inducement for a closing of ranks within NATO as had events in Europe in 1949, the year NATO was founded, following Moscow's Sovietization of Czechoslovakia; or it could be explained by the crusader mentality: hit the communist where it hurts, not out of political necessity but from moral superiority. The one an illusory hope, the other a crusade —both tailor-made for destroying NATO and us with it.

An integral part of this Western reaction to the Soviet invasion of Afghanistan was the official pronouncement that détente was one and indivisible throughout the world. We are all living proof that this overinflated statement is wrong. Europe has enjoyed the blessing of relative détente for a decade now, even as in other parts of the world the greatest of tensions still reigned, again and again erupting into war, with the direct or indirect complicity of the world powers. What purpose, then, does so blatantly false a statement serve, even as we earnestly hope that it will never come true?

Insofar as this false statement is not part of the crusaders' propaganda arsenal, it probably comes from an uneasiness, still with us, over the fact that the Soviet Union is now able to vie on equal terms with our Big Brother as it meddles directly and openly in the gray areas between the respective spheres of influence of the world powers. It may well be true that Afghanistan will miscarry as Vietnam did before it for the other world power; but even if not, the mere attempt is sufficient for us to take heed. In view of this unpleasant fact of life, it is like whistling in a dark forest to helplessly yet defiantly proclaim that détente is indivisible, and that if the Soviet Union behaves as it did in Afghanistan, it will mark the end of détente everywhere. In any case it cannot be in European interests, and the Americans would be wrong if they really thought that it was in theirs.

Détente must indeed remain divisible. As long as we are unable to enjoy it the world over, our morals, however, must be indivisible. The naive or cynical introduction of moralizing factors into the politics of the world powers, even where there is little or no difference to be noted in their respective policies, hardly strengthens such moral constraints on world politics as do exist. Bismarck knew this. It merely renders us susceptible to totalitarian views, which may be found in the West as well, where they undermine the superiority of our system, whose real strength derives from our being able to think something through to its conclusion without the fear of committing an ideological sin. In the gulf between politics as practiced and their moral pretensions, those in power in both East and West have already lost many souls, especially among the youth.

Thus via Kabul we arrive at the first two conclusions that, as

A Peace Policy for Germany

I see it, can be drawn from the existing situation and applied to a Social Democratic peace policy:

First conclusion: our politics must absolutely, with no qualifications, be based on the realization that the Soviet Union is a world power enjoying equal status with the United States of America.

Now, it is pointed out in the West that Moscow enjoys a superiority on any potential European battlefield and hence is more than just an equal. But quite clearly a notorious feature that still severely mars Western thinking is not being able to come to terms with the irksome and disturbing fact that today the Soviet Union can act both politically and military in its vaguely defined spheres of influence almost the world over just as the Americans have or could have done in the past. One world power will here and there assume the number-two position; but then the situation can always be reversed somewhere else. But even being relegated to a number-two position would considerably, and perhaps decisively, enhance the risk of conflict, always present in any case. The situation tends continually toward eruptions of belligerency in surrogate wars, in which more and more often and more and more openly the great powers confront one another head on. There are few remedies to deal with this. A chance, if not a guarantee, might lie in the gallant realization that the Soviet Union is not only an A-1 world power but also has a right to look to its own interests. Any other attitude will sooner or later bring war to Europe.

The second conclusion for a Social Democratic peace policy to which Afghanistan brings us is: contrary to the claim of indivisibility, which has become orthodoxy, we must pursue a policy that will keep détente in the world divisible.

Détente is not a unilateral concession to the Soviet Union that can be rescinded punitively without harming ourselves as well in the process. The cornerstone of a Social Democratic peace policy must remain our undaunted readiness to sally forth from our cramped little island of détente in Europe to win ever new lands for that cause; otherwise both sides will be the losers. That is the alternative to allowing all that has been achieved so far to be reduced to nought again by the many occasions for tension, of which there may well be even more in the days to come. It is not true that such decisions are made in Moscow alone. A corrollary to the equal status of the two world powers is that the West has a hand in such decisions as well.

Poland strikes the second keynote for my attempt to define our interests. For over a year now Poland has put to shame virtually all of our presumptions about the course of any change in political power in a Warsaw Pact country.[d]

To be sure, politicians and journalists have thought of one hasty explanation after another, only to replace it with yet another, for every step along the way to Kania and then from him to Jaruzelski, and from Walesa before the last Solidarity Congress to Walesa since then.[e] At bottom, however, we have all month after month at least once thought: now that's the end, it can't go any further, now the point has been reached.

A few basic realizations can perhaps be retained intact among so much uncertainty. The most important seems to me to be that a war would long since have broken out if we had relied on the traditional instruments of international politics customary not only in an earlier period but extending far into our century as well. The temptation to fill a vacuum and, after new territory had been won, to stabilize the new situation would have been too great. Despite the present state of the Polish economy, things have still not come to that, nor will they either, we may hope, although, of course, not only Moscow but we too will presumably have a say in the matter.

The lucky reasons the worst has not yet occurred—from

d. This talk was given about six weeks before the militaty takeover in Poland. Gaus thus refers to a situation in which Solidarity had not yet been declared illegal, although the economic and political crisis and the impending power confrontation with the free trade union were already perceptible.—R.S. and M.V.

e. The reference is to the debate on the attitude of the Federal government and the Social Democrats toward the impending winter supply crisis in Poland. Later, both the government and Willy Brandt, chairman of the Socialist International and the SPD, adopted a very cautious attitude toward the military coup in Poland, an attitude Gaus adumbrates here with uncommon perspicuity. The American government, on the other hand, and the conservative opposition in West Germany polemicized vehemently against this approach. The SPD is traditionally in support of free trade unions and free elections in Eastern Europe, as well as of a stable security policy in Europe as a whole. These two goals have often come into conflict with one another.—R.S. and M.V.

here on, perhaps I should add, those for whom a European war is not the worst will no longer be able to follow me—have nothing at all so cheering about them; indeed, they are rather homely in their self-resignation. We have not had to die for Danzig in 1980-81 because:

- As a member of the Warsaw Pact, Poland belongs to a de facto sphere of influence, something that should be cause for reflection for those of us who might be inclined too rashly to advocate breaking up the blocs in Europe.
- In a military conflict in Europe, it is by no means sure that total annihilation of both belligerents could be avoided, something that should at least be kept in the back of their minds by those whose armament program has made a regionally limited exchange of strikes a theoretical possibility, whether intentional or not.

These two factors were also decisive reasons why in 1953, 1956, and 1968 no war broke out. We Germans, the Hungarians, and the Czechoslovaks, who live at the center of the probable battlefield, still have the bitter taste of these dates in our mouths; but we have survived. To the two peace-keeping factors of earlier times must be added a decade of détente in Europe, which has meant a much higher intervention threshold for the Eastern superpower; thus Poland has enjoyed a greater margin of freedom, at least for the time being. Without the last decade Poland would long since have turned into a repeat of 1968.

Suffice it to say here that in the past ten years, both sides have accumulated a valuable stock of vested interests in the new *Ostpolitik*, which the Social Democrats have played a leading role in shaping; the Soviet Union would seem to be just as little interested in frittering away this reserve, for it knows, of course, that intervention in Poland would set Europe back more than a decade. For reasons stemming mostly from détente (and let us hope that détente remains strong enough to continue in this role), Moscow has thus far refrained from direct intervention in its allied Polish neighbor. The experiences of 1968 showed the Soviets that an invasion would be no cause for war. They know almost to the point of certainty that given the least opportunity, the West would mark time, weapons at their sides.

We *dare* to say this because those at the top in Moscow know it anyway: we *must* say it so that the facts destined to determine Europe's survival for a long time to come are not frivolously discarded in our political consciousness in favor of emotional self-deceptions that would inevitably cause the collapse of our political morality. Otherwise, we would stand there on the sidelines in the event the Russians were, ultimately, to intervene, doing nothing more than canceling visits and recalling our ambassadors, even as we self-effacingly mouthed pious phrases in the media. The alternative would be war.

Although there is no belying such realizations, no effort is needed to show their obviously shabby side. Who would not be willing to intone songs of freedom at the top of his voice? In both their origins and leanings, the Social Democrats are after all closer to "Solidarity" than many West German mood-makers. who currently are delighted with strikes, as long as they are in Poland. Why must the position of reason in this country always be so cheerlessly lackluster?

And so my third conclusion for a Social Democratic peace policy: we must sit tight with the fact that peace in Europe, strengthened by relative détente, will for the unforeseeable future be tied to the unconditional recognition of the status quo and the current political tenancy.

Dreams of a rapid decline of Soviet hegemony in Eastern Europe, which were aroused by Poland, will remain dreams or become nightmares. Only catastrophe walks on nimble feet and could rapidly be upon us in the form of war. A world power is never so weak that it would abdicate with a whimper without taking others with it. On this point, at least, our ally Mr. Weinberger is mistaken.

We in Europe must get used to the idea of living with communist-ruled states for a long time. A long time does not mean forever; NATO and the Warsaw Pact will also not exist forever. But "a long time" means, for every responsibly thinking and acting politician who contributes to shaping moods in electoral campaigns, always keeping in mind that no European future can link up with the past of a Europe that knew communists only in the underground, not in office.

Like it or not, a full recognition of the status quo in Europe is the first step toward its gradual change. If these changes take

A Peace Policy for Germany

place too quickly, if they are unduly hastened, even indirectly, by a primitive anticommunist crusade mentality in the West, Europe would again enter into the prologue to war. I do not mean to reject change, nor do I harbor an errant belief in the status quo. No European state, in either West or East, has remained unchanged in the past ten years. I do believe, however, that it is necessary to break with a verbal Western radicalism that applauds precipitous and perilous change, a kind of change that no longer seeks to balance interests but rather sets its sights on the defeat of the other side. Western Europe needs a stable Eastern Europe to survive, and vice versa.

Fourth conclusion: even as they are aware of the great, and quite likely even insurmountable, difficulties that would be in the offing, German Social Democrats should nevertheless try to develop an overall European economic plan for and with Poland through the Bonn government (in which it has a share, so we hear) or through the party.

The objections are obvious: the arrogance of the world powers, in this case the Soviets, who know what self-help is only because they are so big and so powerful. For the West it is an urgent necessity, if we really want to help, not to take the state of the Polish economy as a point in favor of our own system but rather to be as discreet as possible. Indeed, help is already being offered.

The United States of America—the third point of reference in our analysis—has given itself a government whose domestic program must be repulsive to Social Democrats in the light of their historical experience and their record of intercession for the weak and disadvantaged. Of course, the decency of their hearts forbids Reagan's followers even to consider the idea that their tax and social policies increase the need of the weak and disadvantaged instead of relieving it. On the contrary, the way they see it, Reagan's program means giving new life to the America of unlimited possibilities.

Europeans know this is not so. For example, in the large American cities they can see problems just like our European problems, which can hence no longer be solved with the venerable prescription from the American pioneer days: individual go-it-alone gumption, supported by good neighborliness. Reagan's attempt to return his country to what by European standards were the ideals of the midnineteenth century could leave his Western European allies more or less untouched. The Americans are in their shoes, and we are in ours. But the current American get-tough resolve—I say it without any sarcasm—to bring the good old days back forcibly into the present, and to transform them into the future, is rooted in an intellectual posture that goes beyond domestic policies. We are participating in the American experiment; we could easily become a part of it, without any deliberately evil intention of Washington's.

This observation is not meant as an abrogation of the alliance with the United States. It is probably better if I directly state my position with regard to the topic of my talk: I am for NATO and the Warsaw Pact; I am against communism and against the anticommunism that sets the tone in Germany. No, we shall not leave the American-led North Atlantic alliance. On the contrary: we refuse to participate in a dismemberment of the Western alliance such as the Bonn opposition is currently practicing with their smooth and facile accommodations to the foreign policy positions of the present Washington government, which for the time being is marked more by a go-for-broke mentality than by any insights into the political facts of the world.

If we want to preserve the NATO pact, we must ask what an alliance is still worth when its military experts proceed to take the next armament step, rejected, moreover, by the majority of the peoples of the alliance, without the elected political experts having made a prior decision. It is certainly not politics, nor political behavior with regard to the task at hand, if politicians seek the cure-all solely in disarmament talks, formulated in military terms, and then military experts, in and out of uniform, once again have the last word after these talks have come to a quite likely unsatisfactory end. Without repoliticization, and that means without extensive demilitarization of the rearmament question, the only end in sight is the Vietnamization of NATO: the bureaucracies of the NATO partners understand one another in their inner sanctums, far removed from the peoples of the defense pact.

A few years must pass before we, allies of the United States, will have to face the consequences of the fact that Reagan's

A Peace Policy for Germany

ideals were not able to solve America's problems. These future headaches will also have a significance for international politics. At present the United States is moving away intellectually from many of its Western European friends by its restoration of faith, unbroken by the experience of suffering, in the neighborliness of virtually everyone. Many of us like this. Others shudder about the age difference, again become evident, between the old and the new worlds.

With all my heart I can't imagine, however faintly, that the Americans, the government or the people, want a war. But an intellectual and emotional inclination to war that has nothing to do with a lust for it also belongs to those factors that could be conducive to its outbreak. Europe was so inclined in 1914; in 1939 it was not. It is born of an undifferentiated feeling of unquestioning confidence in one's own cause and strength, but above all, of a sense that now things simply can no longer go on the way they are; now the only thing that will help is to give oneself a liberating jolt. Experiences of war in one's own land discourage such an inclination. For Reagan's America, Alexander Haig was in fact basically right when he had said that war was not the worst thing imaginable.

I cast no stones his way. Indeed, the Chinese and many of the young nations and peoples probably also think as well that war is not the worst of things. NATO's problem, which has come into a more general awareness through its decision to rearm, indeed lies in the fact that its partners have fundamentally different attitudes toward war in both their thoughts and even more so in their sentiments. Reagan and his government exaggerate these differences. They certainly do not consist in a love of peace on this side of the Atlantic and lust for war on the other. If matters were all that simple . . .

No NATO member wants war; all want peace. But there exists a fundamental difference, more unconscious than conscious, between many Europeans and many Americans precisely on whether war is politics continued with other means or is the end of us all. Who should be surprised at the difference? The United States has been waging wars as a world power since 1945 and, unfortunately, will quite likely continue in the future to have to make war. Nineteen forty-five is further away for Americans than for Europeans by at least two wars.

When the Atlantic pact was established in 1949, this difference in orientation between Europe and the United States did not yet exist. At that time the matter was quite simple: if the Soviet Union were to attack Western Europe to expand its sphere of influence beyond East Berlin and Prague, the West would strike back with its mighty American whip. In this political, not military, strategic concept, which has helped decisively if not exclusively to create our thirty years of peace, the differences in the views of the NATO members about war were still minimal; they did not even exist just after World War II. Our first sin against the modest, unequivocal simplicity of the politically shaped NATO strategy of 1949 was committed with the development of flexible response to any attack from the East.

The fifth conclusion for a Social Democratic peace policy is in my view the following: even as disarmament negotiations between Washington and Moscow are in progress, talks should be carried out within NATO at the highest political level on how Western Europe could once again be put, by an unambiguous statement from Washington, under American protection through immediate total response, with the heaviest weaponry. We must return to the times before flexible response was invented. A politicians' rebellion against the colonels and military experts is needed.

Obviously the United States cannot give such a guarantee of security for any part of the world other than Western Europe. Worldwide only Western and Eastern Europe belong to clearly delimited spheres of influence of the two world powers. Europe is not Afghanistan or the Near East. For many idealistic and material reasons, we are a region and a structure which, if one will, can be defended wholly as our own territory, i.e., this is not merely a friendly theater of battle. Of course, in the NATO talks we have proposed on the restoration of total defense through the threat of total annihilation of the other side (peace cannot be put in nicer terms), Western Europe would have to be prepared to support the defending power, the United States, in all the gray areas of the world, after a consensus was obtained among the sovereign partners outside of NATO, i.e., without

A Peace Policy for Germany 113

the compulsion of a treaty. Perhaps American's European partners could even contribute their historical experience and their experience with détente to reduce the present dangerous admixture of ideology in international politics.

Anyone who wants the status quo in Europe to change in a way different from or no more rapidly than what a recognition of the status quo can achieve through a long-term process of evolution could accept the protective guarantee we are suggesting, which goes back to the origins of NATO. We Social Democrats should follow with utmost attentiveness the arguments which will perhaps be used to dismiss the proposal for top-level political talks within NATO, denigrating it, ridiculing it, or rejecting it for military-technical reasons. These arguments are certain to have an influence on the position taken by many Social Democrats on the modernization decision.

The sixth Social Democratic conclusion from the current situation is, for me, our appeal to the impatient ones in our country that they refrain for now from making their overriding goal the breakup of the blocs in Europe and the neutralization of the two German states that this would seem to make possible. Such a demand would be as little in line with the actual situation as Konrad Adenauer's claim in his day that Bonn's ties to the West would ultimately, indeed in the not too distant future, result in the amalgamation of the Soviet occupation zone into the Federal Republic of Germany. The existence of clearly defined blocs in Europe is today the only chance for regaining as complete a guarantee of protection as possible for our own interests and for those of others. The European status quo, the basis of our peace, can tolerate no hasty change; no second step must be made before the first. Not only would a too rapid effort lead into the dead end of political sterility, but in addition, any campaign now for the neutralization of the two German states would make it easier for the NATO establishment to disregard the demand that it cease striving for a further differentiation of the weapons system and rather return to the credible threat of total retaliation. Efforts can only be from bloc to bloc.

However, the Western proposal of a nuclear-free zone in central Europe is possible without dissolving the blocs that have made Europe politically calculable.ᶠ If we could return to the officially declared security of total massive American retaliation, we would also gain the political margin of action necessary to place détente in Europe on a new level through the withdrawal of nuclear weapons from the center of the continent.

I repeat my appeal that the reasons presented for rejecting such an incentive be inspected carefully; they might after all be part of the emperor's new clothes.

In the Federal Republic of Germany—the fourth cornerstone of my description of the present situation—the majority of the citizens have for all practical purposes come to accept the partition of Germany. For many, thirty years after the founding of the two German states, it is the prevailing sentiment that Germany is Germany enough if it is no greater than the Federal Republic. This attitude is not normal; if I were a foreigner, I would suspect this outward forthrightness of Germans on the partition question. I attribute the general nonchalance in Germany on the German question to the way we have politically overtaxed ourselves and our neighbors for almost a hundred years now. Anyone who thinks that we have overcome the spiritual devastation of National Socialism, which culminated the anomaly of our existence, is wrong.

One day West German indifference to the national question will give way. We will then have to take care that new, dangerous anomalies in our political behavior do not arise out of illusions. German Social Democracy, a patriotic party, had the courage when it entered office in Bonn in 1969 to initiate a policy toward the GDR that was oriented toward realities rather than the clouds. The past ten years have brought respite to our divided country and helped to preserve more substance than

---

f. Gaus is here advocating a position first formulated by Rapacki in the '50s: a nuclear-free zone in central Europe, not as a step toward the ultimate dissolution of the blocs but as an intrinsic element in the bloc system. Rapacki himself attached far-ranging hopes to the plan, even going as far as the end of the German partition. He was thus one of the pioneers of the idea of a reconciliation between Poland and Germany. However, the Rapacki plan was geared to the existing military system. Gaus's proposal, however, contains a further, more specific note: the initiative should be undertaken jointly by both German states: he thus underscores the historical search of both German states for a peace policy: a challenge to both Helmut Schmidt and Erich Honnecker.—R.S. and M.V.

even we sometimes know. Man has a short memory.

There is no way back to Bismarck's Germany. Even if some time in the future there should be a unification of the Federal Republic and the GDR, the resultant state would be completely different both internally and externally from Bismarck's state. We must accept the implications of this more bravely than before.

My wholly personal conclusion, number seven here, for a peace policy of German Social Democracy is: we must adjust our policy toward the other German state—to the outermost limit allowed by the Constitution and the Karlsruhe decisions[g]— to the fact that in the foreseeable future, i.e., for as far as one can reasonably plan politically, there will be no reunification. I say this as a person who in six and a half years of work in East Berlin saw the dreadful consequences of the division more clearly than is possible from West Germany; as a person who in my time there acquired a very concrete consciousness of the German nation, formerly but a pallid and alien theory for me; and as a person who thinks that Germany must be the center of our policy. We must presume that there will be no reunification so that we can make full use of every opportunity for our divided country.

Is it totally impossible to discuss with the GDR whether the two German states might not jointly, each bound to its alliance, venture the proposal of a nuclear-free zone in central Europe?

Why should there not be more direct negotiations between the Berlin Senate and East Berlin, after carefully sounding out the three guardian powers and the Federal government? This need not lead to a loosening of Berlin's ties to the Federal Republic if, after satisfactory official clarification of our legal

g. The decision by the Federal Constitutional Court that the basic treaties negotiated with the Soviet Union and the GDR were constitutional, with the qualification, however, that they must stipulate clearly that the reunification of the two German states must be the goal of the Federal government and that the treaties are in accord with this goal. This requirement was solved formally by an exchange of letters on the Treaty on the Basis of Relations with the GDR and on the Moscow Treaty with the Soviet Union that were considered as constituent parts of the treaties themselves. The Federal Constitutional Court was drawn into the picture originally when the CDU/CSU appealed to it after suffering a defeat in the Bundestag on the treaty issue.—R.S. and M.V.

status (to which the GDR would then oppose its own conception), we were to negotiate development plans for the entire city in as many areas as possible.

The abandonment of the illusion of unification in our lifetime will help us to realize, and to draw conclusions therefrom, that the configuration of states that emerged after 1870 in central Europe has not only had its good but some of its worst years as well. German policy is not a question of how things would look if they could be embellished to our tastes. To think through German conditions to the end would bring imagination back to our German policy and free it of illusions. Treaties could be drawn up, with patience and a long breath, that would link up to the political forms that had once been so abundant in the part of Europe called Germany. The German nation, as I see it, is dependent—"fortunately," I should add—on its neighbors for approval of all the fundamental changes for which it strives. Thus radical changes in the current state of peace in central Europe are ruled out—except those caused by war. The idea presented here of a new interpretation of the cohesion of Germans, now living in their separate ways, should do more justice even to this fact that the insistence on using terms now lacking any content.

CHAPTER

8

THE POLITICAL BACKGROUND OF THE RAPACKI PLAN OF 1957 AND ITS CURRENT SIGNIFICANCE

Ulrich Albrecht

A political solution to the problem of European security

Politicians in the Bundestag were free to accept or reject missiles. But the vast majority of our popular representatives chose not to exercise this freedom. They were not interested in seeking alternatives. On the other hand, even the few parliamentary critics of the NATO double-track decision (see pages xii and xxix) have been more than ready to don their expert's caps and discuss weapons like five-star generals. What is eerily lacking is a political—not a military—discussion of European security.

The result of such a discussion would surely be a broad front against more weaponry. But hardly anyone seems disposed to undertake such a discussion. Accordingly, the following pages are offered as a rough sketch of some arguments that might emerge from such a discussion were it to occur.

European security has become a problem because of two powers, the Soviet Union and—however startling this might be to some people—Germany. Soviet policy after two world wars, as well as much of Western European politics, has been guided by one overriding aim: making a third German aggression an impossibility. Contrastingly, some of the policy measures of the German Federal government over the years could quite easily be construed as an attempt to regain for Germany the role of a key European power (though it is quite unlikely that that was the conscious intention of the different governments that have held office). These are serious claims and must be backed up. In a word, the core problem is the Soviet Union's need for security.[a] If this need can be met, the West's security problem will be resolved as well.

When Stalin decided to move the Polish border far to the West after World War II, the reason had little to do with blind expansionism, as many Germans like to claim. The major political consideration was to solve the key Soviet security problem by creating a new Polish national state (on the ruins of the old one that had been destroyed by the Germans), with the Soviet Union acting as midwife. Stalin made a cynical, although extremely illuminating, remark to General de Gaulle in 1944: since the new Polish state was to arise on the former territory of the German Reich as far as the Oder and Neisse rivers, any hopes for a reconciliation between Germany and Poland would be permanently stifled, and the greatest threat to the USSR would be quashed. "Poland has regularly served the Germans as a corridor for attacking Russia," commented Stalin at that time. "That corridor must be blocked, and it can best be done by the Poles themselves."

A new constellation of powers in Europe based on détente

As a solution to the Soviet security problem, this argument appears persuasive enough on the surface. However, Stalin could not foresee that the *Ostpolitik* pursued by the SPD-FDP coalition would fundamentally alter the premises on which he had based his assessment of the German-Polish situation. That assessment had been valid throughout the twenty years of CDU governments, during which time it had been consistent FRG policy to demand the return of the eastern territories "under Polish administration." The Poles, meanwhile, regularly found themselves forced to second Soviet policy, which they were

---

a. Albrecht formulates here a position, shared by others as well, including Günter Gaus, which if carried to its logical end is in direct opposition to NATO military doctrine. The Soviet Union's security interests are regarded as legitimate and historically rooted. The conditions for a rational political solution must be created.—R.S. and M.V.

more or less compelled to do, in any case, by the similar political systems in the two countries and the circumstances surrounding the birth of the new Polish state. The most recent political developments in Poland—the formation of a free trade union and the articulation of far-ranging emancipatory aspirations—are only conceivable, and indeed could have become a reality, only in the political setting created by Brandt's *Ostpolitik*. Polish differences with the USSR (they are per se no more anti-Soviet than the West German peace movement's opposition to American military policy is anti-American) suggest that Polish politics could be guided by other priorities than the rigid division between East and West.[b]

Stalin's decision contained a moral miscalculation. He thought that by shrewdly shifting the border, the hate between two nations would be perpetuated and the Soviet Union would finally be able to lay its concern about the Germans to rest. The Poles certainly had sufficient grounds for hating Germans: six million Poles had been killed in the war, the Germans had proclaimed the annihilation of Polish identity to be one of the aims of the war, and the Nazis attempted to destroy the very foundations of Polish culture by exterminating the Polish intelligentsia. But what had seemed unthinkable given this background occurred nonetheless. The Poles, like Germany's neighbors to the West, declared quite convincingly that as far as they were concerned, bygones were bygones, and the Germans were forgiven. A gesture of this magnitude transcends anything that governments can plan and do, as it does historical experience in Europe or anywhere else.

The Sovietization of Eastern Europe causes security problems for the USSR

But Stalin made a political mistake as well. The creation of a

---

b. This talk was given after the military coup in Poland. Albrecht is not contradicting himself when he speaks of the continued existence of and totally altered situation in Poland and Eastern Europe. The birth of Solidarity and the crisis in Poland are seen merely as symptoms of a general structural problem in Eastern Europe; the seizure of power by the military simply postpones the matter.—R.S. and M.V.

new national state, whether Polish, Czech, or whatever, as a barrier to any future German retaliatory wars did not necessarily call for the establishment of the Soviet political system in such a new state. Given the uncertain prospects of the policies pursued by the bourgeois democratic governments in the Eastern European nations, Stalin opted against political good sense (which would have meant forcing those governments to pursue policies that respected Soviet priorities, as in the case of Finland) and, on the bird-in-hand principle, carried out a brutal Sovietization of the countries occupied by the Soviet Army. People's democracies surrounding the Soviet Union would, so went his reasoning, in fact be easier to control and would provide more direct protection against a German war of reprisal than any security zone, which could always opt for neutrality.

The Soviet decision was not as freely made as might seem from the way we have described it. The ideological cold war, which had erupted into the open in mid-1947, provided further grounds for Soviet decisions to fall where they did. In France and Italy communist ministers were forced out of the government. In Poland the noncommunist Peasants' Party, the largest political force in terms of membership, disappeared from the scene. But it was not until the American provocation of depriving its ally, the Soviet Union, of the spoils of victory in World War II that the decision was evidently made in Moscow to Sovietize the nations surrounding the USSR.

These countries—the GDR, Poland, Czechoslovakia, Hungary, Bulgaria, and Romania—were all "people's democracies" modeled on the Soviet Union, and by the late forties they were tightly bound to the USSR: there was henceforth no other way that their societies could go. Later on, however, all these nations were to mount impressive efforts to retain some independence from the Soviet Union and to resist being swallowed up by it—to become just one more Soviet republic. The net result was that the decision to install the Soviet system in Eastern Europe has brought the Soviet Union no extra security at all; indeed, the effect has been exactly the opposite: because of it the Soviet Union feels less, not more secure. The majority of the socialist countries have experienced internal systemic crises in the postwar period (the GDR, Czechoslovakia, and Hungary), and Poland has even gone through several. Each of these crises shook East-West relations and signaled a continuing state of insecurity for the USSR in its European bastion.

The fate of Czechoslovakia, like that of Poland, graphically illustrates the Stalinist concept of security and its devastating actual consequences for security. In the immediate postwar period a democratic regime was formed in Prague. Its foreign minister, Masaryk, had lived for many years in the United States, and the government enjoyed far stronger American support than did Poland. The 1948 overthrow of the Prague government evoked strong associations in the United States with Hitler's behavior after the Munich Agreement, just as the Soviet invasion of Afghanistan was to do thirty years later. Dictatorships, so it was said, were never satisfied with what they had, and the lesson then as well as now was that only the showing of a resolute front could prevent a world war. Whether the USSR had only encouraged the 1948 overthrow of the Prague government or had actually stage-managed it, one thing was clear, namely, that neither then nor now has this policy brought the Soviet Union more security. On the contrary, it has earned for the Soviet Union the United States' permanent hostility. There are two points worth noting here. First, in 1945 and for a long time thereafter, the United States was the only power that could seriously pose a threat of war for the USSR. Second, the antagonism that has since developed between the two continental powers, the United States and the Soviet Union, did not appear so obvious in 1945. In the light of the threat to its security, the Soviet Union might have adopted a policy of encouraging isolationist trends in the United States to shift American priorities away from Europe.

However, Soviet policy in central Europe carried on the heritage of the Austro-Hungarian Empire, struggling against the nationalisms of the Poles, Czechs, Hungarians, Bulgarians, Romanians, and various other minorities. Austria's attempts to play the counterrevolutionary policeman in central and southeastern Europe brought about its downfall. The Soviet Union has a somewhat different power situation to deal with there; but the prospect of being the dominant power in the region for the foreseeable future, of never achieving total security, of having political relations with the Western powers continually taxed by this problem can certainly not be a very heartening experience for Moscow either.

Finlandization: an alternative policy for Eastern European security

Unlike in central and southeastern Europe, to the north there is a border zone where the Soviet Union can feel itself secure, and where the population beyond the border manifests little fear of a Soviet invasion. This is Finland. A quick glance at history shows that this has not always been the case. Northern Europe once had problems similar to those of central Europe, but a completely different political solution was found.

In the first thirty years of Soviet existence, Finland was a source of danger of the first order for Moscow. Earlier, tsarist Russia had annexed Finnish territories (Karelia); there was thus a territorial problem as well. The independence of the Finnish Grand Duchy within the Russian empire was steadily being eroded. Finland declared its independence in 1917, initially with the Bolsheviks' agreement. In the Civil War, from January to April 1918, the Finnish Communists, with Soviet support, attempted to take control of the country. In Finland, however, the Whites were victorious, aided militarily by the German Empire. The Finns chose a German prince as king, conscious of Germany and Russia as the two antipodes of power in continental Europe (he later renounced the throne when the German Empire was defeated and the monarchies within it fell).[c]

A second border conflict between Finland and the Soviet Union was resolved by neogitations between 1920 and 1922. The secret amendment to the Hitler-Stalin pact of 1939[d] was

---

c. In 1916 the Finnish labor movement gained a majority among the population. After the February 1917 Revolution in Russia, Finland declared its independence and concluded a separate peace with the German Reich in 1918.—R.S. and M.V.

d. More correctly, the "German-Soviet Nonagression Pact" of August 23, 1939. This treaty permitted the USSR to build up a system of alliances that included Finland. Its conclusion marked the breakdown and temporary end of efforts by the Soviet Union to clarify its security interests with the Western Powers (France, Great Britain). The partition of Poland and the Winter War between the USSR and Finland were the results.—R.S. and M.V.

yet another confirmation, in Soviet eyes, of the view that the Germans and the policies they pursued would be the deciding factor in northern Europe as well: Hitler gave Stalin (why, indeed?) a free hand in Finland. After renewed territorial claims, war broke out in December 1939, and after dogged resistance the Finns were forced to give up Western Karelia, the Salla region, and other parts of the country in the Peace of Moscow in March 1940. The Soviet Union was hardly made more secure through the acquisition of these territories. When the Germans attacked the Soviet Union in 1941, the Finns attacked too, to gain back what they had lost the preceding year. The fate of Finland was sealed with the German defeat. The disputed territories, as well as other Finnish territory, passed once and for all into the hands of the Soviet Union with the truce of September 1944.

So far history had followed its usual pattern. Hoards of refugees streamed from East to West (10 percent of the population was resettled), and tensions were expected to continue with Finnish attempts at reunification, on the one hand, and Soviet attempts to establish another people's democracy, on the other.

But events took a different turn. Despite a strong Communist Party, Finland remained a parliamentary democracy. The greatest achievement of Finnish politics, however, is that of having persuaded the Soviet Union that its vital security interests were compatible with the existence of an independent, Western-oriented Finland. The other Scandinavian countries contributed to ths solution with their astute politics of consolidation. Sweden, despite earnest entreaties to join NATO, remained alliance-free, not because the Swedes were so enamored of their own neutrality but, among other reasons, to relieve some of the Soviet pressure on Finland (with all of Scandinavia in NATO to the west and the Soviet Union to the east, the Finnish situation would have become far more delicate). Although Norway and Denmark are members of NATO, their refusal to permit the stationing of nuclear weapons on their territory in peacetime helps to further buffer Finnish policy toward the East. Thus the Soviet Union has several trustworthy security guarantees on its northern European border: Sweden is not a part of a military alliance directed against it, and in normal circumstances no threat of nuclear weapons exists in Denmark and Norway. The Soviet Union got what it wanted in vain from Poland: namely, that a historically notoriously dangerous route of attack was blocked.

In contrast to Poland, this was made possible by a voluntary decision on both sides. In recognition of what had been achieved, the Soviet Union reduced its claims. In 1956 the important naval base Porkkala (near Helsinki to the southwest, a tremendous security problem for the Finns) was returned, and in 1963 the Soviet Union made concessions on the Saimaa Canal, which had formerly been Finnish. Not that Finnish-Soviet relations have been a source of pure joy—the stubborn Soviet desire for "military negotiations" has cost the Finnish government much anguish (the Finns were able to put off these negotiations). Furthermore, foreign observers have often cast doubt on the independence of Finland's foreign policy and claim that the Soviet Union, with its preponderance of power, has "Finlandized" the country.

However, the crux of postwar Finnish-Soviet relations remains that both sides have found a viable means of coexistence.

The idea of a nuclear-free zone in central Europe

The north is not an isolated case. Once the Soviets were assured that the Finnish solution was viable and Soviet soldiers withdrew from Porkkala, the USSR also approved the Austrian Treaty and withdrew from its occupation zone in Austria.[e] The new Soviet leadership went to Belgrade, accepted the Yugoslav path of nonalliance, and even assumed blame for the break in relations of 1948. European politics on the whole seemed finally to be getting somewhere: military confrontation, which had burst into the open in the Korean War, could not, it seemed, yield to the more supple and versatile art of politics. Proposals for a fundamental change in central Europe came from both East and West. Poland suggested a nuclear-free zone in central

e. After World War II the eastern part of Austria was occupied by the Soviet Union. The Austrian government fought for the conclusion of a treaty and the end of the occupation regime. The breakthrough came in 1955 when the Soviet Union declared itself willing to restore Austrian sovereignty on the condition of Austria's "perpetual armed neutrality." The ideas of and hopes for neutrality for both German states or a reunified Germany also refer to this Soviet-Austrian arrangement—R.S. and M.V.

Europe, in the first place undoubtedly to eliminate the threat of atomic weapons stationed in Germany, but also, in all probability to acquire a margin of freedom from Soviet policies and to gain political support domestically after the crisis of 1956. The Czechs immediately subscribed to this proposal. In the West, George Kennan, diplomat and scholar, became popular with his idea of "disengagement." In the capitals of Western Europe positive efforts were under way to come to grips with how the problem of central Europe could be solved along such lines. (In England, for example, Winston Churchill, Anthony Eden, and Field Marshall Montgomery all supported some form of disengagement and neutralization, and in the Labour Party proposals were made by the opposition leader Hugh Gaitskell and by Denis Healey, later minister of defense.)[f] These ideas came to nought because of two powers: the United States and the Federal Republic of Germany.

The reaction of the United States and the Federal Republic of Germany

The Adenauer government wished in no way to imperil the alliance with the West; it wanted nuclear weapons for defense against the East (and had to settle for a compromise—American warheads carried on German delivery vehicles). The majority of German citizens supported the government. The attitude of the Americans was more important, however. They decided against the disengagement idea. Although President Eisenhower and Secretary of State Dulles had also come to see, briefly, some positive aspects in the proposal for neutralization of Germany, at the decisive moment the view prevailed that any tendency in such a direction would run directly counter to American interests. A loose system of European states would drastically reduce U.S. influence, and the United States would lose its hold on German politics. Furthermore, there was the fear in Washington of a swift Finlandization of Europe by the Soviet Union, and to Americans this meant free and independent states

f. On this point see the discussion and references in the introduction. —R.S. and M.V.

would be lost to the Soviet Union. From the Finnish perspective exactly the opposite was the case. The independent policy steered by it between East and West had preserved the Finns' freedom. An innovative European policy, even a Finlandization, would, however, have been of no special significance for the Western European countries (they quickly regained political stability after the war). Such a path would have been most interesting for the smaller Eastern European states. Even conservative Europeans like the Frenchman Pierre Hassner shared this view; Hassner summed up the problem in the argument:

> As long as NATO and the Warsaw Pact exist, Finlandization is the worst that Western Europe has to fear, but also the best that Eastern Europe can hope for. It would mean an evolution (especially as regards the Soviet attitude) from a total, tyrannical concept of security to an open, more elastic one that would permit the distinction between military power, diplomatic influence, and ideological line-toeing. If it is said that Finland is the name of the game in Europe, this only means that military considerations are a part, but only a *part*, of the picture.

The vital interests of the Eastern European countries do not lie in defending the Soviet Union or helping to bring Soviet policy to bear, but rather in keeping themselves out of the antagonisms between the superpowers so as not to be drawn into a nuclear war. Beyond this they hope to keep as free as possible of the deforming pressures exerted on them by the political role of the Soviet Union. The current regimes may hope to achieve some domestic stability by steering such a course. To their populations, who for most of their histories have had to tolerate much worse political conditions, such a course should be extremely popular.

Key problem for a new European order: German unity

The key to turning European politics in a new direction, focused above all on achieving more security, lies with the Germans. They would have to abandon the taboo of German unity. In the '50s it was believed in all quarters that any lasting solution to the German problem would have to include reunification. Since a reunified Germany would carry too much weight for either of the two military alliances to allow it to fall into the hands of the other, neutralization seemed to be the most promising way to go. The neutralist opposition in the Federal Republic supported neutralization precisely because through it reunification seemed a possibility.

Reunification in whatever form had always been unpopular outside of Germany; it was never realistic. All of Germany's neighbors to both East and West would find themselves saddled with enormous additional security problems if a unified state with the historical notoriety of Germany were formed in middle Europe, for it would be a potential power in a class all of its own intermediate between the superpowers and England or France. In December 1980 the *New Yorker* magazine had this to say:

> Historically seen, partition has been the normal condition of Germany. Unity was an affair of less than one century, and it was filled with catastrophes. Unified Germany caused two world wars and the moral horror of national socialism. It caused chaos in Europe many times over because it was too large. The basic problem of Europe since 1971 has been how to get along with the threat that a united Germany would entail. The answer was finally found in 1945 with great losses. It consisted in a new partition of Germany. As far as one can see at all into the future, it can probably be said with absolute certainty that this will be an irreversible decision.

Germans must come to grips with whether the states and territories that exist today on German soil—the Federal Republic, Berlin, and the GDR—as well as the Austrians could live together in separate German states as they had done in the century before unification. The borders have remained, with many annoyances; but the chances for a rapprochement among Germans—not of Germany—one that went beyond those borders in a way that would be meaningful for the daily lives of the populace, would then be quite different from those existing now, under the present bloc structure. Seen from the standpoint of European security, the German states—the FRG and the GDR—would be politically more viable than a reunified super-Germany. The problem of imbalance in central Europe would be solved, and the whole of Europe could then begin to evolve in a more balanced political setting, such as exists in Western Europe with the three medium-weight powers, the FRG, France, and England. Although one hardly dares say it—in West Germany at any rate—the fact of the matter is that every other country has a fundamental interest in keeping Germany divided, and this applies to the superpowers as well. For Germany's smaller European neighbors the issue is openly seen as a matter of survival. If Germans could be made to realize this, all Europeans could draw a deep breath in the knowledge that henceforth the real geopolitical significance and the implications of the surrender in 1945 had finally been grasped in Germany as well. Conversely, anyone who clings to the idea of a united German Reich, and with nuclear weapons as well, will invariably provoke bitter tensions in European politics.

Indeed, the fact that these speculations on a reunified Germany still have a timeliness in our nuclear age exacerbates the security problem of all Europeans. No one would know how a reunified super-Germany could be kept from acquiring its own nuclear arsenal. Such a Germany would get these weapons exclusively as a deterrent, and indeed that would be creditable as well. But such an atomic power would then begin to "Germanize" its neighboring territories, along just the same lines as "Finlandization." Indeed, it would perhaps not even be necessary to have our own nuclear weapon production to initiate this process, which is the common fear of all Germany's neighbors.

The NATO modernization decision blocks a solution to the European security problem

With the stationing of missiles following the Brussels decision of 1979, the Federal Republic of Germany made graphically clear that in contrast to Austria, for instance, which also borders on the East, it considers more atomic weapons desirable for its own security and places its own security problem far above that of others. But we can also turn the question around and ask whether, for example, Denmark, with its control of Baltic Sea access, is not in more serious peril in a war than Schleswig-Holstein. Despite all the agreements in NATO headquarters in

Brussels on the forbidding military situation, the Danes, steadfastly and correctly, they feel, hold to their policy of permitting no nuclear weapons to be stationed in their country. The modernization decision, it is concluded, threatens to effectively block any political solution to the European security problem. Conversely, the abrogation of the decision and an explicit abandonment of the demand for reunification would be conducive to a better political climate as regards the security situation in Europe, but it would also charge the air sufficiently to enable this climate to be utilized.

Then the Soviet Union and its Eastern European allies would have the trickiest problem of all on their hands. The legal status quo, the existing borders, would be unaltered by a new European policy; indeed, that is the aim of everyone except the Germans. But the military status quo would be changed. Even this seems amenable to a consensus, even if some of those concerned would have mixed feelings. How the political status quo would be influenced by such a development remains an open question. Added security against war could entail sacrifices of position in other areas for the Eastern European regimes, especially if they are unable to maintain control of the changes that would thereby be set in motion.

For the smaller Eastern European countries the key question is how they can contribute to a new course in European policy that would be in consonance with their own interests but that would enhance rather than diminish the security of the Soviet Union itself. In all probability this can be brought about only if the leading role of the communist parties in these countries is not challenged while they are not permitted to retain a monopoly on the shaping of policy. The recent developments in Poland provide a perfect illustration of the degree of freedom permisssible in domestic policy under certain circumstances. Economically, the Eastern European countries would still continue to give priority to their joint efforts in the "Council for Mutual Economic Assistance" (CMEA), if for no other reason than that they naturally turn to each other because their similar economic structures give rise to similar problems. Despite ideologies, both sides should be able to maintain effective links, such as have existed for years now in trade between the two Germanies, with their opposite communities. With a network of economic relations even the gravest of economic problems, with their destabilizing effects on security, could find simple solutions.

The problem of mass loyalty in Europe

For the participating Eastern European countries, such a reorientation of European security policy would provide an answer to the unstated crucial question: can the Eastern European regimes count on mass loyalty? They have so far been able to avoid this question owing to the presence of the Soviet Union, with its instruments of power. A viable European policy requires a creditable answer to this question. It would also, however, provide a singular compensation: if the communist governments can demonstrate with such a broadly conceived new approach to the European question to their populations that they could abandon their fear of war and their anxiety over foreign rule, they would find their people open to reason about quite a few things; and support, currently nowhere evident, for the present rulers in Eastern Europe would become a reality. Although a political scientist would be extremely hard put to present objective evidence in support of these arguments, the level of political maturity and basic social experience, so to speak, in the Eastern European societies appears to be high enough that this difficult path could be embarked on. That is, it could be if other governments in Eastern Europe, like Poland before December 13, 1981, were to permit autonomous trade union movements to exist; if social forces such as the churches were publicly granted a role in grappling with major issues, including the keeping of peace; if the intellectuals outside the party were given a chance to speak out; and if the monopoly control over the press were slackened and the universities given autonomy. Poland again sets the example: these are the facts of life there already, if not yet formally so, and the quality of political life has undergone a dramatic change, even though, indeed, the formal structures continue essentially unchanged. One can validly invoke the guarantees of basic rights given in the constitutions of the socialist countries of Eastern Europe, or (to mention Poland once again) one might cite the speech by Stanislaw Kania before the Central Committee of the United Workers' Party in October 1980; what was happening was

> a mass workers protest not against socialism but against the violation of the basic principles of socialism; not against the power of the people but against bad government; not against the party but against the state and its policies. This is not a protest of wage laborers but a call to battle by a class that believes it is sovereign in this republic.

Such a view contains the key to the security problem in Eastern Europe. The Soviet Union will only be secure if the regimes in Warsaw, Prague, and Budapest are secure because they enjoy the demonstrable support of their populations. But these regimes must be secure in themselves through a show of their own efforts within their national borders and must not rely on the Soviet Union. A Poland which of its own free will considers the security of the USSR to be a cause worthy of being defended, and which on this point enjoys the support of the Western powers, would solve Stalin's problem of blocking the German invasion routes. If Poland is put out of action, the problem would only be worsened.

If we can once again belabor the analogy with Austria-Hungary: suppression of the nationalist aspirations of societies like the Polish, Hungarian, or Czech will in the end invariably be at a tremendous cost. The Soviet Union does not have the resources to bind these nations to itself or even to assimilate them so that it would one day see its security problem solved. On the other hand, its military superiority is sufficient to maintain its present control for a long time to come. In weighing the risk of what would actually harm its own security more—a stubborn continuation of the Stalinist security policy or a new approach— Moscow seems to have unequivocally opted for the second alternative. However, the Soviet government's disarmament proposals have not yet had to pass any test because, quite simply, the West has been unwilling to try them.

Current Soviet defense policy deals with Russia's classical security problem just as simplistically as in tsarist times, and just as then it remains unsolved. The Russians have always been obsessed by the fear of military encirclement and of being routed on several fronts at once; they knew their own weaknesses, their economic problems, and the problems of their political system. Enemies were seen to the south, in British pressure from India to Afghanistan; to the West, where the Germans and others encroached on the mammoth empire in central and southeast Europe; to the north, where Finland offered a vast deployment area not far from the old capital city; and to the East, in the Mongols. These notions of a threat were no chimera; they were the fruit of centuries of experience. The interventions of the Western powers in the Civil War and the German invasion in 1941 were only the most recent additions to this experience.

The counterstrategy was simple: to exercise control as far into the forward reaches of its own territory as possible, to strike without mercy when the situation required it, and not to worry too much where the future might lead. Afghanistan fits the pattern perfectly. If Europeans want no more Afghanistans, they should have an interest in altering this defense model.

Stalin's decision to move Poland's borders westward (or the earlier decision, in 1944, to halt the Red Army at the Vistula and wait until the Germans had put down the Warsaw Rebellion) was based on the old political practice of reprisal. The NATO strategy of mass vengeance (the nicer term "retaliation" is normally used) not incidently takes its cue from the same factor. On the other hand, the German *Ostpolitik* of the past decade has extensively neutralized this factor. A further, second step is necessary, however: application of the principles of détente to military security matters. The first efforts in this direction were made in Helsinki, even if today they are largely discredited.

Conclusion

A new concept of European security would have to revolve around the withdrawal of American and Soviet soldiers beyond their own national borders. This would be backed up by a mutual guarantee of the existing borders and the integrity of the European countries. Details would be negotiated by diplomats.

In the fifties the principal American objection to such a plan was that the Soviet Union would have to withdraw only a few hundred kilometers over excellent highway and railroad communications, while the U.S. army would have to bridge the ocean. This is a logistical argument, not one of principle. In the age of long-range missiles, long-distance air bridges (with the possibility of using previously stockpiled munitions), and satellite reconnaissance, its weight has considerably diminished. The military argument can be turned in favor of a new European security policy: many Europeans west of the Soviet Union ought to be able to defend themselves against the USSR with traditional weapons; after all, they are far superior to the Soviet Union in population, economic strength, and technology. Should American nuclear protection be seen as indispensable, and the American soldiers in West Germany regarded as a kind of nuclear hostage by the Western Europeans, no more than a few GIs would suffice to perform this peculiar function.

A more detailed description of military policy should the arms race be curbed is not the purpose of this article. We merely wanted to discuss the role of politics in keeping the peace; and politics must, indeed, soon assume this role.

War can be avoided in two ways: through deterrence based on large weapons and by politically shaped developments (in former times this was called statesmanship). The missile race is trapped in its own dilemma; we are now in a strategic crisis. It is devilishly dangerous to attempt to prevent war by a missile crisis. That leaves recourse to politics. These arguments are not utopian. They are an alternative to today's precarious peace through deterrence. The question is to anticipate the inevitable and to determine whether something politically positive can be fashioned from it; in a word, it is a job for "statesmen." But it seems in Bonn only politicians are on the loose.

PART III
ALTERNATIVES

Introduction

Since the wide-ranging research carried out under the direction of Carl Friedrich von Weizsäcker at the Starnberger Institute on the consequences of a nuclear and conventional war in central Europe, there have been more systematic discussions of the forms and feasibilities of "alternative" defense models. In the Federal Republic this research is closely linked with the name of Horst Afheldt, a close colleague of von Weizsäcker and author of a classic study of the problem (see *Verteidigung und Frieden*, Vienna, 1976).

The security studies done at the Starnberg Institute were ignored in the public discussion on security policy for almost a decade, dismissed as a curiosity. Only recently has thinking returned to the practicability of Afheldt's suggestions. Afheldt does not come from the left; although he inquires into the prospects for surviving a war of aggression from Eastern Europe, he bases his arguments on acceptance of the current situation.

In Part III of this book we present the four most important currents in the present discussion on alternative security and military strategies.

Egon Bahr ranges furthest afield in his Heinemann prize acceptance speech. He outlines a program for truly new security policy for the SPD in the '80s and '90s in three points: (1) removal of all nuclear weapons from the inventory of those nations of Europe that do not own them; (2) creation of an approximate conventional balance in Europe; plus at the same time, however, (3) retention of the existing alliance commitments and guarantees. In going this far, Bahr breaks with the security postulates that have been policy in the Federal Republic since the mid-'50s. The nuclear component is drastically downgraded, and security policy is consciously based on a "negative security guarantee" in the sense that no nuclear weapons would be aimed at or used against states that renounce the use, acquisition, and production of such weapons.

The article by Klaus Bloemer heads in the same direction. He takes stock of the Western European alliance policy against the background of the discussion in the United States and the Soviet Union. Bloemer is clearly inclined in favor of a transformation of the existing alliance system into an independent Western European defense community, and he presents abundant material to illustrate the crisis in the NATO system. The preservation of the existing alliance structures that Bahr sees as essential is not incompatible with Bloemer's argument. On the contrary, the implications of Bloemer's analysis fit neatly into Bahr's views—indeed, they follow necessarily from them. A concept of "joint security" in Europe, i.e., for both the Eastern and Western European alliance systems, requires a shift in the locus of political power in the Western alliance: a security policy explicitly for Western Europe must be established. The national interests of France and Great Britain play a key role here. Bloemer sees possibilities for a regrouping within NATO, which has been driven into deep crisis by current American policy, making a reordering in power relations within NATO an urgent necessity.

The article by Professor Andreas Buro and the security proposals by the Committee for Basic Rights and Democracy pursue the argument at another level. Buro embodies the arguments of the noncommunist left-wing socialist current in the peace movement. For him an alternative security policy would necessarily entail a change in social and economic structures. Although his concept of an alternative security policy remains vague and rather nebulous, it does represent a broad trend in the Federal Republic that must be taken seriously. This is because in the years ahead, we can anticipate that it will gain ground among Social Democrats and in the trade unions, which in the face of increasing unemployment, rationalization, and automation and the dismantling of social welfare facilities and programs even as arms expenditures are increased will be forced at least to give such a concept sober consideration.

The security proposals of the Committee for Basic Rights and Democracy, which Buro had a hand in compiling, represent another option for the peace movement. While Egon Bahr's arguments are meant to be the basis for a new government policy, the proposals by Buro and the Committee assume that the movement itself will shape a new peace policy. The apparent contradictions among the proposals disappear on closer analysis, in a balanced stages model that follows quite closely the arguments of Bahr and Gaus.

Option 3 of the Committee for Basic Rights and Democracy draws on Afheldt's defensive response model, outlined in this volume by Thomas Trempnau. However, Option 3 is based on a totally defensive model and thus parallels a discussion currently going on within the Bundeswehr and its colleges and training schools (as well, we might add, as within the CDU/CSU, where the first signs of sympathy for a weapons system conversion have appeared). Afheldt's proposal calls for the fundamental conversion of the Bundeswehr into technocommando units. However, to be an effective security policy, this proposal requires far-ranging social changes, e.g., for one thing, for security. It requires broad and direct participation by the population, as in "social defense" in Austria, Switzerland, Sweden, and Norway.

Afheldt's model also has points of resemblance with the position of Professor Theodor Ebert, who has been active for decades in the church peace movement. His criticism of the idea of technocommando units in the last article in this volume is a consistent argument of radical pacifism. Nonetheless, for both Ebert and Afheldt a fundamental change in attitudes and the readiness of the people themselves to repel enemy attacks are requisite conditions for German security. While Afheldt stresses the technical aspects and defensive military technology, Ebert emphasizes the action and the will of the populace. Ebert's position is in the pacifist tradition going back to Gandhi and Martin Luther King, and it also draws on the experiences of the defensive struggle against totalitarian rule in Eastern Europe. It is therefore by no means accidental that those elements in the peace movement that are strongly Soviet influenced emphatically reject these arguments.

All the authors in this section do have one basic point in common: they all accept the need for a security policy to defend the Western European social system, which must itself undergo some fundamental social and economic transformations.

Rudolf Steinke

CHAPTER
9

PEACE: A STATE OF EMERGENCY
Egon Bahr

Everyone wants security. This elementary desire has existed as long as history. To be secure one had to be strong. Those who acquired allies were even more secure. Of course, most secure were those who conquered potential enemies, i.e., eliminated dangers to themselves. The potential enemies, though, armed themselves and acted in just the same way. The practical result describes the history of war.

Today we are living in an age of mutually assured destruction, as the Americans have called it. This capacity has eliminated victory and the hope for victory. We realize this in abstract terms. Actual behavior, however, still follows traditional thinking. We are party to discussions on first strikes, surprise attacks, the advantages of the first use of nuclear weapons, whether wars can be limited or can feasibly be waged.

All these discussions derive their meaningfulness from desperate calculations about how to win a war if one must be waged. The hope of preventing war seeks reassurance in preparations for it and the capacity to wage and to win it. The classical formula "if you want peace, prepare for war" has since its coining failed to prevent literally thousands of wars.

Until now the destruction caused by war could be repaired. The irreplaceable human lives that we do not want to forget have been covered over by time.

A nuclear war would be a fundamentally different thing; it could exterminate all mankind.

A nuclear war is irreparable. Mistakes would no longer be correctable. It must therefore be our overriding aim, politically and ethically, before God and man, to prevent the end of mankind. There is no value that transcends this, no principle that is higher, and no interest that should not be subordinate to it.

Communists and capitalists, believers and nonbelievers, rich and poor, men of all colors must accept this first commandment of human life. "Peace is a duty," said the Pope. Gustav Heinemann[a] spoke of the emergency case of peace and had in mind the sociopolitical conduct of our state; Heinemann's words apply globally in the most literal sense.

The realization that neither side is any longer able to achieve a military or arms advantage that the other could not make up within a short time means security can only be mutual. Only if both sides accept this will they find the mutual strength to bring the race to a halt without one side thereby gaining any advantages over the other. It would then be a common achievement to stop the introduction of new types of weapons. They would also find that overall it would cost less as well. Mutual security leads to disarmament.

Indeed, both here and in America there is a sense that the old recipes and old strategies are perhaps no longer working. The SPD has concluded a strategy debate in Munich, while in America McNamara and others have raised the question whether the West should not renounce the first use of nuclear weapons. In France the strategy prevailing since the time of de Gaulle is being reexamined. In view of our problems I find this both natural and correct and would like to see my reflections here thought

---

a. After 1945 Gustav Heinemann was the leading representative of the Evangelical Church in Germany, a member of the CDU, and a vehement critic of rearmament and Adenauer's foreign policy and approach to the German question. He came from a quite prominent industrial family (his father was confidential clerk for Krupp). He was one of the cofounders of the CDU in Essen after 1945. From 1949 to 1950 he was Federal Minister of the Interior in Adenauer's cabinet, and he later resigned from the CDU because of Adenauer's defense and foreign policies. In 1957 he joined the SPD and was later a member of the Bundestag and again Minister of Justice in the Cabinet of the great CDU/SPD coalition of 1966-69. In 1969 he was elected Federal President, a clear signal of the impending shift of power in the Federal Republic. The Gustav Heinemann prize is awarded by the SPD Central Committee. Its awarding to Egon Bahr is also a sign of accord with Heinemann's politics.—R.S. and M.V.

of as a contribution to this international discussion.

An important general guideline is in order: as long as we have no new model, the old one must remain. As long as there is no new strategy, the old one must be kept. No radical unilateral acts can bring us more security.

Mutual security also means that we in the Federal Republic of Germany are assured security only in and through the alliance with America and not without her. Mutual security is the opposite of a "leave me out" philosophy. Individuals can withdraw; a whole nation cannot. Not even America could achieve security over the long term if left to itself. Mutual security means neither being without arms nor pacifism.

Mutual security must be dead against everything that could be used to disengage the destiny of Europe from that of America or impose unequal risks on the Americans and us. Here begins the discussion on the renunciation of the first use of nuclear weapons. NATO has of course retained this prerogative because it sees no other way to deter or halt a conventionally superior aggression. The East has several times offered mutual renunciation of the first use of nuclear weapons. This has always been rejected because of Eastern superiority in conventional weapons.

I found the proposal by four Americans, McGeorge Bundy, George F. Kennan, Robert S. McNamara, and Gerard Smith, interesting because it recognizes the special situation of the Federal Republic, with our very special risks, and spells out an interest that is also ours: the nuclear threshold must be set as high as possible.[b] We must not allow ourselves, as it were, to slip into a nuclear war because of smaller and smaller forward-based nu-

---

b. This proposal challenges the doctrine of nuclear deterrence on a number of points with regard to Europe and finds that the threat of escalation lacks credibility. It deals, in particular, with the security interests of the Federal Republic and advocates abandonment of the NATO flexible response doctrine and a return to total response, as did Günter Gaus a few months before in his speech reprinted in this volume. In addition it calls for an abandonment of the first use of atomic weapons by the American government and opposes forced conventional armament in Europe. The proposal (originally presented in *Foreign Affairs*, January 1982) became very influential in the West German discussion. George F. Kennan was awarded the German Book Industry's Peace Prize at the Frankfurt Book Fair in October 1982 for his contribution to it.—R.S. and M.V.

clear weapons. This has always been an argument against the neutron bomb, as well as against other tactical weapons whose use would have de facto to be decided on quickly at some lower level in case of emergency, without any real possibility for ascertaining a political consensus.

I can accept renouncing the first use of atomic weapons if there is a rough equality in conventional weapons on both sides, not before. I have come to the conclusion that the present "triad strategy,"[c] as it is called, must remain as long as a balance in conventional arms backed up by treaty and subject to inspection does not exist.[d]

But to make nuclear war on the crossing of the nuclear threshold as impossible as possible has a quite high priority. For me it is high enough to accept its implications as well. We would have to be willing to spend more money for conventional weapons if that were the only way to achieve it. In such cases one must be clear on priorities.

However, in the public debates it is quite astonishing to see that talk of a balance in conventional arms is always understood to mean a buildup in conventional arms. An obvious suggestion would be to negotiate with the Warsaw Pact nations to achieve a rough balance in conventional arms by disarming to a lower level. If that were done, the German Bundeswehr would not have to counterbalance the Soviet Army. For if we take total troop figures for NATO and the Warsaw Pact, the imbalance that must be made up is not overwhelming. Of course, in such calculations we must go beyond the regions specified for the Vienna MBFR negotiations. I would have to count the troops in the Soviet Union and in America, as well as the time necessary for both sides to bring in reinforcements if needed to reestablish an approximate balance. The host-nation-support agreement just con-

[c]. Conventional, tactical nuclear, and strategic nuclear deterrence of the Soviet Union in Western Europe are the three points in the "triad." The escalation stages are seen as flexible, rather than rigid, hence "flexible response."—R.S. and M.V.

[d]. Bahr objects here to unilateral consessions for which he sees no essential function. The study by General Christian Krause in this volume should, however, be seen as buttressing Bahr's position, since Bahr also presumes a rough conventional balance, which, however, must be subject to controls and established in a treaty at the lowest level possible.—R.S. and M.V.

cluded points the way. Perhaps we should limit efforts to central Europe and initially leave the north and the south in their current states. But then, of course, the French armed forces would also have to be taken into account; in case of war they would certainly not be regarded as anything other than the enemy of the aggressor and a part of the alliance. I would then have to deal with various asymmetries, and a considerable Soviet tank superiority, which of course could not be so fully offset by a considerable conventional antitank capacity that we would no longer need any tanks.

But the decisive factor is not to achieve numerical equality in all sectors as much as to reduce the offensive superiority of the other side to such an extent that an attack would not make military sense.

At this point a glance at the interests involved is in order. It seems to me that for more than a decade now, the behavior of both superpowers shows that they have given priority to preventing a global nuclear conflict. On the principle of first things first, they have concentrated mainly on neutralizing the greatest destruction potential, i.e., they are striving to achieve a balance that rules out engagement on the assumption that both sides will behave rationally in view of their mutual vulnerability. The SALT process demonstrates this. Nothing comparable exists at lower levels.

It is in the interests of both sides to prevent war; if this is not possible, it is in the interests of both sides, whatever they might declare to the contrary, to wage the war outside of their own territory to the extent possible. There is no need to criticize this. We would think the same way if we were sitting in Washington or Moscow. Indeed, it is even in the general interest that all of humanity is not exterminated if Europe should be devastated to the point of unrecognizability.

Interests do not lie, it has been said, and hence it is right that Europe should have an interest in achieving the same state of balanced security the two superpowers are striving for. This is being done in two ways: the first is to bring all military instruments together in a cramped, integral whole, which acts on the domino principle, as it were; if one tile falls, so do all the others. The threat of escalation to the ultimate extreme is safe because the fear of the abyss has the effect that no one will throw the first stone. This is what the NATO triad aims to achieve. Europe does not want to allow America the freedom to decide when to put its own existence on the line, but rather wants to link the United States indissolubly, in an almost automatic manner, with Europe's own destiny. If this were achieved, it would be the ultimate in attainable security, so long as the balance of terror remains effective.

But the United States has in fact rejected this option since it abandoned the strategy of mass retaliation with the declaration that the threat of using the ultimate weapon in the case of a limited attack is no longer credible. We should not forget that doubts about whether America would tie its own fate inseparably to that of Europe were probably the decisive factor in de Gaulle's decision to develop France's own strategic and military nuclear deterrents. No one can force America to place its own existence on the line if it does not deem it to be directly threatened.

The strategy of flexible response has two faces. On the one hand it threatens an ineluctable deterrence, and at the same time, it proclaims its interest in doing only what is necessary to provide stages for stopping. If one tile falls, the others need not all necessarily fall as well. The current NATO strategy thus links the two poles. It makes disengagement and engagement, limited war and unlimited war, conceivable.

I have no doubt that in an emergency, efforts would be made to limit the situation, even if the Soviet Union threatened the contrary in its strategy. Oversimplified, Soviet strategy says that a war in Europe is not limitable and retains the prerogative to engage all means deemed necessary to survive a life-and-death struggle; this cannot be done without striking a critical blow to its principal enemy, America.

Nonetheless, it is likely that the attempt will be made to limit a war in the interests of both sides. The likelihood that this attempt will succeed is roughly nil, for many reasons that I will not go into here.

The second way in which Europe would come to enjoy the balanced security the two superpowers are striving to establish for themselves is by establishing a conventional balance that would make any attack senseless. But here we encounter the serious objection that renunciation of the threat of a nuclear first strike could make war once again seem wageable. It can be argued that it was the inconceivability and incalculability of the abyss that had deterred war, so that we should fear that if the dread of war is removed, conventional war once again becomes possible.

Given our high population density, the extremely vulnerable structure of our civilization, and the firepower and precision of modern units, a conventional war in the midst of Europe would be dreadful, crippling, and unacceptable. The small size of our territory makes it truly a nightmare to think that electronically controlled machinery of destruction consisting of a hundred or a hundred and twenty divisions would be rampaging for weeks and months on end, mostly on our soil, in the assurance that the territories of the two superpowers would remain untouched. This could be the perfect disengagement.

A sober analysis would seem to leave Europe only with alternatives that are all in different ways unacceptable.

Any new approach to the mutual security of the peoples and nations of Europe must begin with the facts: there are four nuclear powers in Europe, two different alliances, and different conventional and nuclear armed forces. It would be unrealistic to demand that the nuclear powers undertake their own nuclear disarmament. A nuclear-free Europe is an illusion. No unanimously adopted resolution could induce the four nuclear powers to get rid of their nuclear weapons.

There is a second reality as well: the nuclear powers decide on the use of their nuclear weapons solely on their own responsibility, which they will not share because no one shares the power to decide about his own existence with anyone else; at least no nuclear power does so. This does not apply to nonnuclear powers.

When nuclear powers decide, they are deciding about our existence; we never decide about theirs. This inequality cannot be eliminated. It is a destabilizing factor in the alliances that we need because no one can withdraw from them. Indeed, if the roof of European security begins to burn, it is of no use to withdraw into a neutral corner.

The following proposal for mutual security should be considered:[e]

e. The following three points are identical to Bahr's minority opinion in the Palme Report.—R.S. and M.V.

1. All nuclear weapons should be withdrawn from those countries in Europe that do not have them.

2. A rough balance in conventional forces should be created between NATO and the Warsaw Pact.

3. The two alliances should remain as they are, with their commitments and guarantees.

On point 1: This would not make Europe nuclear-free. The nuclear weapons would remain in the hands of the four nations that have them. A nuclear-free zone would be created, threatened by or under the protection of nuclear powers that have weapons of varying range which they could use should a conflict break out. But the danger of escalation would be reduced: the use of dangerous weapons would be unnecessary where there are no dangerous targets. The entire discussion on the limitability of war and the lowering of the nuclear threshold would become irrelevant.

On point 2: A nuclear-free zone in Europe would require a balance in conventional forces, i.e., that any superiority against which nuclear weapons could be deemed necessary should be eliminated. A nuclear-free zone in Europe is not realistic if there is no readiness to achieve a balance in conventional forces, since neither side must have an advantage over the other.

On point 3: In the interests of stability and security, the alliances remain indispensable. Their governing principle—that the violation of the borders of one alliance partner is to be regarded as a violation of the security of them all—also fits the notion of mutual security. Mutual security can only be achieved *with* the alliances and dominant powers, not in opposition to or without them. Moreover, the neutral nations of Europe enjoy the stability that the alliances guarantee.

But first, this proposal must be tested for its compatibility with the interests involved. The two superpowers might ask whether such an arrangement would not result in a sharing of risk because the possibility of an exchange of nuclear strikes solely between themselves could become greater. But first, they do have SALT to deal with this; second, the risk to the nonnuclear countries remains owing to the threat posed by their geographic position, i.e., the direct threat stemming from the destructive force of modern conventional weapons.

Second, all nations, both nuclear and nonnuclear powers, must see the possibility that in the case of war, nuclear weapons would ultimately be aimed at Europe and be launched from outside the continent. No one should close his eyes to this.

But what would the advantage be to the nonnuclear European powers if in the case of a war they still faced the threat of nuclear weapons? The answer is that the nuclear powers, at least the United States and the Soviet Union, can already reach almost every point on every continent with their missiles; and moreover, in the case of conflict they would of course also have the option of making strategic use of nuclear weapons that were not stationed in Europe.

The difference from the situation obtaining today would be that there would be no targets that would attract a nuclear strike. We must, however, all realize that there is no mutual security that can dispense with the nuclear umbrella—which at the same time is a nuclear threat as well. A situation in which nuclear weapons have been abolished is science fiction, however much this remains a goal that would perhaps be within reach when the doctrine of mutual security had become established and proven and had replaced the doctrine of deterrence.

Something else would become conceivable and meaningful if this proposal were to be implemented: the negative security guarantee that the United States, Great Britain, and the Soviet Union presented to the first special General Assembly of the United Nations in 1978.

The United States declared that it would use no nuclear weapons against any nonnuclear nation that had signed the nonproliferation treaty, except if the United States, its armed forces, or its allies were attacked by a nuclear power or its allies. Great Britain made basically the same declaration.

The Soviet Union declared that it would never use nuclear weapons against countries that renounced the production and acquisition of such weapons and did not have them on its territories.

The commitment imposed by such declarations, which need not be formulated any differently, would bring additional stability, i.e., security, for a nuclear-free zone in Europe. At the same time, the deterrent force of the nuclear umbrella would remain.

A number of points of dispute within the alliance would then become irrelevant: specifically, the development of ever smaller nuclear weapons, battlefield weapons, and neutron bombs, since to develop and produce them would make little sense if the territory on which they could be stationed and, if necessary, used were no longer available.

The objection that one cannot simply discard what has cost so much to produce is not acceptable. The production of weapons is not too costly to us for more security, and their abolition would cost far less. Those who correctly demand that the Soviet Union and its allies discard weapons with no consideration of what they cost must be ready to do the same themselves.

The task of small nuclear weapons could also ultimately be the solution to a problem which all nonnuclear nations, including the West German government, have long demanded from the United Nations, and will soon demand again—a total test ban.

Almost exactly twenty-five years ago the German Bundestag unanimously voted in favor of a ban on further nuclear test explosions. Even then it was justly stated that the destructive potential already accumulated was enough. Today France and England have roughly the same nuclear explosive power as America and the Soviet Union had at that time.

Throughout all these years the nuclear powers have continually come up with excuses to sidestep the united consensus of the nonnuclear nations. They always needed just a few more test explosions, this time in the ten-kiloton range and below, to develop even smaller warheads, which are inevitably less frightening. It could be that the nuclear powers will find it within themselves to conclude the comprehensive test ban treaty only when the nonnuclear nations refuse to permit the fruits of their research to be stationed on their territory.

For more than twelve years the nuclear nations have not honored their commitments to reduce nuclear armaments as per Article 6 of the Nonproliferation Treaty. They should not be surprised if this has effects on nonnuclear nations over and above its implications for the universality of the nonproliferation treaty.

As long as signals are not attuned to strategic disarmament, and by this we mean more than the good-will declarations we have heard long enough without any deeds following, the nonnuclear nations will be compelled to consider the only means available to them in this context: they can decide whether nuclear weapons are to be stationed on their territory. This is the only point on which the nonnuclear nations are sovereign.

But once again there is the question of interest here: there can be no doubt that America would ever permit Europe to fall into the hands of the Soviet Union unharmed. One can also be sure that the Soviet Union knows this. Deterrence would remain with us. Indeed, there is no disengagement if a conventional balance is created and the alliance holds.

The principle of no nuclear weapons in nonnuclear nations would only mean that those nations of the alliance on whose territory nuclear weapons are now stationed would be in the same situation and enjoy the same protection as those alliance nations which have refused to permit the stationing of nuclear weapons on their territory in peacetime, e.g., Norway and Denmark.

The American argument might be that American troops must not be deprived of the capacity for self-defense with tactical nuclear weapons. But we would answer that American troops would then merely have to fight under the same risk and the same conditions as German troops and all others. Their risk would then be no greater than ours. As regards the security structure, the nonnuclear partners in the alliance would be in a situation similar to that of the Americans, French, and English in West Berlin: the risk for the victim of aggression is the same, and in the end the risk for the aggressor remains incalculable, i.e., too great. This works in Berlin and would certainly work for Western Europe.

President Reagan backed up his most recent disarmament proposals with, among other things, the argument that the most destructive and destabilizing weapons, intercontinental missiles, should provide no occasion for miscalculations. Thus he seeks to base stability and security on the calculability of these missiles.

For Europe we have the opposite situation, a deliberate insecurity of the region within the triad structure. Of course, however, Europe must strive for the same security from miscalculations. Nuclear freedom for nonnuclear nations would accommodate this without removing the old threat that exists between the two superpowers.

There has, moreover, been a development in weapons technology that permits the insertion of another step or stage between the tactical and strategic levels. Each side has submarines whose missiles can reach the enemy without having to be fired from its own territory. The refinement and expansion of this potential through sea-based cruise missiles is becoming more and more a factor that works toward establishing a new balance below the intercontinental level; this balance would be marked by making the time factor within which both sides are vulnerable roughly comparable. If this development is pursued, the renunciation of tactical nuclear weapons would by no means be equivalent to an abrupt escalation to intercontinental weapons without any intermediate stage.

If START works, i.e., if miscalculations become impossible by human standards, a disengagement from above is just the same theoretically as disengagement from below would be if one were to rely on a conventional balance. This is why strategic medium-range weapons stationed in Europe should be brought into a balance that also rules out miscalculations.

Other balances are theoretically conceivable: short-range missiles, then tactical nuclear combat weapons before we come to conventional weapons. Common sense cannot cope with all this. The shorter the flight and the early the warning times become, the greater are the risks of becoming the victims of technical errors or mistakes to which human beings must respond because and as their instruments tell them they must.

Further points from other views within the alliance could be added to the list: whether a bonus might not be given to those who believe that they must begin; whether the early rather than the first use of small forward-based weapons was not a more direct danger. The Palme Commission[f] report devoted special attention to this latter point.

f. An independent commission for security and disarmament questions established in September 1980 in Vienna. Prominent former politicians from East and West have participated in its work, e.g., Olof Palme (Sweden), Georgii Arbatov (USSR), Egon Bahr (FRG), Jozef Cyrankiewiecz

Thus the principle of no nuclear weapons in nonnuclear countries would ease the situation in the alliance and so strengthen it. It is a principle simple to negotiate and easy to verify.

This leaves the stage of the land-based strategic missiles stationed in Great Britain, France, and the Soviet Union and the sea-based strategic missiles of the four nuclear nations below the intercontinental level.

The nonnuclear countries could leave it completely in the hands of the nuclear nations to bring these levels into a stable balance free of miscalculations by the four nuclear countries themselves. It is after all in the common interest to maintain the apparent contradiction with which we must live: to prevent nuclear war, but at the same time to be capable of waging it. This is the nuclear umbrella, and it will remain.

There is also another interesting aspect. Today, we face the technical negotiating problem that Geneva must see to it that no new race with short-range missiles begins while negotiations over the longer-range missiles are in progress.

If tactical nuclear weapons are left out of the negotiations, efforts in Vienna to achieve a balanced troop reduction could turn out to be merely cosmetic. In other words, everything is interrelated. Nothing can be regulated without taking into account the other factors. The principle of no nuclear weapons for nonnuclear countries would in formal terms bring both items in the negotiations, i.e., conventional and nuclear weapons, down to a manageable level. The matters dealt with in the Vienna talks would of course expand.

Let me repeat: we must not give the existing devices away as long as we can only talk about new weapons but do not have them. In other words, Geneva and Vienna and the new negotiations to reduce strategic weapons must be given their chance. The fundamental premises must remain intact.

But we must open up a perspective that once and for all will

(Poland), and David Owen (Great Britain). The report of the Palme Commission was intended for the special UN session on disarmament in July 1982. It may, however, also be regarded as a guiding document of government policy for the Social Democrats currently in Sweden (Olof Palme has again assumed the post of prime minister there) or in the future in the FRG.—R.S. and M.V.

again put political considerations above military considerations, that gives due considerations to the material constraints without yielding to them, that relieves us from the oppressive world of small tactical advantages, and finally, that restores to Europe its natural forces; we must get out of the cramped situation that has kept us bound so long, to the point of numbness, to the old strategies. Of course, unbiased reflection means being able to accept better ideas and to consider every relevant objection.

Finally, we might ask who would in fact be harmed by freedom from nuclear weapons among signatories of a nonproliferation treaty? No nation and no person, as far as I can see.

Such a solution would cause positive changes in the political climate in the world and significantly reduce the danger of a collision course. The very intention to undertake negotiations on such a point would give the world new hope and give all of us more security.

CHAPTER
10

THE ALLIANCE IS TO BE MODERNIZED— REFLECTIONS ON A EUROPEAN DEFENSE ORGANIZATION

Klaus Bloemer

Two different analyses of Germany's alliance policy and *Ostpolitik*, undertaken from two quite different approaches, have recently made their way to the broad public and have arrived at almost parallel conclusions. Günter Gaus, once secretary of state in the Federal Chancellor's Office under Willy Brandt, made the off-the-hip statement in *Der Zeit* (January 22, 1982) that NATO was in a crisis from which it would not emerge unchanged. Accordingly, he has called on the alliance leaders to seek ways to restabilize the military alliance by setting up equal decision-making levels for the entire territory. "Western Europe, which has experienced its de Gaulle, will have to discuss this question thoroughly, and the sooner the better, with its ally the United States." At about the same time, *Der Spiegel* (1982, no. 4) published extracts from a study by the planning staff in the Foreign Office which contained the recommendation that the "coordination of security policy" among the Federal Republic of Germany, France, Great Britain, and Italy should observe the basic rule that such coordination should strengthen the alliance by creating "a second, European pillar of support and be regarded by the Americans as constructive rather than divisive." More than ever before, the new situation requires European cooperation in security policy, which includes defense, we read in another passage in this paper, compiled for internal use in Genscher's Foreign Ministry.

This option contains yet another surprise: a few months earlier, when the foreign minister was in Strasbourg soliciting support at the European Parliament for the stages model in a "European Act" (November 19, 1981) that would include security policy as a topic for political cooperation, he added explicitly: "It must be clear that this does not mean military coordination among the ten, as is presumed in a number of quarters. The military aspect of security policy remains the affair of other organizations."

Nonetheless he left open the question of whether he was still inclined to give priority to the institutional status quo of NATO, or whether he would be prepared to pursue the deliberations on a resuscitation and review of the Western European Union, which the French government has recently again set into motion.

In any event, on the same day and in the same place, Willy Brandt welcomed the German-Italian initiative toward the establishment of a political union and came out quite explicitly in this context in favor of giving more say to the European states in the Atlantic alliance. The SPD chairman was even more direct three days later in an interview with Dutch television: We Europeans must make a greater effort to become independent, self-aware, but also reliable partners in the Western alliance. We must seriously consider whether everything that was correct in defense policy over the past thirty years need remain just as correct for the years to come. "We must be prepared to call it into question and be challenged on it."

Thus there are signs across the German political spectrum of a concern with the at times taboo but ultimately inevitable question of whether and to what extent the alliance can be functionally restructured so as to accommodate to the shift in gravity that has taken place within a generation between this and the other side of the Atlantic. Germans are particularly motivated to undertake such initiatives to prevent the emergence of neutralist and nationalist tendencies that might be fueled by the growing criticism of U.S. foreign policy by Western Europeans.

The question of accommodating the rationale of the alliance both to the demands of American global strategy and to the needs of a European politics of regional self-interest would then indeed by no means seem to impugn the alliance as such. It is not that Western Europe would perhaps be well advised to keep equal distance from both superpowers; rather, we would like to see a reform that would reduce the alliance's sensitivity to troubles through a multilevel network of trans-Atlantic ties. By allocating responsibilities and powers in accordance with geopolitical perspectives, such a reform would enable the pluralistic societies of the Western nations to become more in tune with themselves, structurally more flexible, and on the whole outwardly stronger.

Common values

For a foreign alliance presumably founded not only on shared ideals but also on common interests (see Eagleburger, July 12, 1982, in Bonn), an accord merely in negative and defensive terms, i.e., in terms of a common rejection of actually existing "socialism" for its own vital interests and a policy of preventing the expansion of Soviet influence and power, is simply not sufficient. The shared values, of crucial importance for the alliance, as the Americans are continually pointing out, ought nonetheless be expressed in some minimal consensus on common principles and related action vis-à-vis the rest of the world and the rest of mankind. It seems imperative, therefore, that an open and publicly waged debate, undertaken in order to modernize the organizational aspects of the alliance, begin with a stocktaking and a definition of the political and philosophical premises on which the alliance is based. A clarification of how the Americans see their future role, in coordination with currently prevailing Western European views on political reason and morality, must be achieved if we are to effect the regeneration of the alliance that is necessary if the West intends to be prepared to meet the strategic challenges of the next decade.

Reforms and the alliance

Naturally, the political strategy of a restructured Western alliance will contain gray areas where there is an agreement to disagree; however, such a situation should be interpreted as one of the causes of the emancipation process rather than as its result. The NATO council would no longer be under the inevitable disciplinary pressure of the leading power, the United States, and thus subject to the vagaries of the government in office at the time in Washington or of the shifts in mood of the Congressional majority. Hence the security policies of the allies in Western Europe would no longer have to be fit as smoothly as possible into the armaments program and the global operational planning of the Pentagon. Instead, in the future a European Defense Council, acting on its own responsibility, would decide on a regional security policy that included military components and then would coordinate this policy with its American partner in a permanent consultative and coordinating committee.

The question is merely whether and when the Americans will be able to muster the willingness, and the European allies the courage, to take concrete steps in this direction so as ultimately to achieve a more effective alliance on both sides of the Atlantic. This topic is already being discussed by and through the media —more in the other Western countries than in the Federal Republic. One advocate of a European defense policy, the British Common Market delegate Christopher Tugendhat, observed quite trenchantly: "We will be more likely to be partners in a successful alliance and achieve the requisite support of the public if we proceed in a European spirit rather than as individual nations in disagreement."

This fully accords with the growing realization in Bonn as well that any insistence on special national interests, whether politically or economically motivated, merely causes more irritation in the alliance and, in the particular case of the Federal Republic, is all too easy to interpret as a confirmation of *"incertitudes allemandes."* Continuity and consistency in Bonn politics would also be much better served if our special concerns were situated in as much as possible a European context.

An argument made in the context of the European Community would also mean that the Americans would not be so easily tempted to concentrate their political pressure in NATO on the Federal Republic as the most vulnerable of their European allies. Indeed, the American attitude toward its European allies has seldom been so multifaceted and indefinite: on the one hand the Americans threaten to punish their involuntary wards by a "denial of their love," so as to force them into greater compliance and broader acknowledgment of Washington's leadership; yet on the other hand, they are seriously busy seeking means to reorganize and resuscitate the alliance to give the United States greater mobility in protecting its worldwide interests.

The desire to be relieved in one way or other of its burden plays a key role in American thinking with regard to Europe, and herein lies the great chance over the long term to create more propitious conditions for the development of a "European Europe" via an autonomous defense policy based on U.S. consent. Dieter Dettke (NATO Memorandum 4-81) pointed out that greater flexibility in the alliance would reduce the impression of it being an imperial alliance, which is hardly conducive to the furthering of Western influence in the world; this alone should be sufficient argument to make a European defense option a plausible aim to the Americans.

The United States does not have a mature strategic program

In its official proclamations so far, the Reagan administration has shown no signs that it might be inclined to give up the political and military hegemony the United States enjoys in the closed organizational structure of the alliance; the downright doctrinaire zeal with which it is pursuing the stationing of U.S. medium-range missiles on Western European soil, without allowing the alternative, say, of a sea-based deployment to be even weighed, is an indication rather of the opposite.

That nuclear weapons are political weapons—with a political effect beyond one's own allied front in this case—is once again demonstrated: the American medium-range missiles on European soil serve the purpose of binding the allies firmly into the web of Washington's global strategy.

For such a huge, insular, sea world power as the United States, it is probably an alluring idea to establish a pincer grip on the continental Soviet imperium on its European flank in the west, and in the east through the potential represented by China's huge population and Japan's strength as a major industrial power, and thus to bring it to its knees if possible. However, this worldwide strategic dimension has little in common with NATO's original defense mission; the alliance system was indeed conceived as a cornerstone of European security (and on the whole has in fact performed its role well), but not of a policy aimed at bringing the rest of the world into line with American principles and interests. How such an aim is actually to be achieved without the Asiatic host remains to be seen.

However realistic the prospects of such a game plan, and however much or little it does in fact correspond to Washington's real intentions, it must be quite enticing to a government in Washington, inasmuch as it would naturally strive to make up for declining domestic prestige by being assertive in foreign policy and by affecting a demonstrative style of leadership within its alliances. This also explains the American pressure on Western Europe, and especially on the Federal Republic, with its sovereignty limited by the German Treaty and the troop agreements and its hands further tied by its commitments to Berlin. Reference to a possible new version of the Mansfield Resolution to withdraw troops from Europe is being heard more and more often from American emissaries, and indeed might even be able to obtain a Congressional majority considering the current latent isolationism in the United States. We are presumably to take this as a friendly warning, and perhaps even as a threat, to bring us into line in foreign policy.

The administration and its party allies on Capitol Hill have mobilized a media lobby throughout the country that follows the flagship *Wall Street Journal* on the East coast, which attacks, usually in emotionally charged terms, the irresoluteness, cowardliness, and unreliability of the Western Europeans, hitting hardest, however, at the "Germans on the front lines," calling them defeatists and potential turncoats. The Pulitzer Prize winner William Safire even goes so far as to call for a withdrawal of GIs from the American Sector in West Berlin as a means of pressure. Invectives of this sort are echoed on both sides of the Atlantic; but if anything, this can only further burden and ultimately destabilize the alliance, not strengthen it.

There are a number of signs that behind these disciplinarian tactics, the White House, the State Department, and the Pentagon have no mature, binding, and coherent strategic program. An alternative line of thinking is expressed almost as a second choice, as, for example, in statements by the "West Coaster" Caspar Weinberger, who recently confided to journalists before a visit to Stockholm that Sweden was actually not a neutral nation because it had its own powerful armaments industry and a relatively strong defense system. The U.S. secretary of defense could therefore hardly refrain from chiding the Germans and other Western Europeans for a latent neutralism or "self-Finlandization" if they were to decide on an autonomous defense system of their own—while still in an alliance with North America at that—more in line with their economic and technological capacities.

The Western Europeans should also take seriously Weinberger's comments, made in mid-February at the Munich Defense Conference, on the need to strengthen conventional defense forces. They could quite easily be read as a rethinking of the NATO doctrine, still in force, of flexible response, which permits a first use of nuclear weapons stationed on European soil and so conflicts with the principle, upheld by a number of American authorities (McGeorge Bundy, Averell Harriman, George F. Kennan, Richard W. Allan, etc.), that nuclear weapons are there exclusively to deter the enemy from the use of his own destructive capacity.

The NATO commander and chief, U.S. General Bernard W. Rogers, however, pointed out unceremoniously in Munich that the armed forces under his command might in an "unlucky situation be the ones that would have to begin a nuclear war" if they were unable through their strengthened conventional potential to foist the decision onto the other side. To be sure, the general had declared to the press a few months earlier that the NATO troops in Europe were in good enough condition to ward off an attack from the East with conventional weapons alone; but his most recent statements seem to point in a direction that would fit quite well into broad ideas on an autonomous European defense policy, namely, the discarding of the NATO concept of a nuclear integrated, staged response.

Proposals made by the former vice commander-in-chief of the

U.S. army in Europe, Arthur Collins, in *The Baltimore Sun* (September 9, 1981) might be instructive here. The former army general rejects mainly the introduction of neutron warheads into the European defense system because he sees them as militarily counterproductive and their political explosiveness as a mortal threat to the alliance. Instead he would like to see the billions of dollars required for the production and storage and potential stationing of these weapons used to procure the most up-to-date conventional antitank and antiaircraft weapons. He would like to see all tactical nuclear weapons withdrawn from the front-line defense areas, so that only air- and sea-based deterrents, ready for immediate engagement against any enemy attacking with nuclear weapons, remained far back in the hinterlands. The large number of soldiers now used to defend the front-line nuclear weapons sites would then be available to supplement conventional antitank weapons; reserve units and territorial units, equipped with manual antitank weapons, would then take over a crucial role deep within the defense territory.

The arguments of this American military expert, with long European experience, indeed show the way for strategic rethinking; unfortunately, they have not prevented the production and further development of the neutron bomb, which is now in progress in Texas. Furthermore, large sections of the NATO artillery and missile-bearing weapons stationed in the Federal Republic are to be technically modified to be able to launch neutron bombs. Dismaying and confusing verbal hocus-pocus is practiced to minimize the horror of this latest monster; the common and quite apt term "enhanced radiation" is supposedly to be replaced, cynically enough, by the phrase "reduced blast" to lessen its effect on the public.

But it would be wrong to draw only negative conclusions for the future of the Western alliance from this mass of contradictory words and actions, or to see no chances for a turn away from a "war-oriented foreign policy" (Jimmy Carter) that inevitably must dominate the North Atlantic defense organization. In a speech at the Friedrich Ebert Foundation on December 2, 1981, in Bonn, Richard Burt, director for political and military affairs in the U.S. Department of State, answered a question he himself had asked that could indicate that the United States, overburdened with its own problems, would not turn a deaf ear to a concrete European proposal: "Has Western Europe in its striving for unity developed to the point where it can maintain its own defense without foreign aid? If such a development should be manifest in Europe, I can assure you that the United States would put no obstacles in its way."

American doubts

Influential American commentators and scholars are ever more insistently expressing their doubts whether it is really wise and consonant with joint Western interests to adhere to the traditional alliance structure. Thus William Pfaff (November 14, 1981, *International Herald Tribune*) joined the chorus of displeasure and pomposity that is pillorying in such shrill tones the Western Europeans and their purported readiness to capitulate, a symptom of the instinctive isolationism and nationalism among conservative Americans who have wantonly charged that there is an effort to dismantle the alliance. On the other hand, NATO is pictured as a superannuated alliance structure that should be replaced by a "better security arrangement" in Europe as quickly as possible. However, such a process must not drive the nations on the two sides of the Atlantic apart but rather must be pursued with the positive aim of ratifying Western solidarity anew on the basis of true partnership rooted in mutual trust. NATO's *raison d'être* must be questioned, it is argued, if for no other reason than that the confrontation with Russia in Europe is of a completely different sort than it was thirty years ago. Now there is a problem of mutual security for all of Europe, including the Soviet Union.

The editor of the arch-conservative *Chicago Tribune*, Stephen Chapman, puts it even more tersely: "There is no longer any convincing reason for the continued existence of NATO. The responsibility for defending Europe is now in the hands of the Europeans." In *The Washington Post* Carl Rowan (January 10, 1982) observed that old military alliances often die long before their architects admit it. Many Americans, even liberals, simply do not want to see that France and the Federal Republic of

Germany have a different view of NATO and the United States than the Americans. Given all these mutual disappointments, the time would seem ripe to consider whether NATO might not already be moribund. Rowan therefore calls for replacing an ailing NATO strategy based on an assumption that has since become invalid, namely, that France, Britain, West Germany, and the others must follow the Americans, even if only out of fear.

Finally, in *The Wall Street Journal*, Professor Walter Laqueur (January 4, 1982) writes that it is simply laughable to pretend that everything has always gone smoothly in the alliance; this fiction can be maintained no longer. America should get a clear idea of the extent of its common interest with Europe in the world of 1982 and no longer seek to create the impression that it is more European than the Europeans themselves. The question of the future of the alliance is now on the agenda of history and will not soon vanish from it.

In *The London Times* (February 16, 1982) Zbigniew Brzezinski observed that both NATO and the Warsaw Pact are the products of conditions that existed in the late '40s and early '50s. "The time has come when we must ask whether these two arrangements, in terms of their internal nature or the relations between the two alliances, still have historical validity in every respect."

The lifting of taboos on NATO has begun—in America

The leading Harvard expert on Europe, Stanley Hoffmann, has presented an especially concrete and constructive discussion of the topic in which he focuses on the key weak point of NATO —the ultimately exclusive decision-making authority of the United States on the use of nuclear weapons within the Atlantic defense system. At the American-European Conference in March 1981 at Princeton, he called for a new alliance strategy that would gradually create a Western European defense organization; this would mean an upgrading of the conventional role of Western Europe, while at the same time the nuclear potentials of England and France would have to be integrated. But if the United States now demanded that the Europeans take a greater hand in their own defense, former American resistance and objections to a reorganization of NATO and to a European defense community would be deprived of any justification.

In an article written by Hoffmann for the winter 1981-82 issue of *Foreign Affairs*, he addresses the question of nuclear autonomy for Western Europe even more directly; indeed, in 1965 Henry Kissinger argued for the same thing in his book *The Troubled Partnership*. Taking up the TNF problem and the divergent security policies within the alliance, Hoffmann postulates that a Western policy aimed at deterring the threat of war with the Soviet Union by political and military means should no longer be determined by Washington alone. Thus the European allies should also be able to participate actively in negotiations on arms control insofar as they concern a European theater. The formation of an independent European deterrent power should be contemplated; it could complement the French medium-range missile systems by procuring similar weapons of American production if they were taken out of the control of the United States or NATO (which is the same thing) and placed under that of a Supreme European Command. A prerequisite for this, however, would be the creation of a "European Defense Directorate" in which the Federal Republic would have a hand in deciding not only on the use of nuclear weapons but also on their production and hence their collective possession; this would also per se ensure that Bonn could not produce or control such weapons independently.

With regard to the German question, Stanley Hoffmann says,

> Is not a Federal Republic with increased military responsibilities, exercised and contained within a European organization, preferable to a Federal Republic tempted by neutralism and nationalism? Would such a development, in the last part of this century, really be considered by the Soviet Union as a genuine threat, given the absence of any West German revanchism and the restrictions that would contine to limit Bonn's military sovereignty?

And Moscow?

Unfortunately one would still have to assume that in its ideologically rigid political inflexibility, Moscow would entertain strong reservations about any form of Western European independence in military matters (they have long had such reservatins economically with regard to the Common Market), especially when this inevitably would have a nuclear component. The Soviets regard such a project solely from the standpoint that it would strengthen overall Western potential.

However, it would be wrong to consider such Soviet imaginings, if for no other reason than that it would be at variance to our understanding of a security partnership; indeed, ultimately the meaning and purpose of autonomy in Western European defense policy would consist in making the political and military conduct of this community of nations not only more binding for our American allies but also more calculable for the Soviet Union.

The attitude of Western European allies

As regards the attitude of our Western European allies, especially our French neighbor, toward the project of an independent defense union in alliance with North America and the related problems of nuclear policy, there is no need to go all the way back to similar proposals made by de Gaulle in the mid-'50s, which are quite close to the ideas formulated by Stanley Hoffmann. On January 29, 1982, the sober weekly *Paris Match* reported—although it has remained unconfirmed—the following under the heading "Tomorrow's Headlines": During his sudden and unexpected visit to Paris early in the year, Federal Chancellor Schmidt was supposed to have suggested to French President Mitterrand that Pershing II missiles be stationed in France. Schmidt is reported to have said: "The United States is prepared to turn over control of them to you."

Such an offer would in itself have been a revolutionary act because it would have gone beyond the agreement on American-British cooperation on nuclear arms concluded in the Bahamas in late 1962, and thus it would herald a fundamental turn in U.S. alliance and nuclear policy. Had France reacted positively to the offer, an important precondition would have been created for the establishment of an autonomous European defense policy. In an interview with *Corriere della Sera* in October 1981, Mitterrand had declared: "I understand the peace movement quite well, especially in the Federal Republic. It is a country denied the right to possess nuclear weapons, yet its territory is covered with weapons, the use of which depends on others." (Mitterrand said almost exactly the same thing on October 19, 1981, in *Time* magazine.)

Helmut Schmidt picked up this point in an interview with *Nouvel Observateur* (January 30, 1982): "In this respect the Germans are not in the same fortunate position as the French, since the French president alone decides on the use of the nuclear weapons based on French soil. There are weapons on German territory whose use depends on the decisions of other governments."

Clearly, such a highly unsatisfactory situation as this could most easily be changed through a European defense union, whose members would have a de facto territorial identity of interests. European deterrent weapons from the ABC arsenal are fundamentally of another political quality than American ones, for example. If, in addition, a European defense council, as the supreme security policy-making body, had control of these weapons, which would be under the command of a European supreme commander, then the question of their stationing would become politically so defused that it could be dealt with largely in terms of military expediency.

Pierre Lellouche, of the French Institute for International Relations, who has close ties to the Foreign Ministry, addressed the possibility of placing French and British medium-range missiles on German soil in the spring edition 1981 of *Foreign Affairs* and did not rule out an arrangement in the broader Western European context. However, statements by Prime Minister Pierre Mauroy at the Cadre Academy in Paris on September 14, 1981, set the tone for the French government's attitude, which leans heavily on continuity in foreign policy and is thus based on a broad national consensus. In his speech he took up the question of the "overall geopolitical zone to which we are tied" and called efforts to reorganize and consolidate on a European scale urgently necessary to overcome the obstacles in the way of creating a "mutual military defense area in Europe." Mauroy noted that aggression against France did not first begin "when an enemy encroaches on our sovereign territory." In the American concept of deterrence at self-selected stages, Europe could "be only a rung on the ladder of violence and not one of the principal purposes of its defense. For the French this is an unacceptable eventuality, an eventuality which should give Europeans cause to reflect on the prospects for a political entity that controls its own defense" (*Europa Archiv*, 1981, no. 21).

The date of this declaration makes clear that the French government was not speaking under the impress of the German peace demonstrations, the *Ostpolitik* dialogue, or Bonn's stance on the events in Poland, i.e., that it was not being guided by a current concern over the possible loss of its military threshold as a result of purported neutralist trends when this forceful declaration of faith in a European union was made.

Mauroy's programmatic comments were later followed by similar statements made by leading government figures, members of parliament, and top-level officials in the Socialist Party of France, and they were bolstered by commentary even in conservative newspapers. It is more than surprising that this deluge of advances, which quite obviously were meant primarily for Bonn, has been hardly noticed by the German public:

- "I am in favor of putting the European dimension to use. . . . We will create the institutions we need" (Foreign Minister Cheysson, October 10, 1981).

"We must give Europe the means for its own defense and make the continent into a social, industrial, economic, scientific, and technical unity" (Chévènement, Minister of Technology and left-wing socialist spokesman at the Party Congress in Valence, October 1981).

- "How can Europe be denied this strategic dimension and independent defense?" (Jospin, First Secretary of the Socialist Party, October 21, 1981).

- "Reagan's comment on the possibility of a limited nuclear war made the question of Europe's security a leading topic of discussion at all levels of leadership in France" (Darinot, Chairman of the Defense Committee of the National Assembly).

- "Although France today has an independent defense, it regards the commitments entered into in the Treaty of the Western European Union as absolutely binding on itself" (Lemoin, Secretary of State for the Ministry of Defense, on German television).

• "It is becoming increasingly obvious that Europe must itself find the means for its own defense and survival" (Claisse, on French radio).

• "Indeed, the circus games engaged in by Moscow and Washington are being played over our heads. They should strengthen Europeans in their joint resolve to equip themselves with autonomous nuclear and conventional weapons..." (*L'Aurore*, November 19, 1981).

Counterarguments

The main objections heard in Germany and other Western European countries to a revision of the Atlantic alliance, in which a militarily integrated NATO would be replaced by an autonomous European defense system, are the following: first, the massive presence of U.S. troops on the continent is the surest guarantee that the United States would automatically be drawn into the fray in case of any military aggression from the East (the hostage theory). Second, a withdrawal of American troops would require compensatory measures from the Europeans that they could not manage financially. Third, a buildup of the German army would be necessary, giving the Federal Republic a military preponderance that would be difficult for its neighbors to accept.

The first argument implies a fundamental mistrust of our American allies, which they do not deserve insofar as the standards of national security, coupled with the interests of a world power, are at all a governing factor in their politics; the other side of the Atlantic, where the other half of total Western potential has been amassed, has plainly an existential significance for the United States. Thus if today the wartime host-nation support agreement contains Washington's explicit assurance that it will send six divisions to defend Western Europe in case of crisis, there is no obvious reason why similar or even larger expeditionary units should not also be made available if the five U.S. divisions now stationed here were transferred back to the United States or elsewhere. Clearly, American communication staffs would be attached to a supreme European command, and American sea and air bases, as well as depots, quarters, and other logistical installations, would be kept in readiness on Western European territory. However, the decision on whether and when military weapons would be engaged could then not be made unilaterally by the United States but only after a resolution by the European defense council in coordination with Washington.

The second argument, of an overstrained budget, was refuted quite impressively by the president of the Italian Institute for International Relations, Cesare Merlini (*Europa*, 1981, no. 24), with his proposals for a "radical reform" of the Common Market into a community capable of acting politically: "The Europe of the Ten spends for defense approximately two-thirds of what the United States spends, yet only a few on this side of the Atlantic know this. The lack of even the smallest measure of rationalization, to say nothing of integration, makes the difference in strategic effectiveness enormous."

Thus it is not a lack of money, nor of personnel reserves, nor of technological capacities, but the lack of organization of existing resources that must be overcome to create the material basis for an autonomous European defense force.

The former director of the Stockholm International Peace Research Institute, Robert Nield, now professor of economics at Cambridge, in an article for *The New York Times* came to the conclusion that a defense system that shifted its focus to electronically guided weapons for antitank and antiaircraft defense and (following the Swiss or Yugoslav model) otherwise decided in favor of decentralized territorial defense, backed up by deterrent weapons with second-strike capability against nuclear attacks, would by no means necessarily entail greater outlays if the reprogramming also included the abandonment of costly prestige weapons systems.

The third argument, concerning a German preponderance, would be deprived of much of its force by a structurally modified defense model that provided for a mobilization of operational reserve units from the civilian population. Furthermore it should be possible to bring the British, French, Belgian, and Dutch troop contingents stationed in the Federal Republic, now totalling 150,000 men, up to about a quarter million.

Social consensus

The Swede Neild, currently teaching in England, points out that the Western European peace movements have also recently begun discussing alternative defense models that place greater stress on conventional defense, as has also been recommended by a number of military experts. The common denominator could perhaps be the point made by the Copenhagen political scientist Anders Boserup, as instructive as it is simple, that an improvement brought about in defensive capability by the procurement of additional, exclusively defensive weapons could not possibly be regarded as a threat by a potential enemy. The arms race could thus be stopped even without negotiations.

The appearance of this reference to a conceivable social consensus of Western European dimensions in America's leading newspaper was certainly not accidental. Nor would it be too presumptuous to think that a domestic consensus, ranging from Eppler to Strauss, could also be achieved in the Federal Republic on the prospects of a redefined Western alliance on the basis of a Western European defense union (*An Outline for Europe*, 1966: "Europe's security must be guaranteed by Europe itself"). The views are perhaps indeed the same in France, where we can read, for example, in the newspaper *Matin*, which is close to the government, on February 23, 1982: "More and more sympathisers for the project of a European defense system are being found in all political camps."

A survey by the periodical *Capital* recently showed that 80 percent of West Germans, 75 percent of the French, and 59 percent of the British were in favor of a Western European Union. The popular views that these figures express should encourage the governments of the major EEC countries to undertake initiatives. In a speech on February 19, 1982, at Georgetown University in Washington, the Italian Foreign Minister Emilio

Colombo proposed a European-American friendship pact. Such a treaty, expanded to a support pact, could establish a new harmony in the West that would derive a lasting quality from the mutual respect of different interests.

The quintessence of such a broad alliance reform is perhaps reflected in a statement by François Mitterrand on German television on February 23, 1982, on the question of an autonomous European defense system: "If we want to make Europe more independent, we cannot do so if we are in conflict with the Atlantic alliance that guarantees our security. On the other hand, we do not want to build up this stable unit of Western Europe as a kind of outpost against the Eastern camp. I do not think there is anything positive to be gained by adding to the already severe tensions burdening the world, and especially Europe."

CHAPTER
11

PRINCIPLES AND PROBLEMS OF ALTERNATE PEACE STRATEGIES

Andreas Buro

The NATO strategy of deterrence and the arms race have grown into an unwarranted risk, especially for the peoples of central Europe. This has given quite a boost to discussions about alternative peace policies, although as yet no alternative strategies or even programs have been presented. Perhaps the first task is to establish an agreement on principles and basic attitudes. My discussion of the latter is based on the following assumptions:

- Alternative peace strategies are incompatible with the arms race. They must set their sights on ending it, initially for a single country, then a region, and finally, the world over. Their ultimate aim, therefore, is disarmament. All prior experience with disarmament and arms control negotiations (the latter were unquestionably an integral part of the arms race) indicates that no new directions such as these can be achieved through multilateral negotiations by the major powers, which have themselves sustained the arms race.
- A world partly or even wholly disarmed is still not free from conflict. It is not sufficient, therefore, to call for disarmament alone. It must be linked as well to efforts to develop nonmilitary ways of resolving conflicts and forms of defense, as well as to social, economic, and political reforms designed to reduce the sources of international conflict.

There is no security without risk and no absolutely sure road to disarmament. Security presumes jeopardy. The goal of alternative security strategies is therefore to reduce risks, to weigh risks in terms of the advantages sought, and to accept containable risks where structural changes can be achieved politically to reduce the causes of conflict. Through such a modification of risk, security strategies become peace policy strategies because their primary aim is safeguarding peace.

Although I do not overlook the major differences between the capitalist and bureaucratic ("real socialist") societies, I nonetheless am aware that both West and East, NATO and the Warsaw Pact, entered firmly committed into the arms race system after 1945 and utilized the "worst case" rationale to build up their military kill potential. There is no question of a camp of peace and a camp of war, as is repeatedly heard in many quarters. To put the arms race behind us would require major changes in both NATO and the Warsaw Pact alliances. The peace movement must therefore address its criticisms to both East and West.

Reduction of the causes of conflict—an essential component of any peace policy—of course also requires social and economic changes, especially in our society. Thus we must neither concentrate solely on military policies nor neglect them in favor of a one-sided emphasis on social changes. Alternative peace policy strategies must therefore relate to the existing society and the forces moving it, yet at the same time actively work for change in all areas of relevance to such a policy.

Are interim stages of arms conversion and dismantling necessary as stations on the way to total disarmament and a civil defense system?

I do not believe that disarmament alone is sufficient. Nonmilitary ways to settle conflicts and civilian forms of defense must also be developed at the same time. The question for the peace movement is whether it should set its sights directly on the conversion from today's policy of deterrence to nonviolent social defense, or whether interim stages involving conversion to other types of weapons systems and partial disarmament might not be more realistic as part of a probably long reorientation and learning process. An answer to this question should consider the following points:

• The experiences of the peace movement since World War II shows that none of the relatively broad-based movements was able to maintain a long-term focus on nonviolent forms of defense. Questions concerning weapons systems and weapons deployment, such as disengagement, nuclear-free zones, etc., soon moved into the forefront. Apparently, the idea of a nonviolent peace policy had not yet found sufficiently broad acceptance.

- A compounding factor is that experience with nonviolent models of conflict resolution and defense is still on a rudimentary level, and what has been learned in other countries is only partly of value here. Thus we must first broaden our own experience through nonviolent actions and convey this experience in a convincing manner to the public at large.

- Nonviolent social defense is a complicated and slow social learning process of major dimensions; the peace movement therefore cannot be indifferent to how military strategies and weapons develop in the interim, or to the fact that the arms race and a continued adherence to a policy of deterrence merely magnify insecurity, heighten risk, and create structures that increasingly obstruct our efforts to achieve disarmament and develop alternative peace strategies.

Even those sectors of the peace movement that see themselves as primarily pacifist must also address the question of the development and implementation of alternative military security strategies, without of course losing sight of their own goals. They must become knowledgeable on military questions, just as the ecology movement developed expertise in the areas of its immediate concern.

But interim military answers pose problems for the peace movement. Such solutions could also easily develop a dynamic of their own that would in turn create barriers to further progress toward disarmament. The peace movement must therefore find credible criteria for evaluating military arms conversion and disarmament proposals, so that the road to disarmament and nonviolent social defense is not barred structurally and psychologically.

Stages on the way toward total disarmament

The arms race is not just a process of action and reaction; it has its own dynamic rooted in socioeconomic developments in each camp. Still, an arms buildup requires legitimation in terms of an alleged enemy threat. If the threat is clearly nonexistent, any further arms buildup loses its legitimacy. An initial interim stage, therefore, would be to reduce and ultimately to eliminate one's own threat to the security of the other side. This means renunciation of nuclear deterrence and all offensive weapons systems. A no-threat policy toward the other side requires putting oneself in the others' position and experiencing their fears. In the process false stereotypes of the enemy are eradicated.

Renunciation of a strategy of threat means withdrawal from the arms race with first- and second-strike weapons and conventional offensive systems and a shift to defensive weapons, acceptable to any potential enemy since they would be no longer coupled with offensive weapons. The second stage would thus entail a switch to weapons systems that would permit withdrawal from the offensive arms race. Since the arms race derives most of its dynamic from the latter, a partial, perhaps even regionwide breakthrough of the barriers in central Europe that have hitherto always blocked any steps toward disarmament would perhaps ensue.

Continued participation in the defensive arms race by the superpowers or the other nations in the respective alliances entails the risk that military-industrial interests will assume their own dynamic and that the military will revert to the ideologies and strategies of deterrence. Therefore a third major consideration is that steps toward disarmament in these interim stages must not be determined by military calculations alone (total defense against any type of attack) but also by a concept of security that stresses peace and socioeconomic factors. Strategies aimed at reducing conflict must therefore have priority over military ones. The gradual abolition of the threat to the other side has priority over perfectionist military capacity. The road toward further disarmament will remain open only if primacy is restored to political objectives above the spurious dictates of military necessity: the elimination of ideological stereotypes of the enemy has priority over a presumed strengthening of the defensive will be steeping the population and the armed forces in ideology; democratization of the military, by giving it, too, a say in peace policy strategies, has priority over pervasive hier-

Alternate Peace Strategies

archization and centralization in the name of greater military striking power.

To establish the primacy of politics requires interim stages aimed at reducing conflict in other areas as well. If dependence on raw materials and export markets is a major factor creating tensions throughout the world, it is vital that social structural changes be considered that could reduce such tensions. If militarization of the Third World contributes immoderately to heightening tensions between the two power blocs, then whatever weapons' industry that is still needed must be structured in such a way that arms exports no longer carry any economic incentive. The call for conflict reduction and its social and economic implications at the same time open the way for the peace movement to strike up its activities in daily life and to transform it, instead of concentrating solely on the struggle for changes in military policy.

Finally, a last point of relevance to steps toward arms conversion and disarmament is their practicability. Most importantly, these steps must be such that any country could implement them largely independently. They should not be dependent on or blockable by international negotiations. After all, alternative peace policies are not intended to subserve other policies; they are programs for improving the security of one's own country over the long term and reducing the risk of annihilation. To act unilaterally a nation must be secure in its autonomy and be able to rely on its own intrinsic strength rather than on the impetus the arms race can give it. This does not, however, rule out multilateral consultation, the exchange of information, or a readiness to cooperate, on the basis of the points enumerated here, to strengthen general security on the road toward total disarmament.

A strictly defensive model as an interim stage

A strictly defensive model that is not identical with Afheldt's views of wide area defense by technical commando units (see pp. 187-96) will include a proposal to abolish nuclear weapons and to renounce deterrence based on threat to the other side (the idea is described more thoroughly in the book *Frieden mit anderen Waffen*, edited by the Committee for Basic Rights and Democracy, rororo aktuell, November 1981). Important aspects of this model are a military defense organization with nonnuclear weapons systems, strict renunciation of all weapons systems that could be construed as a threat to other societies, pushing for social and economic change in one's own society as a means to reduce factors conducive to conflict, and efforts to develop nonviolent forms for resolving conflicts.

This strictly defensive model only partly meets two of the points I mentioned. As in any military interim solution, withdrawal from the arms race is restricted to offensive weapons systems alone. Further development of defensive weapons may be necessary, however. Although this would no longer constitute an arms race in the usual sense, the development of weapons might still tend to exceed the defensive limits placed on them or even constitute a challenge to the primacy of seeking political solutions to conflicts insofar as it would yield to the dictates of military technology. Even though positive experiences with a strictly defensive policy would strengthen those forces pushing for further disarmament, it cannot necessarily be assumed that this policy would in itself be seen as a compelling reason to pursue disarmament further and to move for transition to a system of nonviolent social defense. Therefore, even a strictly defensive model will not go far enough if it is not coupled with those forces pushing for democratization. Thus the peace movement must attempt to galvanize a dynamic social learning process in the nonviolent resolution of conflicts. But it can do so only if it makes consistent use itself of nonviolent forms in its struggle for an alternative peace policy so as to create the psychological and organizational foundations for nonviolent social defense and for a conscientious effort to reduce conflict. By not disdaining military questions it can have a hand in shaping alternatives while at the same time itself developing into a nonviolent alternative.

CHAPTER
12

FIVE PROPOSALS FOR A NEW SECURITY POLICY
The Committee for Basic Rights and Democracy

Our five proposals must be seen against the background of the criticism of the concept of security in the NATO alliance and our more realistic analysis of threat. They too, of course, entail some risks. Security without risk is unobtainable. However, we think the risks entailed by these proposals are much smaller than the risk of war conjured up by the recently amended NATO concept and the modernization of weapons it calls for. These proposals are of course not polished programs for action. They are intended merely to provide some reasonable guidelines for achieving the overriding goal of disarmament and peace. The proposals are several because, first, there exist various ways to tackle the problem, and second, because intermediate stages must be formulated between the currently prevailing deterrence model and a situation in which there would be no armaments and no arms spiral, in which conflicts could be resolved in nonmilitary ways. Hence the proposals by no means coincide always or on every point. Although they may be in part contradictory, they also overlap and hence hang together. The first two proposals aim for disengagement (a nuclear-free zone) and neutrality; they thus begin at a relatively basic level and require mainly changes in the military armaments and the political concept of the Federal Republic. They give way to the third proposal, which is geared primarily to a purely defensive model, and which requires much more extensive changes in domestic policy. The defensive concept would have to be radicalized, or indeed abandoned, if exclusive reliance on the instruments of civil defense became possible, as called for in the fourth proposal. Unilateral total disarmament is one of the implications of an abandonment of the strategy of deterrence and is therefore outlined in the fifth proposal as the most categorical alternative.

Option 1: A nuclear-free zone

If the two superpowers are unable to desist from their frenetic arms buildup, and if the threat continues to grow through more and more and ever more sophisticated ABC weapons, what could be more reasonable than to try to keep the superpowers as far from one another as possible and create as broad as possible a nuclear-free zone between them? This merely reproduces the key thoughts of the plan put forth in the '50s under the catchword of "disengagement," signaled by the names Kennan on the one side and Rapacki on the other. The wrappings have recently been taken off these plans again, with modifications, of course, as befits the times, through an initiative organized by the Russell Peace Foundation. Europe would become a nuclear-free zone from Portugal to Poland and would then be more than merely a corridor. Such a zone would undoubtedly have feedback on the two blocs and their alliances, on the ideologies of hostile adversaries, and ultimately on the military strategies of the superpowers themselves. It is in the Federal Republic's own security interests to push resolutely and zealously for disengagement, which would be a real contribution to détente and a step toward peace.

Option 2: A policy of neutrality

The concept of disengagement, which is not in principle incompatible with NATO, does not necessarily entail neutrality, however much this might be suggested. A limited neutrality backed up by military force could strengthen the buffer function of a nuclear-free zone and allow those nations within it, particularly the Federal Republic (which of course is our primary concern), to define and assume a peace-keeping role of their own. Such a

Proposals for a New Security Policy	181

neutrality would of course have to be a contingent neutrality, i.e., some elementary level of armament would still be maintained. A policy of neutrality would therefore not necessarily have any broader economic and political consequences. The Federal Republic could remain a member of the European Community and still retain its political orientation to the West. Thus we are not speaking of a neutrality of the Swiss type: highly armed, but as a matter of principle free of ties. A policy based on neutrality with an elementary level of armaments would rather enable the Federal Republic to pursue an active peace policy without being laid open to the charge of wanting to play the role of an expansionist middle-sized power, or even great power, backed up by military might. Not only would such a policy strengthen détente, but beyond zonal disarmament it would actively contribute to putting political negotiations in the place of an arms buildup and maintaining stereotypes of presumed enemies. Finally, a neutral Federal Republic would be disengaged from the dangerous lurchings of the American security campaign and U.S. involvement in the arms race.

Option 3: The strictly defensive model

If the option of neutrality were chosen, it would almost necessarily lead to the question of how the neutral status of the Federal Republic could be secured against aggressors, still a possibility, from without. The defensive model offers a solution and provides as well for the Federal Republic to pursue a peace policy within NATO, which of course would also have to change its present course. The strictly defensive model is compatible with subnuclear military policy inasmuch as it does not seek to abolish armaments and the military but rather to limit both to defensive weapons and defensive strategy (which would mean decentralization). The military concept and the weaponry would make clear in unmistakable terms to any potential aggressor that the Federal Republic neither desired nor was capable of any aggression, of whatever sort. But it would also be made clear that an attack on the territory and the citizens of the Federal Republic would not simply be accepted but would be resisted with all the means of defense at the country's disposal. Thus any potential aggressor would also have to assume the risk of considerable losses as well as skirmishes and problems without end. The strictly defensive model, more integral to the politics of peace than it is of a military nature, would remove the Federal Republic as a source of fear in international politics. In adopting this model unconditionally, the FRG would be making a material contribution to disarmament and to the disarmament discussion in other countries, and its field of political action would be widened. The strictly defensive model would, of course, require West Germans to undertake an even deeper rethinking and an even more radical rejection of old, worn-out notions of security than Options 1 and 2. Neither domestic policy nor foreign policy could then be based on an ideology of a presumed enemy. The Federal Republic and its citizens would finally have to find a positive identity of their own in the security question. The economic and social implications would also be considerable. Not only would steps have to be taken to ensure that the apparatus needed for defense—the weapons industry and weapons research—did not become a state within a state and evolve a dynamic of its own, there would also be active contributions made eliminating the causes of conflict through radical readjustments both internally and externally. The defensive model could thus be an important interim stage toward ultimate total disarmament.

Option 4: Nonviolent resistance

Nonviolent resistance is based on the following premises: first, it respects the human being in every enemy and endeavors to draw out this humanity through appropriate actions and responses. He who makes use of destructive physical violence not only destroys his adversary, he tends himself to become inhuman in the process. Where is this better demonstrated today than in the arms buildup on both sides with the absolute weapon? Second, nonviolent resistance seeks to make clear that security, and indeed the security of existence itself, is the concern of each and every individual in society, and that one cannot relieve oneself of this burden by relying on other persons or institutions in these matters. No one can delegate his security and not ultimately suffer the consequences. In other words, it is incumbent on each and every one of us to ensure that the society in which he lives and wants to live remains secure. This deeply democratic impulse of nonviolent defense means—and this is our third premise—that resistance must be organized democratically. The most important implication of this premise is that the humanist scruples of nonviolent resistance must always include the enemy (i.e., the needs of the enemy must be studied and respected wherever possible). Only those interests may be defended that do not place the freedom and equality of those with other views and interests in jeopardy. Nonviolent resistance, or civil defense, demands a lot of its adherents. Understood rightly and put in general terms for the whole of society, it calls for no less than a long and arduous process of reeducation of man himself, of man conditioned for hundreds and even thousands of years in different forms of the friend-enemy ethic: "an eye for an eye, a tooth for a tooth"; "if you don't want to be my brother, then I'll smash your skull"; "he who wants peace must prepare for war"; etc. For these reasons it would be difficult to introduce civil defense as a general principle for the whole of society. The repeated claim, however, that it is humanly impossible (i.e., against human nature) is in fact wrong. If some day ways are found to resolve conflicts without the threat and fear of destruction, then that day society will for the first time become truly human. We must not underestimate the perils of trying to put through the concept of civil resistance in present-day circumstances—especially if we want to avoid them: there is the risk that the moral caliber required by nonviolent resistance would be too much for the individual to bear; and there is the related risk that an elite of moralistic "warriors" would emerge and establish their rule even more thoroughly and forcefully, if more sublimely. These and other perils should not in any sense, however, be construed as arguments against the effort to make the means of nonviolence a universal tool for the resolution of conflicts. Both individuals and society in general would not thereby be deprived of their defenses, but they would have to relinquish the power to destroy others. Freedom from fear, insofar as it is produced by men in their physical circumstances, would then become a real possibility. Other groups and even whole societies as well would ultimately be swept along in the wake of nonviolent resistance, and even a modern Nero would be unable to undertake a nuclear arms buildup against societies organized on the principle of nonviolence and at the same time justify such policies domestically.

Option 5: Unilateral disarmament

The fifth option is effectively an explicit statement of the ultimate aim of all the other options without describing in detail the various steps and stages along the way. This option obviously cannot be implemented in a trice and assumes much more than the other options, particularly the first two. But it would serve no purpose here to sketch the contours of a remote utopia. A more relevant task is to outline a course that could be pursued today, a goal not only most devoutly to be wished but also most zealously to be pursued. The proposal of complete unilateral disarmament is based on two considerations: first, the fact, which history has demonstrated a thousand times over, that the modern state, and modern states in general in their competition with one another, is constantly generating the causes and reasons for war as well as war itself. The distinctive characteristic of the modern state is its "monopoly on the legitimate use of physical violence," i.e., through the police domestically and through the military outwardly. This concentration of violence in the hands of the state makes for a precarious peace on the home front, enforced by the state, while outwardly it engenders the organized use of force, or the threat of its use, by a state in the pursuit of its own self-interests. Total disarmament would make it possible to alter fundamentally the way the state is organized and eliminate one of the causes of war: namely, the international Darwinism of economically and militarily motivated power-hungry states, the bases of which must always contain an element of instability. The proposal is also, however, based on the unequivocal message of the arguments of the disarmament debate since 1945. If a country or a bloc does not unilaterally begin to disarm in conformity with the goals set down in the UN Charter, then behind all the profusion of words will always be arms, arms, and more arms, and nothing more. The Federal Republic must take the initiative for the sake of the security of its citizens.

This initiative must be coherent, i.e., the various steps it entails would all have to move in the same direction. Of course, as we have said, total and unilateral disarmament has a number of preconditions that must be met. In particular, West German citizens must be persuaded that the lack of arms will not leave them naked and exposed but indeed ultimately more secure than under a deadly, oppressive nuclear protective mantle. But total unilateral disarmament would also have a contagious effect on other countries, which would then find it more difficult than under the preceding options even to justify repressive measures domestically in the name of defense. They would have to disarm as well.

The first steps in a new policy

The five options all represent different approaches. Their distance from the realities of the day also varies in increasing order from option one to option five. They do not, however, overlap in the sense that each subsequent option embraces and supersedes the preceding one. They are partly contradictory, yet also partly complementary; and insofar as they begin at different levels and set different numbers (again in increasing order from option one to option five) of preliminary conditions, they can also be construed as indicating in rough terms the sequence of steps to be pursued to achieve the ultimate end common to them all: prevention of war and elimination of its causes. This means above all disarmament, however much it may vary in scope and in kind, and hence security, genuine security, for the Federal Republic and other countries. Finally, it means striving positively for peace. With these ends and present dangers in mind, the first steps are, accordingly:

Prevention of "weapons modernization," which is merely a vehicle for drawing the arms spiral even tighter; efforts to persuade the West German population that disarmament is squarely in their interests without any ifs, ands, or buts, which means, as a first step, a nuclear-free zone; efforts to give our citizens a say again in deciding questions of their security, to give them an opportunity to discuss the various options, and not to allow them to be blinded to the real dangers by an ideological anticommunism; and finally, efforts to change the Federal Republic so that it will take the lead in disarmament and the pursuit of peace—all these things only the citizens of the Federal Republic themselves can achieve.

The Federal Republic must indeed be the initiator. Nothing would inspire trust so much as steps toward disarmament taken independently. Nothing would secure peace in real terms for the Federal Republic and its population better than having the courage to entertain the cause of peace and say no to an expansion of the military complex, weapons technology, and the formulation of strategies that instill a sense of false security. He who desires peace—and this applies more than ever today—prepares for peace himself in his own backyard.

CHAPTER
13

HORST AFHELDT'S DEFENSIVE RESPONSE MODEL

Thomas Trempnau

Preliminary comments

In his study *Defense and Peace—Politics by Military Means*,[1] Horst Afheldt of the Max Planck Institute in Starnberg presents a detailed study of the current NATO strategy of flexible response. He concludes that flexible response cannot achieve its aim of "preventing war through deterrence,"[2] i.e., securing peace, because on the one hand it fuels the arms race and thereby increases the risk of war, and on the other, the strategy of deterrence is not credible: the military responses programmed into it would lead to the the destruction of what was supposed to be defended.

In view of the "irrationality" of this strategy, Afheldt calls for its abandonment and outlines a second-strike defensive response model, i.e., renunciation of all offensive weapons such as tanks, bombers, etc., including tactical nuclear weapons, but not longer-range nuclear weapons (strategic nuclear weapons). Furthermore it includes renunciation of the type of defense referred to as "forward," which is a part of the flexible response strategy, i.e., renunciation of front formations. In its place Afheldt proposes a network of technocommando units, as he calls them, extending throughout the entire Federal Republic (outside of the large cities). Each of these commando units, numbering about 10,000, would be locally based and would have the task of *autonomously* defending its territory with the most modern high-technology defensive weapons if any attacker of the Federal Republic tried to advance into it.

Afheldt has thus developed not only an alternative strategy to flexible response but also a concept that would require a thorough reorganization of the weaponry and structures of the Bundeswehr.

In the following we shall describe Afheldt's essential criticisms of flexible response as well as the main features of his alternative model of military defense. We are not concerned here with evaluating Afheldt's model. After presenting it we will merely pose a few questions that seem either not to be solved by his model or to be inherent in it.

Criteria for a politics of peace by military means

"In its security policy the Federal Republic proposes to protect the freedom and independence of our country against military threat and political pressure and to maintain the peace" (*Weissbuch*, 1973-74, cited in II, 639).

Starting from this postulate of security policy expounded by the Federal Minister of Defense and the assumption that "The securing of peace without military means in our times is an illusion," Afheldt attempts in his concept to solve the problem of "how military means can serve the political end of ensuring peace and in the long run abolish force and violence within the community of nations."

The prevention of war by military means is the attempt to "deter the enemy from the use of his armed might." Deterrence is an appeal to reason. However, it is not in every case certain that decision-makers will behave rationally, as indeed examples down to the most recent past have demonstrated (e.g., Johnson's escalation of the Vietnam War in 1965, see I, 136), so that a policy of peace by military means must guarantee "that the consequences of misconduct on either side can be met with the broadest countervailing measures possible...."

Therefore Afheldt regards the buildup of a military balance "to preserve peace through deterrence" as *necessary* but not *sufficient*: for neither can a military balance reliably prevent war, nor can the striving for such a balance be maintained without jeopardizing peace.

What conditions must therefore be met for a peace policy backed up by military means to make war unlikely over the short and middle term, and over the long run, to serve the cause of world peace?

"The broadest criterion for armaments to prevent war is stability. Generally undisputed criteria for peace, crisis, and war follow from this goal of arms control."

First criterion: "To make war as unlikely as possible" ("stability in peace").

Both sides abandon attempts to force the adversary to capitulate by threat of military means.

- A security policy must aim for disengagement from the arms race "through an *independent* defense strategy that deliberately does not use the same means as the adversary (e.g., antitank defense instead of tanks)."

Second criterion: "No benefits from prevention or preemption" (no advantages from a preventive or preemptive first strike—"stability in crisis").

- "The position of neither side should be essentially improved by it being the first to start a war in the case of crisis."

Third criterion: "The means and strategies of defense must safeguard our social and economic structure" ("stability in war").

- The use of military means is *rational* only if one's own strategy ensures that the conflict can be resolved while still keeping violence and destruction within limits "in which war can still be regarded as a rational means of politics for one's own side."
- Strategy must ensure that what is to be defended is not destroyed.
- "Practicable (rational) military options can be a precondition of credible deterrence. Thus deterrence becomes contingent on the practicability of the threatened options."

Basic principle: "If the enemy has weapons that can cause unacceptable damage and cannot be repelled, a rational strategy requires ensuring that the enemy is not presented with militarily rational or indeed decisive options for the use of these weapons." That is, no "targets the destruction of which would yield military advantages" may be formed (I, 99).

Fourth criterion: "NATO's nuclear weapons must be given no military tasks."

- "The enemy must be offered no possible uses for his nuclear weapons that are militarily rational or indeed decisive." A "militarily rational use" of nuclear weapons by the Warsaw Pact could be to destroy tactical atomic weapons stationed in the Federal Republic and thus force NATO (if a conventional attack by the Warsaw Pact cannot be stopped) either to escalate early into a strategic nuclear war or to capitulate (in NATO strategy tactical nuclear weapons have the task of "making escalation to the strategic level credible by constituting an intermediate stage between conventional war and a strategic nuclear war"—II, 652).

● Thus in the deterrence policy of NATO, nuclear weapons would retain only *political* tasks, for example, as threats to get negotiations started to end the war.

● The U.S.'s precision guided submarine-based nuclear weapons are sufficient to this end, so that no ground- or air-based nuclear weapons would be necessary in the European NATO countries; this would help to implement the principle of setting up no targets for enemy nuclear weapons.

Fifth criterion: "Use of military means only if an attack is successful."

● The military means of NATO must with no equivocations be usable only after an attack by the Warsaw Pact, i.e., NATO's weapons must permit only defensive response operations. For "the capacity to wage a war without a prior attack, i.e., the capacity to attack the territory of the Warsaw Pact, is incompatible with the principle that military means are to be used solely and exclusively to safeguard the peace and security of our country," i.e., only those weapons may be built into plans which cannot reach the territory of the Warsaw Pact and hence cannot threaten it.

Sixth criterion: "Modern technology favors defense."

● Modern technology not only provides the possibility of improving the weapons systems, it should also be used especially to develop strategies that can only be used in defense after a successful attack (second-strike defensive response).

Criteria for a peace policy and flexible response

Current NATO strategy conflicts with each and every one of

Afheldt's criteria for a policy of peace with military means. In the following I will discuss the most essential points of irreconcilability.

First: The forward defense provided for in flexible response could rapidly force the Warsaw Pact to a preemptive strike in a crisis. Preparations for this type of defense mst be undertaken promptly so that an enemy attack can actually be stopped in a forward position, at the border of enemy territory. This means: thorough mobilization and perhaps even a preventive attack at the slightest sign that an attack is being contemplated. The commander of the allied forces in central Europe, General Schulze, makes this quite clear: "The enemy offensive must be countered where it is most vulnerable, at the start of the attack, before it gains momentum." And: "Waiting until the enemy's intention can be more clearly discerned must necessarily lead to a surprise attack." Finally: "If a forward defense is to be practiced, it requires the political will not only to act promptly at the first signs" but also to act in fact (II, 641 and note 9).

Second: the nuclear weapons stationed in the Federal Republic could force the enemy to a preventive first strike. This also reinforces the tendency for a crisis to escalate.

Third: the flexible response strategy entails the creation of targets the military destruction of which must necessarily appear both advantageous and imperative to the enemy, e.g., nuclear bases, as well as the line of defense (front), with the corresponding massing of troops and weapons and logistic installations (barracks, airfields, etc.) in forward defense. They are spread throughout the entire territory of the FRG, so that the whole country would become a battlefield from the very first days (II, 642).

Fourth: the current strategy would be conducive to the destruction of what was to be defended. As a tendency this makes flexible response a suicidal form of defense (I, 169). From this it follows that:

Fifth: "There are no rational war options," and the overriding strategic defensive aim of West German security policymakers, namely, the protection of the "freedom and independence of our country" (see above), cannot be achieved with the flexible response strategy.

Sixth: "A deterrence strategy that operates with nonrational combat units can be empirically demonstrated to lead in practice to an arms race" (I, 177) and hence to the destabilization of peace.

Models for a new security policy in Europe

The aim of Afheldt's alternative military defense model is to demonstrate that the above-outlined criteria for a policy of peace by military means can in principle be met. It is not his purpose, however, to claim that this is the last resort but to encourage reflection and the working out of other models that might meet these criteria just as well or even better.

Afheldt's model contains two different types of military means: the nonnuclear technocommando units and nuclear weapons, reserved for exclusive use as a means of political coercion.

The technocommando units and their mission

Size: about twenty men in each technocommando unit to combat the enemy's tank formations; finally, up to sixteen additional men for air defense and other tasks.

Stationing: each commando unit covers an area of about twenty square kilometers within the FRG; large cities are not covered and hence could not become "combat areas" in the case of war.

Needs: excluding large cities and high mountain areas, about 200,000 square kilometers must be covered by technocommando units, i.e., there would be a need for about 10,000 of them. In peacetime this would require about 360,000 men; to this must be added communications units of 30,000 men for reinforcements in peacetime; thus the total need is 390,000 men.

Arms: precision guided antitank weapons (e.g., Milan missiles), mines, light infantry weapons, semiautomatic and automatic destructive weapons, antiaircraft missiles, minicruise missiles (longer-range target-seeking missiles of at least 25 km range).

Afheldt's Defense Model

Task: the task of the technocommando units would be to render an attack on central Europe and the occupation of NATO territories "politically and militarily as costly as possible" to the enemy ("credible, nonnuclear limited-range deterrence") and to prevent a *fait accompli* so as to give the United States time to bring its military and, especially, nuclear power "to bear" (II, 647). On its territory each commando unit would autonomously attempt as fast as possible to prevent or smash the enemy advance. The civilian population must also be protected, which is why large cities are not to be defended by the technocommando units. (Afheldt discusses the possibility of civilian resistance for the large cities, II, 287 ff.)

Efficiency: each commando unit would destroy a statistical average of three enemy tanks in the case of attack. This would, at least theoretically, absorb the entire Warsaw Pact tank reserve.

The enemy infantry could be held off for only a short time by each individual commando unit and so would conquer each commando area one at a time and knock out their antitank weapons. However, these missions by the enemy infantry would deprive the tank attack of its surprise effect, and the network of tank-destroying commando units would thereby have prevented the *fait accompli*.

Types of nuclear weapons and their function

Since the network of technocommando units would considerably delay the enemy (i.e., the Warsaw Pact troops) but in the end could not prevent the occupation of the FRG, other means are needed to restore the status quo, i.e., to force negotiations to end hostilities. This would be the goal of a "rational strategy of threat and coercion," backed up by the use of U.S. nuclear arms. The threatened use of nuclear weapons can be "rational" only if they are stationed neither in Europe nor the United States, since otherwise again what was to be defended would be destroyed by retaliatory or preventive strikes by the USSR. U.S. nuclear submarines, therefore, would be the sole means at hand for this strategy.

The target of the threats cannot be determined militarily; thus the target of a nuclear threat cannot be the invading Warsaw Pact troops, since our own population, which actually was to be defended, would then be exposed. Rather, the purpose of the threat is derivable politically from the "basic principles of rational deterrence." "In the system of deterrence the target of the use or threatened use of strategic arms is the government of the enemy.... It follows from this that a deterrent threat must entail disadvantages that from the standpoint of the enemy government are insupportable."

But the target of a threat also cannot be the territory of the USSR, since then a counterstrike would hit U.S. territory. This alternative would thus not be "rational" either.

This means that for the specific case of an attack by the Warsaw Pact on Western Europe, which the Eastern European countries would support because of Soviet authority, the aim of the threat could be to place this Soviet hegemony in jeopardy, since that would be "unacceptable" to the Soviet government.

The aim of this strategy could be to dissuade the Eastern European nations from taking part in a Soviet attack on Western Europe: "Every nation of the Warsaw Pact that took active part in an attack on NATO would be admonished: 'After warnings to give the local population opportunity to evacuate the target areas, NATO would begin with minor attacks on the economic infrastructure. If these warnings go unheeded, and if the government did not within a reasonable time desist from the prohibited activities, the economic structure (of the particular country) would if necessary be destroyed.'"

It is Afheldt's presumption that the probable Soviet counterthreat would force both sides to resume political dialogue. The major West German cities occupied by the Warsaw Pact troops could then no longer be the targets of threats, so that the further the Warsaw Pact troops advanced and the more cities they occupied, the narrower would be the Soviet margin for launching counterthreats (I, 265 ff.).

Afheldt imagines that a nuclear war on the territory of the FRG could be prevented in this way because, in contrast to current NATO strategy, NATO nuclear weapons would only strike enemy territory, and the Warsaw Pact would have no targets for the USSR's nuclear weapons. Furthermore the damage caused by nonnuclear acts of war could be minimized because large

Afheldt's Defense Model 195

cities would not be defended militarily, and the decentralized use of technocommando units would cause less damage in the countryside than the current forward defense strategy. In addition, the network of technocommando units would have no targets that it would be of advantage to or even imperative for the enemy to destroy: there would be no concentrations of NATO troops, no heavy units (tanks, etc.), no air force support bases, and no reinforcements.

Problems in the implications of Afheldt's military logic

Quite apart from the social problems resulting from Afheldt's model (entrenchment of the present archetype of the enemy, militarization of the population, etc.) and the unsolved problems of defending large cities (how to defend against enemy bombing attacks on large cities?), the role of NATO nuclear weapons is especially problematic: even assuming that the Warsaw Pact would in fact attack the FRG, this attack would be "irrational" from the outset, since in such a case NATO would threaten the use of nuclear weapons. On what grounds, then, can Afheldt hope that the Warsaw Pact would abandon this irrational conduct after the explicit NATO threat to use nuclear weapons?

What would happen if the "USSR's authority over Eastern Europe" could not be broken, i.e., if, for example, a threat to destroy a Polish coal mine were ignored by the Polish government? Would the threat then be made good? Is an escalation of the war still avoidable in this case? Can one then still be sure that the consequences of the Warsaw Pact's "misconduct" could be contained as broadly as possible by "countervailing measures"?

What happens if the USSR counters with a threat to destroy an unoccupied large West German city? Once it has started the war, would it be ready to negotiate the end of the war, which for NATO would after all have to mean the withdrawal of all Warsaw Pact troops (restoration of the status quo)?

Going further, one might also ask what would happen if the USSR were to counter with a threat to destroy Paris or London or Washington. The problem seems to me to lie mainly in the fact that Afheldt's envisaged use of nuclear weapons as *political* instruments is just as little able to prevent the escalation of a war as the flexible response strategy, in which nuclear weapons would be used, primarily to military ends, on the field of battle. Is a decision between a political and a military use of nuclear weapons meaningful or even possible if in the end the results are the same? Thus the inclusion of a nuclear strategy in a defense model unequivocally calls into question Afheldt's criteria for "rational options."

But beyond this, the readiness to use nuclear weapons in the case of war would at the same time mean heightened instability in a crisis, since to the Warsaw Pact they would continue to constitute a threat.

NOTES

1. H. Afheldt, *Verteidigung und Frieden—Politik mit militärischen Mittel*, Munich and Vienna, 1976, hereinafter referred to as I, plus page references, as well as the abridged version, idem., "Friedenspolitik mit militärischen Mitteln in den neunziger Jahren," in K. D. Schwarz, ed., *Sicherheits-politik*, Bad Honnef-Erpel, 1978, pp. 639-56, hereinafter cited as II, plus page references.

2. The Federal Ministry of Defense, *Weissbuch zur Sicherheit der Bundesrepublik Deutschland und zur Entwicklung der Bundeswehr*, Bonn, 1979, p. 123.

CHAPTER

14

TECHNOCOMMANDO UNITS OR SOCIAL DEFENSE? A COMPARISON

Theodor Ebert

The NATO "modernization" decision, the Soviet military operations in Afghanistan, and the crisis and war in the Persian Gulf have aroused renewed interest among broad layers of the population in the issues of peace and security. In the FRG not only are there more than 50,000 eligible young people refusing military service each year, but peace weeks under the slogan "Peace without Weapons" are well received, particularly among church groups, and "alternatives" to current NATO security policy are being demanded. On the other hand, the optimistic expectation of the seventies that controlled disarmament could be achieved via "cooperative arms control" within détente has vanished. The doctrine of maintaining a balance was seen through by the critics of the arms buildup as the ideology of "modernization."

Critics of "modernization" have brought up a number of alternatives to NATO for discussion, for example, the military alternative of technocommando units which Horst Afheldt[1] has proposed as a model, borrowing on the studies by the Austrian Spanocchi and the Frenchman de Broselet,[2] and the civilian alternative of "social defense,"[a] which has been developed by a number of peace researchers in international collaboration since 1964.[3]

---

a. An explicitly nonmilitary form of defense. It can be seen as the contribution of pacifism to the security needs of the population. Social defense is directed at the defense not of a state but of democratic social structures and institutions. It relies on nonviolent activities across a broad front as well as civil resistance. Its historical models are Gandhi and Martin Luther King, and it regards the general strike as an important means of defense against aggression.

Defense by a network of autonomous technocommando units is based on the consideration that fundamentally only those defense models are rational for us Germans in which we would survive as a nation in the case of war. NATO's forward defense, which would make the FRG and GDR into a battlefield, does not meet this criterion. Afheldt would avoid combat and accompanying conventional or nuclear annihilation strikes by transferring the mission of defense from tanks and aircraft, which are potentially offensive weapons, to about 10,000 technocommando units covering the entire FRG in a uniform network. "Instead of preparing for battle, there would be a series of decentralized combat actions all following the same tactical pattern. The statistical efficiency of these individual maneuvers is well-known. Combat would be replaced by a series of minor actions of known statistical efficiency."[4] The basic strategic consideration is that unlike in World War II, modern precision weapons give "firepower" the advantage over "movement." This was demonstrated by the high tank and aircraft losses in the Yom Kippur War between Egypt and Israel.

This model meets the above criterion of rationality because the light, stationary commando units, made up of about twenty men, are small but strong enough to offer no rational targets for greater strikes with conventional or nuclear weapons; it would be like shooting at hornets with cannons. Furthermore the technocommando units would on principle operate exclusively outside of built-up areas and moreover would not attack the enemy in such areas. The population in such areas would thus have a high chance for survival.

Afheldt's objective with this strictly defensive model employing technocommando units is to restrain a potential aggressor from attacking by dint of two considerations (restraint instead of deterrence): first, it would be made clear to him that a swift overrunning of the FRG in a few hours is out of the question (prevention of a *fait accompli*), and second, he would have a clear picture beforehand of the tremendous losses he would suffer if he attacked (high price of entry).

Social defense is based, first, on the fact that remote-controlled weapons have deprived the territorial state of its original hard protective shell, and that forward defense is totally impossible

Technocommando Units or Social Defense?

in the FRG; and second, that the presence of armed units on a territory does not necessarily imply political control over the social institutions in the area in question. Social defense draws on fundamental arguments put forth by Reichschancellor Cuno on March 7, 1923, in the German Reichstag in reference to the situation at that time:

> Though unarmed in the crude sense of the term, Germany possesses a strong defense in the will of free man. Colonial lands can be conquered with armies, but they cannot extract productivity from any industrial region. It is an insult to the intellect to believe that the seizure of territory is the decisive factor. Let the French stay either days or years in the Ruhr region and bring in foreign colonists to replace the German worker—the curse of infertility will descend upon the enterprise. This is passive resistance, and we embrace it as a weapon of nonviolence in the struggle against injustice and violence.

In 1980 the Soviet leadership as well was forced to realize that a military intervention á la Prague 1968 would not be the way to achieve social control over Poland and solve its economic problems.

By preparing the population for civil resistance, social defense will demonstrate to any potential aggressors that occupation will be at such a high price that restraint will result. The costs to the aggressor will come from:

- personnel costs (expenditures for military and civil occupation forces);
- economic costs (loss of trade);
- political costs (loss of legitimacy).

Both concepts have the advantage that whether it succeeds or fails, the German people will survive the conflict. Advocates of the nuclear deterrence strategy object against both that they make wars possible again because the aggressor has no reason to presume his own defeat; a military conversion to technocommando units or a shift to social defense would have a destabilizing effect on the world situation and hence imperil peace. Only those who consider a catastrophic collapse of the balance of terror to be probable, and no longer regard the domestic manifestations of militarism as acceptable, would accept the risk of such a destabilization. At present this is not yet the majority of the population in the FRG. Since the champions of the military and the civilian alternative models agree in their criticism of the present NATO concept and would find the application of any other alternative to be better than an attempt at forward defense á la NATO, it might be useful to investigate and compare these concepts without too rash a readiness to compromise, but without polemics as well.

Christian pacifists in the group "Live without Weapons" will of course not be able to accept defense based on technocommando units; yet there are good reasons for regarding this model as by far the lesser evil compared with forward defense. Furthermore it cannot be denied that from the pacifist viewpoint, Afheldt's military alternative would have much less resistance to overcome than the civilian alternative. Afheldt retains the official conception of the Warsaw Pact enemy; and while he questions the presence of foreign troops on FRG soil, he does not question FRG membership in NATO. The army would be given new types of arms on a broad scale; but the soldiers would retain a social function, and even the domestic armaments industry could expect orders (if not exactly for the manufacture of aircraft and tanks). On the whole, the present social and economic systems are not radically questioned. These features will make the technocommando unit model more acceptable to broad sections of the population as well as important interest groups than is social defense.

The fact that even groups standing far to the left prefer the technocommando unit model over social defense can probably be explained by their hope that it will be more broadly accepted and by their reservations with regard to the suspected dogmatism of nonviolence. However, I have even met officers who regarded social defense as a more comprehensive and more broadly developed concept. In any event, before the technocommando units are declared a defense strategy, we should take up a few urgent critical questions regarding the implications of this concept for military and political strategy, as well as its social implications.

Although Afheldt himself has discussed a few military problems, like the prevention of airborne landings in political and economic centers, there are three areas which it seems to me still stand in need of clarification:

1. For Afheldt the restraining effect of his model is contingent on the aggressor's losing roughly half of his tanks. However, for such high losses to occur, the firepower of the technocommando units and the precision of their weapons must also be sufficient. How tanks are supposed to be hit on protected terrain, under poor weather conditions, and at distances of up to 50 kilometers seems to me not yet sufficiently clear.[5] However, this problem could be solvable technically (although the moral issue of killing so many soldiers still remains). One difficult problem might be that the aggressor would probably take advantage of the fact that the technocommando units are unable to operate in built-up areas, and hence in the thickly populated Federal Republic the aggressor could advance by hopscotching from one small town to another. In addition there are large towns near the border where the technocommando units could not set up obstructions.

2. Technocommando units have no means to launch a counteroffensive. If they wanted to attack the enemy in occupied localities, they would have to mass themselves, and thus would become an inviting target for heavy weapons, while an attack against them would endanger the civil population. Thus once an area was taken, it could not be liberated by military means.

3. Should the nuclear threat of the allied superpower not be carried out, as for instance in Andreas Buro's adaptation of Afheldt's model,[6] an aggressor could take the time to weed out the technocommando units one by one with his infantry. In this situation the most sensible tactic would probably be to offer no military resistance from the very start and build on the possibilities of civil resistance in occupied areas.

4. In Afheldt's model the technocommando units only have the limited mission of preventing the *fait accompli* of the FRG's being swiftly overrun and of inflicting considerable losses on the aggressor. The time gained and the weakening of the aggressor would be used by the United States to pressure the aggressor to withdraw on the threat of nuclear strikes. The use of this U.S. nuclear covering force does not meet Afheldt's own criterion of rationality, since an escalation to nuclear strikes remains a possibility. Should the FRG's allies drive back the weakened aggressor by conventional means, Germany would become a battlefield in

the second phase of the war and would be devastated.

Even if the military problems of a successful defense against an attack by the Warsaw Pact nations could be solved, we would still have to answer the question whether Afheldt's military tactic is capable of dealing with all the security policy questions. Afheldt himself writes that he is only dealing with one special question: "How must military preparations in the Western industrial nations be structured so that they lead to peace and not to war?"[7] Although Afheldt thinks that the Warsaw Pact nations would respond in a constructive and peace-promoting way to a conversion of defenses, nevertheless, since he is himself a security policy-maker, he examines the worst case of an aggressive response by the Warsaw Pact nations. Why such a pessimistic approach only for the Warsaw Pact but not for our allies and the Federal Republic? Might not the social process pushing for a new security policy lead to new conflict situations in the West, such as we observed in 1968 in Czechoslovakia and 1980 in Poland as the result of social processes? A technocommando defense that was in its very first construction phases, or even just in the planning stage, is not enough to hold one's own against a Bundeswehr that could refuse to go along with the conversion or against allies who would not want to withdraw or might even intervene.

The concept of technocommando units implicitly assumes that it would be instituted by the government as a more rational concept of security after a public debate on security policy. First, a thoroughgoing transformation in security policy is inconceivable without the pressure of a social movement, and second, it is rather unlikely that a social movement in which engaged pacifists would certainly play a leading role would extend its efforts to the concept of technocommando units. However, this concept could be a bargaining position for a government that felt itself pressured by advocates of social defense. In that case it would be important to enumerate both the differences and the points in common in the two concepts.

One important factor is that Afheldt's concept also provides for civil resistance in occupied localities. Furthermore both concepts face similar problems in supplying occupied territories with energy and food.[8] The role of civil resistance in occupied localities is unclear in Afheldt's model. If it could be shown that the price of holding territory would be relatively high, this could give a government the option of forgoing the price of entry of the technocommando units in an acute conflict case, since the lives of many of the defenders would also be lost, and building up the social defense model from the very beginning.

With all due respect to the intellectual achievements represented by Afheldt's criticism of forward defense and the development of the model of the technocommando units, I nonetheless believe that there are two good reasons for the peace movement to commit itself to the cause of social defense and not to a peace policy with alternative military means.

1. Social defense is the more comprehensive concept in terms of security policy. Although it is based on the current stereotype of the enemy, it does look to the social process and conceivable military interventions. Civil defense also could prevent coups d'etats and military interventions by the allies.

2. There is a series of continuous links between nonviolent actions in domestic conflicts and nonviolent resistance against aggressors. Social movements can act independently in the preparation of social defense and need not rely on the support or even the consent of the government.

NOTES

1. Emil Spannochi and Guy Brosolet, *Verteidigung ohne Schlacht*, Munich, 1976.
2. Horst Afheldt, *Verteidigung und Frieden. Politik mit militärischen Mitteln*, Munich, 1976.
3. Theodor Ebert, *Soziale Verteidigung*, 2 vols., Waldkirch, 1981.
4. Afheldt, p. 238.
5. Ibid., pp. 261-62.
6. A Buro, "Sozialistische Politik und Friedensicherung, Thesen zur Einleitung einer überfälligen Diskussion," in *Links, Sozialistische Zeitung*, no. 126, September 1980.
7. Afheldt, p. 15.
8. Th. Ebert, "Energieversorgung im Verteidigungsfall, Uberlegung zur Verträglichkeit verschiedener Energieversorgungsysteme mit Konzepten alternativer Sicherheitspolitik," in Theodor Ebert, *Soziale Verteidigung*, vol. 2, Waldkirch, 1981 (in press).

About the Authors

Professor Ulrich Albrecht

Born in Bern 1941. Degrees in engineering and political science; 1967-72 assistant at the University of Stuttgart and staff member of the Hamburg Institute for Peace Research and the Institute for Strategic Studies, London. Since 1972 Professor of Peace and Conflict Research at the Free University of Berlin. Since 1981 Vice-President of the Free University of Berlin. Numerous publications on peace and conflict research. His two last books, much read in the peace movement, are *Die Wiederaufrüstung der Bundesrepublik* (Cologne, 1981) and *Kündigt den Nachrüstungsbeschluss!* (Frankfurt, 1982).

Herbert Ammon

Born in Brieg 1943. Studies in history and English and American language and literature. Gymnasium teacher in Franken. Since 1975 Councilor at the Board for Foreign Students at the Free University of Berlin. Joint publications with Dr. Peter Brandt: *Die Linken und die nationale Frage* (Reinbek, 1981) and *Wege zur Lösung der deutschen Frage* (Berlin, 1982).

Egon Bahr

Born in 1922. Journalistic education and activity with numerous newspapers in Berlin up to 1950; 1950-60 chief commentator of RIAS Berlin. Regional staff for the Berlin program at the Accra Embassy; Director of the Berlin Press and Information Office 1960-65; Ambassador for the Foreign Office 1967; State Secretary at the Federal Chancellor's Office 1969; Federal Minister for Special Affairs 1972-74. During this time responsible for the negotiations in Moscow. Person primarily responsible for the establishment of the "New *Ostpolitik*" of the Federal Republic. Federal Minister for Economic Cooperation 1974-76; from 1976 to 1981 Federal Administrator of the SPD; currently Associate of the Party Central Committee of the SPD for disarmament questions and member of the Palme Commission. Numerous publications. Last book: *Was wird aus den Deutschen?* (Reinbek, 1982).

Dr. Klaus Bloemer

Born 1921. Essayist and editor. 1951-59 editor in chief of various newspapers in Munich, Stuttgart, and London. 1964-68 in charge of foreign policy questions for CSU Chairman F. J. Strauss; since then member of the SPD; sporadic posts in the diplomatic service in Iran, the United States, Norway, and Switzerland. Numerous books.

Dr. Peter Brandt

Born 1948. Studies in history; assistant professor at the Technical University of Berlin. Member of the Alternative List in Berlin. Most recent books: *Antifaschismus und Arbeiterbewegung* (Hamburg, 1976); *Die Linken und die nationale Frage* (Reinbek, 1981): *Preussen—Zur Sozialgeschichte eines Staates* (Reinbek, 1981).

Professor Andreas Buro

Born 1928 in Berlin. Studies in the natural sciences and work in applied research; later active in industry in the construction of plants. From 1966, after long years of service in the peace movement, particularly the Easter March movement for democracy and disarmament, studies in political science in Munich and Frankfurt. Presently Professor for International Relations at Johann-Wolfgang Goethe University in Frankfurt. Cofounder of the Socialist Bureau and the Committee for Basic Rights and Democracy. Numerous essays.

Committee for Basic Rights and Democracy

Founded in 1976 by leading members of the liberal professions, writers, politicians, etc., in response to the Berufsverbot. Since then it has survived and been responsible for a number of publications of relevance, among other things, to the peace movement.

Professor Theodor Ebert

Born 1937. Professor of Political Science in Peace Research at the Free University of Berlin; editorial board of the journal *Gewaltfreie Aktion* (*Nonviolent Action*); active in the Central Committee of the "Union for Reconciliation," a pacifist organization; member of the Synod of the Evangelical Church of Germany. Numerous books on the historical forms of nonviolent resistance, e.g., *Gewaltfreier Aufstand, Alternative zum Bürgerkrieg* (Waldkirchen, 1976).

Günter Gaus

Born 1929 in Braunschweig. Studies in history and German language and literature; journalistic activity with various newspapers and weeklies; 1965-69 program director of the Südwestfunk; 1969-73 editor-in-chief of the weekly *Der Spiegel*; Secretary of State of the Federal Chancellor's Office 1973; Director of the Permanent Mission of the Federal Republic of Germany to the GDR 1974-81. Numerous books, e.g., *Gespräche mit Herbert Wehner* (1966); author of the television series "Zur Person"; *Texte zur Deutschen Frage* (1981). Now working on a book on his experiences at the Permanent Mission in the GDR and his views on the German question.

General Christian Krause

Born 1918. Professional soldier since 1936. After the war and prison active in various professions, most recently as editor. Since 1957 in the Federal Army (Bundeswehr). 1971-73 Representative of the Staff Department Director for Military Policy and Leadership at the Federal Ministry of Defense. Since retirement in 1978, active as free-lance journalist and member of the Research Institute of the Friedrich-Ebert-Stiftung. Last publicatin: *Das konventionelle Gleichgewicht in Europa* (Bonn-Bad Godesberg, 1982).

Professor Ekkehart Krippendorff

Born 1934. University lecturer for International Relations at the Kennedy Institute of the Free University of Berlin. Editor of the annual publication *Weltpolitik. Jahrbuch für Internationale Beziehungen*, together with Professor Ulrich Albrecht and others at the *Journal of Peace Research*, Oslo. Author of numerous books on international relations and publications in scientific periodicals.

Michael Lucas

An American political scientist and free-lance journalist who lives in West Berlin, he writes for publications in West Germany and the United States. Recent articles include "Die Vereinigten Staaten von Amerika und die Krise des Kalten Kriegs Systems," "Reagans Erneuerung des Kalten Krieges," and with Ekkehart Krippendorff, "Die USA und Westeuropa."

Rudolf Steinke

Born 1948 in Kiel. Apprenticeship in commerce and later study in economics, history, and German language and literature. Consultant with the Senator for Science and Research and later for Günter Gaus; currently consultant with the Bundestag for Peace Policy. Member of the Committee for a Nuclear-Free Europe; earlier spokesman for the International Committee for the Release of Rudolf Bahro; editor of *Bahro-Kongress. Aufzeichnungen, Berichte und Referate* (Berlin, 1978); *Vom Umgang mit der Deutschen Frage* (Berlin, 1980); *Alternativen europäischer Friedenspolitik* (Berlin, 1981).

Dr. Stephan Tiedtke

Scholar at the Hesse Foundation for Peace and Conflict Research in Frankfurt. Publications: *Die Warschauer Vertragsorganisation. Zum Verhältnis von Militär- und Entspannungspolitik in Osteuropa* (Munich and Vienna, 1978); *Rüstungskontrolle aus sowjetischer Sicht* (Frankfurt, 1980).

Thomas Trempnau

Born 1955 in Berlin. Studies in political science at the Free University of Berlin. Since 1980 on staff of *antimilitarismus information*, monthly information publication on armaments, conscientious objection, and activities in the peace movement. Active as journalist.

Michael Vale

On the editorial staff of *Critique* (Glasgow) and senior translator for M. E. Sharpe, Inc.